Dragon Rampant

By

By Robin Hyde

Dragon Rampant
Published by – AG Books
24 Harper St
Wanganui
New Zealand

ISBN - 978-0-473-54135-4

Cover Photo: Watch tower at the centre of Tengyueh, Yunnan, China 1938, by Dora de Beer. Courtesy Alexander Turnebell Library, New Zealand

Foreword

"In the deserted village, sunken down
With a shrug of last weak old age, pulled back to earth,
All people are fled or killed. The cotton crop rots.
Not one mild house leans sideways, a man on crutches.
Not a sparrow earns from the naked floors,
Walls look, but cannot live without the folk they loved --
It would be a bad thing to awaken them.
Having broken the rice-bowl, seek not to fill it again." - Robin Hyde

Born Iris Guiver Wilkinson in Capetown, South Africa. Robin Hyde arrived in Wellington as a baby in 1906. She began writing at the age of nine but it wasn't until attending Wellington Girl's College that her poetry and short stories garnered attention.

She began working for the *Dominion* as a reporter in 1923 at the age of 17. She wrote "Peeps at Parliament" in 1925 but left Wellington to pursue a prolific career reporting for the *Christchurch Sun* and the *Wanganui Chronicle* where she wrote her "Margot" columns and was lady editor. She found it difficult to marry her journalistic work, which paid the bills, and write poetry and fiction, yet she manged to publish *The Desolate Star*, a small collection of poems in 1929 when she was just 23.

She became the lady editor of a small paper called *The New Zealand Observer* in 1931 and lived in Auckland for the next seven years. She became a prominent writer and editor was well-known in her neighbourhood in the North Shore. She would often be seen limping around with books and manuscripts in one hand, and greeting her fellow neighbours with the other according to Gloria Rawlinson.

She published *Journalese* in 1934, *The Conquerors* in 1935, *Passport to Hell* and *Check to Your King* in 1936, *Wednesday's Children* and *Persephone in Winter* in 1937 and *The Godwits Fly* and *Nor the Years Condemn* in 1938. Finally she published *Dragon Rampant* in London in 1939.
Although she won high accolades as a poet and journalist, her personal life was a struggle, full of adventures and unconventional choices.

Hyde's first tragedy was Harry Sweetman. He worked with her father who introduced them when Hyde was 16. Sweetman was the "love of her life" and it was shortly after visiting him in Auckland in 1924 that she was treated for an injured knee which would result in pain and a limp for the rest of her life. Sweetman devastated her when he left for London, a journey that they spoke of going on together. It was two more years before she found out that Sweetman had died shortly after arriving in London from pneumonia.

Hoping that the Rotorua hot springs would help treat her injury, Hyde encountered a young RAF veteran pilot named Frederick de Mulford Hyde in December 1925. They had a brief and intense affair, after which Hyde found herself pregnant. She hid her pregnancy in Sydney where her son Christopher Robin Hyde died shortly after birth.

All of these events played a role in her subsequent bouts with depression, suicide and excessive use of pain killers and drugs. This is also when she began to use Robin Hyde as her "nom de guerre" in tribute to her lost son. These events all occurred by the time Hyde was 20.

Her life wasn't all dark. Hyde had many friends and admirers such as John A. Lee and Prime Minister Coates. She also had her lifelong friend Gwen. Her mentor John Schroder helped compile her first book of poems. She corresponded with literary editor and journalist Charles Marris and young poet Gloria Rawlinson to name just a few.

In 1929, Hyde began having an affair with a very married Lawson Smith and became pregnant for a second time. Some speculate that Hyde had the affair in part to have a child and she refused the money that Smith gave her for an abortion. Hyde once again spent her pregnancy in Australia, gave birth to her son Derek Arden Challis in 1930 and smuggled him back to New Zealand. She must have found being an unwed mother difficult as Derek was placed in a nursing home and then within more than one foster home.

Her tireless work for *The Observer* and her relationship with Joe, a pharmacist who supplied her with drugs, took its toll and Hyde voluntarily checked into "The Lodge" at Auckland Mental Hospital in Avondale. It was during these three years as a patient that she turned her attention to her literary work.

After leaving "The Lodge", Hyde wished to visit England, in similar fashion to her book *The Godwits Fly*. Upon arriving in Hong Kong, however, Hyde was inspired to see more of China. She wrote about these experiences in *Dragon Rampant* after arriving in London in September 1938. London was a difficult and depressing place for Hyde and a combination of lack of money, the upcoming war, illness, depression and drugs may have caused her death on the 23 August 1939 from benezedrine poisoning.

Dragon Rampant is told in typical Robin Hyde prose: lyrical, meandering and soulful. She tells us in great detail of her departure from New Zealand and her experiences on the *S.S. Changte* heading to Hong Kong. She writes of her companion Rene Hoe, a thirteen-year-old Chinese student returning to Hong Kong from Australia. From Rene and another passenger, Mr. Lam, Hyde learns short phrases in Chinese and eats chinese cuisine with chopsticks in second class, a place where very few "Europeans" venture.

Hyde describes Thursday Island, a place where Japanese and Chinese "have forgotten to go to war", Manila and finally, Hong Kong. Hyde stays in Hong Kong for a week giving lively anecdotes about the origins of "tiger balm", the factories that she toured with Mr. Elliot, various people and events such as Chinese New Year and a Chinese funeral. It is in Hong Kong that she hears about Shanghai and decides that "...a place like this Shanghai could perhaps use an ex-journalist for a few weeks."

Hyde saw the change as a practical decision, just another route on her way to England. She thought that she would spend just a few weeks there and report back her findings to *Woman To-Day*. Although, the war was prominent in Shanghai, British nationals were allowed through Japanese port facilities. Her decision to visit Shanghai would be a momentous one. She left Hong Kong for Shanghai on 17 February, 1938.

Upon visiting Shanghai Hyde comes face to face with the realities of war between Japan and China. The battle between countries would become the beginning of the Pacific war and eventually be merged into World War Two after the bombing of Pearl Harbor.

Hyde visits many places in the wintery Chinese north and meets many people, one of which is Rewi Alley, a New Zealander who advocated for chinese peasants and would ultimately become a writer and lecturer for nuclear disarmament. Alley also worked for and wrote about the People's Republic of China. Hyde also meets James Bertram, who would make a significant impact on the remainder of her life. Facing barbaric realities and an assault by Japanese solidiers, Hyde spends close to six months in China, departing for England in July 1938.

A compelling travel story of a lone female journalist, venturing out into a war-torn country. Echoing the hope that China "will keep" and that the Japanese would be expelled from China, Hyde writes about her experiences as an author with a unique voice and perspective. Another masterpiece from one of New Zealand's most distinguished writers.

CONTENTS

Part One

ONLOOKER

Part Two

GAME

Acknowledgment

IT WOULD BE USELESS to try to thank all those friends, Chinese and foreign, who facilitated the passage of a stranger in China. Some I have written of in this book, though seldom under their own names. All did their kindly best to make me understand fragments of the mosaic, and wherever I have failed, the fault is mine.

I know they will believe I have done what I could. China is not a hard country to love, hard and long though any apprenticeship to an understanding of its complexities must be. But I haven't attempted anything so presumptuous as a book about China—only a record of things seen and heard during a few months of the Sino-Japanese war; and, for the rest, faces, voices.

There are some without whom I could not have started this Chinese journey, and those I would like to thank by name: Dr. Wen Yuan-ning, editor of *T'ien Hsia*; and his staff; Mr. H. J. Timperley; Mr. R. Alley.

In London, Mr. James Bertram (author of *Crisis in China* and *North China Front),* for the very great help and encouragement he gave me while this book was at its most inchoate stages.

And, for coming to see me every day in hospital, my friends, Billie, Ena, Pilan, and Lynne.

And two people who sent me Chinese candles, here in England.

Introduction

THE TROUBLE IS, I'M making a fuss, boring people with fuss, thinking over and re-living events instead of using any knowledge of them. In a way, I do try: but that 'I' which is capable of sustained effort is like a person in a railway smash, pinned under the still bleeding, still moving body of another self.

Within the limits of a passer-by's ignorance, I might be of some trivial use to the Chinese people I say I want to help, if I could forget them as realities, and turn them into people on paper, lively as their own war cartoons. The one sane sentence I wrote, among everything scrawled aboard the Dutch boat which landed me at Southampton in Crisis Week last September, was 'The Chinese will keep: China and the Chinese will keep.' But it's hard to adhere to that when you're humourless and westernized enough to wish to affect personal destinies.

Most English people I have met seem to agree that China will keep; even that in the military sense, China, in the long run, will prevail. They think this because there are so many Chinese, and they don't realize how a huge numerical preponderance works out as handicap rather than help. When you have a nation of over 400,000,000 to co-ordinate and prepare for a mass resistance—welding peasants, industrial workers, students, old-style Chinese, recently despised soldiers; 50,000,000 refugees swinging into a movement of exile which makes the Book of Exodus look like child's play; when your charity and overseas collections must try to blanket orphans and wounded men a thousand times as many as the most generous estimates reckon for; or when you have a few millions, instead of a few thousands, to comb for spies, traitors, and plain simpletons; your national score of numbers begins to queer its own pitch. On quality, not on quantity, China must ultimately defend herself.

Most of the pleasant and kindly people in western democratic civilizations want China to win, less for any deep-rooted antipathy for Japan, than because the ghost of the League of Nations still warns them against military aggression. They particularly dislike the bombardment of civilian populations, in which Japan has far outdone her predecessors, Mussolini and Franco. Japan never invented war from the air, she did not originate any of its chief instruments, she will not be the last or most powerful nation to make a large-scale use of it over the world we know, love, and are probably about to destroy. But again she excels herself as a copyist, and is hated for it.

'China must win in the long run,' comfortingly, a little comfortingly, say

9

the kindly people. It might be possible, by writing a story with few politics and no art, to illustrate a few pages from the agonies of the short run; the agony of the drops which show human faces for a single moment before they go over the waterfall.

England, queer and paradoxical England! I think this is still true. While another nation or system of nations, the U.S.S.R., for example, may build up an order of society which will change the whole standing of mankind for the better, at the present moment only the English-speaking races can give 'No' to this pithy little proposition:

'The dulcet harmony of earth's benignant law—
To live, we have to slaughter.'

After all, these people too, the people from whom every ranter in the world expects everything except understanding (which might sometimes be disconcerting), have been sold their own pup. They were told they were getting a democracy. What they got—you in your small corner, and I in mine—was a ruling tradition cast over a demagogue's Paradise. Then their demagogues betrayed them. Then they were informed that they had betrayed their democracy. A good many of them had died for their supposed democracy, while the majority had willingly consented to maimed lives, half-lived. Iron entered into them—the fatal iron of their own civilization— and many of them believed in their own supine treachery, accepted the contempt doled out to them. Their walk turned to a bewildered shamble . . . so bitterly tired, so spent without march, in face of the Fascist or Nazi strut. 'A people without homes will not quarrel with their rulers.' A people without the clothing of self-respect and world respect will not quarrel with their uniforms.

I think alternately of them, 'the insulted and injured' of western democracy, and of the people in China, where democracy, almost disarmed before the coming of its great test, inexplicably has not failed.

Canton, Hankow. Within a few days these cities were gone, neither achieving much of a sunset on western front pages. The point was, suddenly front pages and the demagogue's trick of front page government came a terrific crash. For something else, not having the name of a city, though it has manned a score of Chinese cities, had not gone. Its name was China.

A world-mind divided, a democracy, like the American democracy, the victim of occasionally sincere demagogues, always good-heartedly ready to listen to their sentimentality, their vague plans and ideals, may perhaps stand. But while it remains the prey of so many leeches, how can it frighten even its stupidest enemy into the idea that it has enough vitality to move? Its idealism flows in one direction, its munitions and oil supplies in another.

Can foreigners, other than those in a position to sell munitions, money, and supplies, do anything to help China, beyond the natural will to costless kindliness? Certainly, if they have any faith in China. Since I don't speak of mystical faith, but of the faith of man in man, before faith there must be understanding. And what may be found, perhaps, in this book—an effort towards understanding.

Part One

Onlooker

CHAPTER ONE

In Departure

QUITE SOON NOW, early in January 1938, I am leaving New Zealand: in spite of all the reiterated congratulations, I don't want to go.

Once I was a journalist; then, after some illness, at twenty-seven on the permanently retired list. After that I wrote novels and verses, and the surprising result was that, although I hadn't a penny of independent income, I accumulated £50.

This is a large sum in dollars Mex., more than the life-savings of many a Chinese refugee family. But at that time I had never heard of the dollar Mex.

I had spent a good many imaginary years in England. But I felt tired now, and shy, and wanted to be left alone to write worse or better verses. However, in an outburst of confidence I said: "I'm going to England," and, when I had told everybody, realized quite clearly that I was still in love with New Zealand.

After side-stepping via Panama, via Suez, via Cape Horn, and even via Norwegian grain-boat under full sail (which might have been interesting), I went into an agency which advertised the trans-Siberian route as a sideline.

These agents were pleasant, and not, I think, especially Aryan. I left their office, having paid a deposit on a trans-Siberial trip from Sydney to London, second-class. In Kobe there would be some delay, while I waited to see if U.S.S.R. would decide I hadn't the look of a person interested in sabotage, and let me through. The Russians were also a little tough about roubles, but I thought I could just do it.

After the North Australian ports, the route was by Thursday Island, Manila, Hong Kong, Kobe, Vladivostok, Moscow, Warsaw, Berlin: then London.

One day in Hong Kong, then tranship to Dollar Line for Kobe. So that left out any hope of seeing China, even the smallest tail-end of China.

All the same, what remained was enough to impress. If New Zealanders don't mind my saying so, about some things we are mostly a little green in New Zealand.

For a few weeks I was Sinbada, and enjoyed it vaguely, through being miserable, and thinking: 'Anyhow, I haven't enough money . . . or somebody will rook me in the first port . . I hope that will be at least amusing . . . will they put me in the same cabin with a woman who has three crying babies? What should I wear? I can't afford. . . . . I should have kept still and said nothing, but, of course, it wasn't to be expected I could hold my tongue for five minutes together. New Zealand, I expect liking you is at least partly similar to the fuss curried Colonels make about mangoes, but there it is; illusion or not, you work.'

A letter from Cook's, Shanghai, said: 'She travels at her own risk, and owing to the disturbed state of the Far East the firm takes absolutely no responsibility.' This induced a newspaper office to give me £20 for some travel tales (paid in advance). I stopped worrying about what to use for roubles in Russia, and bought myself some good English shoes for walking cobbled streets at Kobe. Because (stated the writer of an amiable book on Japan) everything else is fine; but nobody can deny anything about those streets.

The very good English shoes are gone now. I sometimes think that where they went, and how, and what they did, was so odd that they can't have lain quiet on their final rubbish-heap.

I was alone and out walking on New Year's Eve. For three weeks I had been staying at a place I liked, but had had to leave in the ordinary way of business. Behind it was a road, dark bushy grounds on one side, and on the other bluegums, stubble, and stream, until it came out by a grey, hard-running level of sea. One cottage, on the stream side, stood isolated. It looked old-fashioned and small, with chimneys like wooden legs, and its windows showed no light.

Only, as I stood at its gate, somebody inside the house was playing a piano—soft, thready bits of tunes, rather carefully joined, as if a child or a ghost played them. I listened until the thread slackened.

I hadn't a thing with me, except a paper bag of plums, and three of those I had eaten on the road. So I carried the rest inside, and put the bag down on the path, where the first one who came out could hardly miss it.

Then I went away, and everything stayed quietly dark and silver.

CHAPTER TWO

Coasts of Many Colours

NOT UNDERSTANDING WHY, I look up; the shadow of a great curve, like a wing, passes over my face and arms—the shadow of Sydney's harbour bridge. It is new since I came here last. By description it sounded a hellish screech of steel, but in early morning, its shadow wine-dark through the porthole, instead of being antipathetic it is like a still song, like a bow drawn without the flickering of arrow; a bow made by man, with man's traffic for its shafts.

Now Old Girl can go ashore, find herself some secluded spot, and take off those corsets. They were beginning to hurt me as much as they hurt her. I'll bet that under her ribs she's red. raw Now the West Coaster can get into his aeroplane, fly harmlessly away and break his neck. And the three silent Japanese wool-buyers, who sat in the saloon, feeling the air with the acutely sensitive tips of their antennm for insult or innuendo, where there was nothing but tobacco and stuffy smells, can stop looking like dignified, wounded ants, find some of their own friends, awake, and maybe even sing.

Old Girl had the lower berth. Her corsets hurt, but she couldn't take them off, even to sleep, because of me.

"I've been 'ad before," she said, staring between the curtains of her bunk, where she rolled groaning, first on one side, then on the other, trying to ease her excoriated flesh.

It was no use blaming the corsetiére, because she had one of those ex-figures on which the steel bones promptly work loose, and their tips prod, under the ribs, and in the small and large of the back. She must have suffered, she tossed so much in her sleep. But I don't see how it was my fault, either. I told her quite directly that I didn't want to steal the money she kept pinned under her corsets, and she wouldn't believe me, preferring to stand firm on the ground that she had been 'ad before. Her old man died of a weeping cancer, and she'd been a good wife and a mother, few if any could say it with as clean a conscience. The trouble was, she was always too good-natured and easily 'ad. She used to wipe her moustache on the back of her hand and stare like a huge crayfish, half indignant, quite helpless. I felt sorry, but fed up, because no matter how often I begged her to take off her corsets and enjoy life she never did.

The West Coaster was different. He erred on the genial side, because the drink was in him. A quiet young fellow at the other side of the table helped me to carry his weight. He was having his first holiday for years, and felt like flying to Melbourne, where he meant to whoop it up at the races. I didn't feel confident that he would live to reach Melbourne if he ever got into a 'plane, because the drink being in him, he would surely do some fool thing, and that would mean Good night, pilot; Good night, West Coaster.

He was like that all the way across the Tasman, making our table notorious; but at heart he was such a decent little West Coaster that neither of us would lend a hand in deflating him. He was the sort who'd shove a handful of notes down the back of a duchess's backless evening dress. He kept cracking at people, quite without malice, but you could see they didn't like it. On the last night, the stewards were all set to throw him out, because he came down not merely in his shirt-sleeves, but with green braces for the defilement of our eyes.

The stewards came up.

"The ladies are in evening dress, sir," contempted one.

"That's right," said the West Coaster, "I felt hot. She's got no reason for feeling hot."

He jerked his head at my black and silver gown. The quiet young fellow and I exchanged a long, deep glance, but decided to back him up, in the name of God and the revolution. We said, if we didn't object to the gentleman's costume, why should they? The stewards, contempting us also, retired, and the West Coaster made remarks about his birthday suit.

And now he can go away to Melbourne, probably like the May-fly, whose dancing ecstasy lasts but one hour—if that.

"You are going to travel in the East?" said the Chinese girl in the consular office. "Then I hope you will come back wise, but not too sad." She was a pretty girl, fragile, but with a spirited face. Chinese visas were not obtainable outside of China. The Japanese chrysanthemum was already on my passport.

Alongside a real liner, the little ship which sailed at mid-morning would have looked like a launch. Two of its second-class passengers were held up by reporters and camera-men. One was a Chinese child, Rene Hsu, returning to her family in Hong Kong after getting an elementary schooling in Australia, which had presented her with a full-blown Sydney accent. She looked about twelve, and had a piquant little face under a white hat with a hat-elastic.

As soon as the streamers broke, she dived below and was sick for two days, coming up to surface with the announcement: "Well, for forty-eight hours I was a very white Chinese." She was quite alone, and dressed western style, and all the time she alternated between being twelve years of age and approximately a Chinese five thousand.

I was the second press quarry. Apparently Australia was as widely mistaken over the abnormality of trans-Siberian journeys from New Zealand as I was.

I like storms; my stomach behaves throughout with sweetest harmony. White rough weather; the few other second-class passengers lie below, very seasick, especially the four nuns bound for Thursday Island, who at moments of lull can be heard shrieking and offering up prayers for assistance. I like having sea and little ship to myself, the waves' movement like the dip of a giant's dance. Always go with the natural things; then, however they show their teeth and snarl, they have no wish to destroy you.

At the end of a passage, the purser, the only European officer on view to Second Class, has a room containing a castle aquarium under the sea. Swimming through its grottoes and empty rooms go tiny blue and sovereign-coloured fishes. These, he says, are nothing; on reaching Manila he will stock up again with little blue chaps and angel-fish, whose rosy streamers wave from gills to tail. But so many of them die. The reason for the high price of tropical fishes, outside tropical waters, is this disheartening mortality. Poor Chinese ship-boys, who make a few cents on their enterprise, bring them on board, feed them tenderly, almost pray over the tubs where they are kept. But the fishes are patriots. Their weird eyes goggle at the foreign devils, their mouths purse up, and the gleam in their scales goes dull.

The ship is Australian-owned, with English and Australian officers; but it seems more like a Chinese ship, the crew, the ship boys, and, after Thursday Island, all the Second-Class passengers except myself being Chinese people. Both crew and boys are Cantonese, but the boys all come from a little island, the crew from the mainland, and they cannot understand one anther's dialects.

Mr. Henry Shih, the Chinese writer (the only Chinese who seems to be fully recognized as a human being), speaks Mandarin and a couple of dialects, and brushes the boys' letters for them, if they want to send letters. But much that Chinese from obscure districts say to him he cannot understand. Besides a minimum number of forty main dialects, there are variations between *hsien* and *hsien*, village and village.

I never made out whether Rene liked the Australian school or sizzled on the edge of hating it. She was less concerned over the girls who did come down and throw streamers than over the ones who said they would, and then forgot.

"They promised."

"Well, it wasn't very good weather."

"An' once they gave me the essay prize, an' one of the girls said I was cheating, but I didn't. An' some of them never came down to the boat at all, after they *said* they would. An' they used to call me Rene, Rene, Bim-Bam-Bini."

Round little face, looking up from the curious thirteen-marble game which nobody else can get out except the Mother Superior of the nuns, who, when she gets up from her nightmare bed, turns out to be a serene woman, young, with steadfast amused eyes and the colouring of a topaz brunette.

Rene flicks away on another curve.

"When I get back to Hong Kong I won't have to do a single thing. I won't even have to pick up a handkerchief if I drop it. A maid will do that."

"What's Cantonese for 'maid'?"

" 'Mu'tsai.' "

"How do you say: 'Where is the shop with the lanterns'?"

"Oh, that's silly."

"Well, what's the word for tea?"

"I think that's 'tong-cha.' I forget."

"Come along down. We want some 'tong-cha'."

There was no need to eat Chinese chow Second Class unless you wanted to, but I wanted to. After two days with Boy Number Two hanging over me like a wounded pelican, fork in hand, I learned some approximation of the use of chopsticks, though never the correct parallel, which is supposed to render any clean feeder capable of picking up single grains of rice. Rene looked in such terror of social disgrace that I made haste in getting a freak grip. It looked rather like scissors in action, but it worked.

The variety of Chinese chow makes European food look tame. It thrives on vegetables and eggs, and though there is meat, solid western dishes, such as steaks and joints, never appear. Sweet and sour pork, eggs with crimson insides, tasting like old cheese, four kinds of seaweed, served either in soups or as a vegetable, tiny mushrooms garnishing eggs, more eggs swimming like sunken moons in soup, bean curd, kidneys arrayed with sliced beans, green onion-tips, pickled shoots of bamboo—trifles out of a majestic menu. Rice is the usual groundwork: I was a one-bowl woman, though it seemed perfectly normal to eat two or three bowls of rice. (In the noodle region of the north, the rice basis largely disappears. The celebrated Eighth Route army are all noodle-eaters.)

Never left out are the little dishes of sauces and relish. You dip the tips of your chopsticks in these. A polite person, qualified as a sufficiently daring trapeze artist with the chopsticks, selects tit-bits from various dishes and passes them over to his friend's bowl of rice. Soup is taken less as a separate course than as an accompaniment. Getting weary of rice, you change to a

18

china spoon—or to the bowl alone—and drink your soup. It is courteous to be very audible about this. Turtle soup can be had at any Chinese hotel or restaurant for forty cents, or less than sixpence.

Chinese people seem unimpressed, in every way, by the turtle. If you really want a knife in your ribs, one way is to associate a Chinese man's female relatives with the turtle: I am told this has an obscene significance, but don't know what it is. Zoology, however, does play an odd part in the intricacies of epithet. No turtles in China, not too many camels in Egypt; a policeman, who is a cow in Paris, and may become a fair cow in Australia, is sexually metamorphosed and appears as a bull in America.

On the little ship, all dishes are designated by number, like the boys who carry them. You ask Boy Number Three to bring you Dish Number Four: but if you wish to be pleasant, give the number plus the full pronunciation of the dish, which Boy will then memorize. The menu cards are switched around rather than altered, and when Boy has learned a sufficient number of dishes by name, he may be shifted to First Class, where the tips are better. Tips are shared out at the end of each voyage.

In Brisbane you see the first toehold of Asia, in the pile-lifted, lattice-carved old balconied houses, rotting above their log-cumbered river; also the beginning of Asiatic influence over tea. Simple days of China, Ceylon, and Indian teas are gone. Now you have many grades, some fabulously expensive; and besides the plain teas begin the flower-teas, jasmine, chrysanthemum, rose, or ko-flower, whose dried yellow petals, floating on pale green liquid, are supposed to bring repose as well as fragrance.

Behind and above Brisbane stew the tropics, the steaming jungle with alligators, scarlet flowers and grey lakes on whose shores glide the snakes. The sugar-mills lie a few miles inland, and at Townsville and Cairns the experimental orchards where every known variety of tropical fruit is nurtured.

Down past Chinese shops and cafés to the Gardens, great thickets of bamboo arching its paths, and birds quarrelling among them. The birds quarrelled in the thickets of the bamboo, with their harsh, almost growling voices: and the birds were not our birds, and a ragged white butterfly blew out of the heart of the bamboos, but it was not our butterfly. The cranes and pheasants and melancholy little birds, dark blue, waded in a mist of grass. And when I came out at the far gate of the gardens there were poinsettias, thrown like a glassful of livid wine in my eyes.

In the afternoon Rene and I took Mr. Keep ashore. Mr. Keep first said he was a missionary bound for the Fly River, then that he was a mission carpenter about to spend three months near the Fly River. The nearer he got to the Fly River, the more he seemed to dislike it. Our first soul-brightening efforts were a failure, for Mr. Keep turned out to have a monomania against gambling, and Brisbane is nearly as full of lotteries, sweeps, and Golden Casket Union booths as Manila. He strode along, quite white and glassy-eyed, muttering. A Chinese-run ship seemed a bad place for him, as the Chinese had at least three mah-jongg schools that I knew of, perhaps more that I never knew. We cooled his feelings by taking him to Koala Point, where after motoring for miles up through the very green, crowded redgums, all dripping with rain, we were at a mountaintop café, offering tea and wetness and koala bears. One for Hong Kong again, one for the Fly River, one for England, high up over a city whose flying jewelled scarves of mist made it look like some dream town, unvisited by any man before.

Townsville and Cairns we missed, because of the hurricane weather, though a launch came out from Cairns bringing a lot of Chinese (who after crossing the plank bridge just rolled into the Third Class hold, and were terrifyingly sick for days) and an immense German.

It was funny that night. Rene and I went down to supper, as usual, and sitting in their overcoats, but without their trousers, were the immense German and two Chinese, one very young. The German and the older Chinese were unperturbed, but the younger one, uttering a sort of squawk, fled. I am afraid we plunged him into shyness for the rest of the voyage, which was bad. He was an American Chinese, going back to his home in Canton, and intending after that to do military work. He had gold teeth, and whenever he forgot his shyness one enthusiasm —skipping.

It seemed a pity the nuns had to get off at Thursday Island, for now we were used to them and liked their quiet ways, though we thought it was bad that they had to swelter in their thick black woollen robes until the very hour they reached the island (which is known to its inhabitants as 'T.I.'). Then they changed into white. But we were glad when the Australians and Thursday Islanders, who got on at Brisbane, left, because they were crabs.

On the wharf at Thursday Island, the Torres Straits policeman, who had never spoken a word since he got on the boat, suddenly unthawed, and pumped my hand like a handle. Well, he was home. I wished he could have melted before, for his occupation was a strange one. He spent much time chasing native murderers on a bicycle—no other means of locomotion proving feasible in his terrain—and as he was a very fat but determined policeman, his stories of bicycle quests should have been worth the hearing.

There are over twenty-eight different kinds and almost all known shades of human people on T.I., and one day I am going back to its stony, shallow-grassed slopes, where the big goats wear handsome leather collars round their necks, and will write an immense history about it, which will have no beginning and no ending. This is fitting, because T.I. has no clear claim to existence. There is no real Thursday Island, the baptismal name having been Thirsty Island. But something slipped at the font, and not only was Thirsty Island sunk without a trace, but a whole series of incorrect derivatives suddenly nodded their coco-nut fronds in the warm sea. Wednesday Island, Tuesday Island, and also, I think, a Saturday Island came into the world, like changelings, all due to T.I.'s misnomer.

The coral gardens, and the rival diving-firms, the blister-pearl brooches and rings, the low street sunken between its flamboyants and its almond trees; good hunting here. I secured a copy of the Torres Straits *Pilot*, which is the tiniest newspaper in the world, and apparently anti-Japanese.

But this is a queer fact. Thursday Island's Chinese and Japanese people had omitted to go to war. Everything was serene, in contrast to the tense atmosphere aboard the little ship, where the boys were still bitterly annoyed and argumentative because they had not been allowed to throw things at a Japanese ship which passed us very close off the Queensland coast.

Who eats of the *whongae* will always come back. But it may be spelt *whaugae*, or *whangi*. It is a small, darkish fruit, and though it was not in season at this time, even hearing the proverb may have helped to make T.I. stick, like a tiny postage stamp, in mind. A Thursday Island boy who took me through the old Chinese and Japanese cemetery up on the hill, to see the fireflies and hear the ghosts, explained about the *whangae*.

The ghosts talk in ancient voices from under their charactered tombs. Their bones are longing to be away, and buried in a true Asiatic soil. But whether their converse would have meant peace or war, I never heard them. The fireflies came instead, pieces of coldly silver blue, that rose out of wet ditches and danced.

So did the mosquitoes. Rene had been to the T.I. cinema, which has no roof, and from which the gigantic voices of Hollywood bawl out of a battered screen, the only covered portion of the place. When rains flood, the crowd—all classes, all colours, though otherwise the white T.I. people have small social contact with the rest—duck for cover. Rene had also discovered some Chinese friends of her mother's, and went to their house: an' the mosquitoes were simply *awful*, but they shut up all the shutters, and put little braziers close to your legs to keep the mosquitoes away. Cure sounded worse than disease.

Rene, and the ship's doctor, who was a Catholic and cared so deeply about the beautiful old cathedrals and jewelled vestments, the storied treasures of Manila; and the bare legs of laundry-boys moving in a circle round and round a great cauldron; and the little Chinese boys who looked at us with solemn eyes from his smiling father's shoulder, when we called down the companionway of the Third Class, saying in Cantonese: "Good morning, little boy!"

Always, on a small ship, no matter where you are, there is a ladder or a stair leading to the Place Below. On fine days Third Class was all right and looked vividly gay. The Chinese squatted on the tarpaulin, or used folding stools. The two Filipinos plaited the wild scarlet and gold threads of belts they were going to sell in Manila. Black shiny gowns characterized the more ancient men, the rest were mostly in coolie blue. Only when it rained this place streamed, and clinging like a small opossum to his father's neck, our little boy was swept with the rest into the sightless hold.

All this time we were getting closer to the Chinese war in more ways than one. At Manila the ship's black sides were painted with large new Union Jacks, and people chaffed the Chief Engineer, who insisted on another flag up top. But the Chief, looking heavy and solemn, said: "Anything can happen in the China Sea."

On deck in the mornings the stewardess read out daily wireless bulletins, nearly all war news. This was for the benefit of the Cantonese boys and crew. English-speaking passengers translated. The boys and crew were wrought up, and at nights the Second Class decks belonged to their white-singleted, sprawling forms. They were supposed to be sleeping on deck; actually they held pow-wows far past midnight, until sometimes the argumentative tension of their voices seemed to snap like a fused wire in my own brain. Every boy was contributing to Chinese war-funds, of which, even aboard the little ship, there were two, belonging to different political parties.

This was the version given by the Chinese writer, Mr. Henry Shih, and from its vagueness he never budged. It was perfectly obvious that he indicated the Kuomintang's war-chest and the Communist war-chest, but Mr. Shih was not given to the mention of names. He was a queer, shy man, now passionately talkative, now very suspicious and morose. He suspected not me, but Rene. I think he found Rene overwhelmingly modern.

"What is she doing, travelling all alone?" he asked sombrely. "She is only a little girl, but a little girl may do so much!"

I said he didn't suspect me; but he had me quite wrong, though not in a hostile way. He thought I was a well-informed friend, perhaps an agent, but on the Chinese side.

I told him I knew less than nothing, but he always cried: "You cannot expect me to believe that!" and went on to discuss an Australian girl who (according to his legend) had come on this same boat, gone to Canton, and died with a gun in her hands. What she would be doing dead with a gun in her hands, as the Japanese anywhere near Canton then possessed the skyways only, I could never guess; but Mr. Shih's introspection and his shy loneliness (he dined First Class, but more often than not in his small office) probably made him imaginative about the war.

It was he who first retailed to me Chiang Kai-shek's favourite quotation: 'China would rather be a broken jade than a whole tile.'

I passed that on to the Chief, who was anti-Chinese, and kept lending me kind books about Japan, written by Frank Hedges.

"Doesn't know the meaning of it," growled the Chief. "None of these chaps do. Just memorize things Come to you for the English. Know" (he leaned forward impressively), "whole provinces in China, inhabited only by tigers?"

I didn't know, and don't know. Mr. Halley, who had only been to Shanghai, and probably never seen a tiger outside a zoo or circus, didn't know either. But I am much afraid of tigers, so, when he was gone, I asked Rene about it, and she said there was once a tiger in Hong Kong, an' a policeman thought it was a big cat, because the people told him it was a big cat. So he went out with just a little gun, an' it ate *him* up. So then the people waited until they got another policeman sent out, an' the tiger ate him up. Finally they thought it must be a tiger, so they sent out a man with a big gun, an' he shot the tiger, who was carried on a striped pole all the way through Hong Kong and Kowloon. An' she knew a school where there was a teacher who hadn't any arms, an' she had to teach by pointing two sticks, because she met a bear once which ate her arms off.

"You've got to be very careful not to change money for a stranger in Hong Kong, not even the littlest bit. If a girl does that, the old woman turns into a witch, an' takes her away to the man whose servant she will be. My auntie knew a lady once, an' her sister was always quarrelling. Once she looked under the bed—it was a Chinese bed—an' she saw a saucer. Underneath the saucer there were big, live rats. If she hadn't found out they'd have eaten all her insides up."

Her mouth suddenly drooped.

"When I get home I'll have to share my sister's bed. Because my sister's home now. But my aunt's gone away. I'm glad she's gone away. She used to beat me with a stick just for any old thing. She had a temper that was *awful*."

I said: "Let's try the marble game just once," and she ran away to get it. At the doorway she stopped, and I thought she was going to say about the girls who called her Rene, Rene, Bim-Bam-Bini.

But she said: "If you eat any ice-cream you buy in the streets you'll go to

23

the lavatory for about SIX MONTHS," and pelted.

Mr. Shih's village got bombed. He was alternately depressed and fiery. He played the violin, but only in his own retreat. I listened for a while one night. Perhaps he didn't know the meaning of that either, but his music sounded otherwise to the casual ear.

Manila. . . . The Philippines have many islands, but round Manila alone many books could be written; a score, perhaps, between the crumbling thickened walls of Intramuros, where the small girls outside the great quiet cathedrals sell perfect trees of artificial lilac, artificial roses. But about Manila now there is nothing I would want to say, except that if I were a Filipino, I would forget much of more apparent and present importance, and remember Rizal, patriot youth, whose name is so curiously alive in the city where he was dead so young.

On the little ship they were taking down the canvas swimming-bath. This was the only place where we ever came in touch with the semi-mythical naiads and Neptunes from First; excepting one time, when Rene and I were invited to the Captain's bridge to see a gun popped off, startling the million-winged clouds of brown and white muttonbirds from their volcanic dot of Bird Island, which had sulphur spilling down its rock like egg on a baby giant's bib. There is no water on Bird Island, and the muttonbirds fly forty miles to a clear source. . . dam' silly as a woman in love, for there were probably nearer waters on the way, if they'd stopped to look. But birds and women, of course . . . creatures of habit.

The invitation was all very well, but to get to the bridge we had first to mount a couple of companionways and cross First's smoking-room. The moment we started through doors of the latter, a long man in assam silk leapt out from behind his newspaper, like dagger from sheath, shouting "Hey! Hey! Hey!" We gave him a look and scooted for the bridge, where we were safe and could see the muttonbirds.

"Never you mind him," I told Rene, "he's just one of the puckered sahibs." But she never took kindly to the idea of First after that.

I loved the sound of the xylophonic Chinese gong, answering sweetly the blows of a muffled stick, and chanting up and down the passages before First went to dinner. Second had cracked a bell. That is one of the small things I would call unreasonable.

In the swimming-bath, we had First on the hip, because corning back from Hong Kong the little ship always carried far more passengers Second than First. Consequently Second was awarded a longer time in the bath. As we crawled over the Equator, it was surprising how First's consciousness of time and space melted, and one by one, pink and brown globules from

24

the upper decks plopped down into the cool water. Rene had her bathing-gown, but wouldn't go in very often. I think it offended her Chinese sense of propriety to be ducked by the Chief (who was a dandy at swimming under water), and hosed gasping wet by the English Purser.

It was in the bath that I heard the cutest little criticism of New Zealand, from an American widow who had been to Gisborne, one of the North Island wool-growing towns. She dog-paddled up, her grey hairs possibly reverent, but hard as iron under her black cap.

"Say, I heard you were a Noo Zealander. Now, I've been to Noo Zealand. I don't like Noo Zealand, and I don't like the Noo Zealanders either. So now Sarly and I, we're going right on to Manila."

Delivered of this, she dog-paddled determinedly back to the steps, and disappeared, never to be seen again.

I'm afraid she had been meeting too many of our right people.

It is dark, hot dark, and the forrard hatch, which disgorged a cargo of onions at Manila, yawns open, shorn of its tarpaulin, stinking very much of onions.

Mr. P. Soo, Mr. Shih, Boys Number One and Number Two, in particular, Barber of the Seven Silences, and Rene Hsu—what am I going to do without you? To-morrow you will be dead; anyhow, you will be gone, which means almost the same thing. I will not miss you, surely, because my very good English shoes are taking me to Kobe, and I know my Lafcadio Hearn pretty well, but only a few small fragments of Chinese verse, as translated by Arthur Waley.

Perhaps I only like you because you are the first Chinese folk I ever met, and haven't snubbed me. And Rene, these last two days, has been drawing back into her shell. She is on the edge of her old and new worlds, an unhappy little girl, looking forward, looking back. She is unloading her own sentimental and bitter cargo. . . . Rene, Rene, Birn-Bam-Bini. But in spite of her small years, Rene is somehow a person of distinction. When Mr. Shih was so upset about some further bombs in Canton, she said: "My auntie says, nobody but God knows the future." It wasn't the platitude, it was her voice which rebuked us both.

Mr. P. Soo, most harmless of all our fifty-eight boys: a little English, like a little drink, having taken at a 'Frisco night-school, he is ravenous for more, and brings baffling 'Englsh' post cards from his Chinese friends to be deciphered. His favourite anxious phrase is: "If, please." One post card refers to a small loan rashly made by Mr. Soo: his friend feels incapable of paying back.

'Oh, my dear fellow, you must creep around the Governor!'

Governor in the paternal or the provincial sense?

I translated: "Your friend is now destitute, but if you are very respectful with your old father and those above you, your virtue will surely be rewarded."

'They only come to you for the English.' It never seems to dawn on the Chief that perhaps I go to them for the Chinese. Not for the Chinese language—too hard a nut to crack in a few weeks—but for other things.

Boy Number One, small grizzle-chinned man, who, when first I came aboard, and was always lost somewhere, used to follow me, giving a gentle little pull in one direction, a mild shove in another. He speaks not a word of English. Boy Number Two, fat and humorous, with the sly look of a Bishop turned jackdaw, speaks fairly well, but is a fat old man, nearly seventy, who sometimes, wearing a tussore gown with a blue dragon curled on its back, goes to sleep in the sun, hidden behind the deck-house. One day I found him like that; the waves mocking by, pale and gay as white children carrying harebells, and Boy Number Two asleep. I could have wept, the sea and the worn-out old man looked so innocent.

They are known only by numbers. Many boys, according to Mr. Hailey, don't know their own names. Both afloat and ashore, they come under the heading of domestics, and regulations governing hours of work and pay-rates do not apply to them. A boy is usually still a boy at seventy, even at eighty. He makes about ten shillings a week, less tips, but helps to support his relations. Mr. P. Soo is helping from his lowly meed to support fifteen relations; he is unmarried, and none of them is a descendant. It is probably true that even in China, few people but Mr. P. Soo would get into such a complete mess. The boys have only half a day's shore leave at Hong Kong, so they seldom get to see their families. The perpetual gambling on the ship is probably the prerogative of lone bachelors without aged parents.

The barber has two words of English: "Sit down." Lest they prove inadequate, he pushes me down. I lie quiet, while he treats every strand of hair. His walls are covered with paper portraits of gods, demons, apostles . . . all the same to me, but I christen them the Seven Silences. A queer frosted picture shows a tiger prowling in the reeds, and over him dances a white butterfly. Of course the name of that is Life. In the barber's tarnished mirror, I have just thought, 'Now my hair looks quite nice,' when he up-ends a crimson bottle, and oil, smelling of tiger-lilies, simply streams. He combs the mess until no hair writhes or revolts, then pins it back severely as Radclyffe Hall's crop. It is not the end. He seizes and flourishes an enormous razor, tilts back my head, and without sign of hesitation starts shaving. When I crawl down to dinner, stinking of the tiger-lily, Rene's brown eyes shine. "Now you look like a lady!"

The barber was usually paid spot cash, and learned a new English phrase in recompense. "Thank you, Sir-Miss." I liked it.

Sharp old rapping voice out of the past: "Will you kindly play your 'Valse des Adieux' with a little less emotion?"

CHAPTER THREE

More Lost Heads than One

SO IT ENDED in an early morning sheerness of rocks, with pine spindling off above them. You couldn't see the Hong Kong forts. A Japanese boat nosed down harbour, under the arrogant eyes of our Cantonese. Sampans and junks matched sails against jade water, sails dirty white, brown, or ripe as wine.

Rene's mother and father were outside in the first wallah-wallah (translation, I believe, 'noisy-noisy'; nature, a small steam-launch). She looked dancingly happy. She asked me if I would like to come and meet them, but I guessed they would rather have no foreign streak in her first day home, and said no. We shook hands, and she gave me her school-badge.

Ricksha-pullers shivered and streamed, bare-legged beneath their wide rain-capes of straw. Newsboys and newsgirls, beggars and shoeshines, concentrated on Victoria's waterfront road, the Bund. Wicker crab-pots and lobster-pots, hanging over the breakwater, kept their scratchy fruit in sea water until a sale was made. This custom seemed familiar. It is what the Italian fishermen do at Island Bay in Wellington.

They call the capital city of Hong Kong island Victoria. For its size, I doubt if any other British city goes in for Victorian and post-Victorian English Royalties on a more comprehensive scale, all together in a family party on the one visible square of grass. And past them, streaming by, proceeded what looked like at least a million very wet Chinamen.

I went to the shipping-office, and inquired about the boat for Kobe. It was overdue. Owing to circumstances beyond the firm's control, it wouldn't reach Hong Kong this day, possibly not the next day.

After that, I walked slowly along, beginning to be in a temper. I had a headache, and my arm, inoculated and vaccinated for cholera, typhoid, and smallpox in the last two days, was up in a hard painful bulge the size of a goose-egg. I saw a jade frog and a Han dynasty bronze mirror for sale, women in shiny black trousers, some with tiny smear-faced babies clinging to their necks (these were refugees, beggars, or both), and western-dressed indifferent Chinese who passed without hurry, and Sikh police, turbanned and bearded, like very large, vain, gorgeous cats.

I didn't know what to do, and all the time my arm was hurting. Bed for the night seemed obvious: but the hotels were all selling on a rising market, owing to the influx of rich as well as destitute refugees.

The rich ones, in their way, were helping Hong Kong along with its 1938 war boom. Two business propositions that flourished most rapidly in Hong Kong, after the fall of Shanghai, were small printing works and chiropodists' shops; the former because the refugees and the politicians wanted to print as much as they could about the Japanese, and the latter, seemingly, because the Shanghai foot is a delicate foot.

Presently I was standing in front of the desk of a Chinese hotel, explaining to a stout Chinese who spoke perfect English that I hadn't yet changed any money into dollars Mex. He was a man of fifty or so, and wore, besides his cream cloth gown, a little black tasselled cap on his head. When he smiled, he had several chins to laugh with him.

On my mentioning money, he said: "You had better give your money to me. I will keep what you don't want to change, and change the rest for you myself. Other people might *sook* you."

In a state of mesmeric trance, I handed over my money, thinking" 'Well, I suppose it's good-bye to all that.' My arm was hurting and I didn't know what to do next, so nothing mattered much.

However, I wronged my host in the tasselled cap. His chins laughed at me when they felt so disposed; but he never did, at any time, *sook* me. On the contrary, he gave me a jade ring and some king mandarins.

Morning; wandering about in the rain, among hundreds of Luise Rainer types, black draped over their patient heads.

'Hao! Hao!' or alternatively 'Wei!' from the ricksha boys, squatting heedless of puddles between their dropped shafts. *Hao* and *Wei* both mean 'Missie come for a ride,' and if you are finally positive you won't, the correct retort is "*Pu yao*"—"No wanchee."

"*Cumsha! Camsha!*" sing-song the black-draped women, the pathetically thin old man whose claw stretches out between two crutches, the small irascible elfin girls, on whose tight black pigtails a twist of pink wool is tied, for ornament and luck.

Cumsha means 'tip.' The street *cumshas* picked up the word from hotel employees and domestics generally. None of the street *cumshas*, old or infantile, will ever be persuaded that the tip principle should not apply to them. But they are good-humoured: and if you really want to be left in peace, you pat your handbag or pocket, according to sex, saying curtly: "*Mei-yu, Mei-yu-la!*" This means you haven't got anything left; with remarkable celerity and still good-humoured grins, the *cumshas* fade away.

The little *shusans* are much fiercer, a tribe on their own account, torn by personal wars, but instantly united in face of the foreigner. They have learned a much worse word than *curnsha:* it is a frightening word, and they keep on yelling it at the tops of their voices.

"Dollar! Dollar! Dollar!"

Cornered by these, my policy was always to yell (but much softlier): "Police! Police! Police!" In the end (an interested crowd looking on, and invariably taking sides with the infant Mussolinis), we usually struck a bargain at ten cents per shoe. The correct rate was two cents for both shoes, but to understand the discrepancy, you must first meet the *shusans*. *Shusan* is what they call their art; they mean, of course, shoeshine. To do them justice, they polish. I never once succeeded, though, in having my shoes polished by one *shusan* alone. There was invariably a determined imp clinging to either leg, not to be removed without physical violence, which might have ended in a riot.

The origin of the Hong Kong *shusans* is quaint. A few years ago, a good-hearted British official decided that half a dozen youngsters who used to pester him were too active and promising for the shiftless life of the streets. So he bought some boot-polishing sets, lined up his army, and issued instructions. Off they pelted, and, contrary to the pessimistic beliefs of most philanthropists, they set a shoe-shining example to the whole of Hong Kong. Like Professor Picard, Tarzan, the Ely Culbertsons, and Shirley Temple, once accepted they went over big . . . so big that they were patronized not merely by the foreigners, but by the Chinese who, when they see a *cumsha* on his way, have a sublime trick of contemplating imaginary navels, and sail past in trance,

But these *shusan* kids were the fashion, and the Chinese came and had their toe-caps shone; they seldom bother about the heels, so maybe they get it at a cut rate. The only trouble was, the success killed itself. At the end of a month, a somewhat distracted Inspector was pointing out to a still good-humoured but also distracted patron of *shusan* that where he had dispensed half a dozen sets, Hong Kong now possessed a minimum of five hundred intensely active *shusans*, average age seven, and already engaged in desperate tong warfare.

The theory is that if you give a *cumsha* man or *shusan* ten cents, you have given him a full day's bodily upkeep. Newspaper-selling in Hong Kong is another racket, for which I blame the British newspaper proprietors, who have a way of bringing out several editions of a day's paper. If nothing exciting has been brought home by their correspondents, then they can always turn from the boneless cupboard to Domei if the Japanese official news service, because something intensely exciting is also happening, according to Dornei ... if Chiang Kai-shek hasn't been critically wounded, or peace declared, another assassin has once again bumped off 'Young Marshal' Chang, whom, for some reason, Domei seems to dislike.

Coming back to the racket, the distribution of newspapers is where art is employed. Sometimes a sad-eyed, black-trousered woman with a grubby baby clinging to her neck, sometimes a cross, wet little fairy of a girl, sometimes a particularly weak and failing old Chinese man waves his paper under your nose. You buy. You buy again. You begin to get wild. You return to your hotel, noting that the insides of the spittoons placed against the lifts have turned yellower than when you saw them last. You put your hands to head or stomach (whichever is your more sensitive centre), slam-a door behind you, and sit, drumming your heels, on the edge of the bed.

Down below, a long way below, but not so far that sound and steam cannot drift up, Chinese life goes on, indifferent. Drizzle by day, drums and fire-crackers by night. You are the foreigner. Nobody loves you. When you cross to the mirror, staring bitterly at the pale face among the dishevelled Medusa locks, you can see no sound reason, not even a pretext, why anybody ever should. So you practise a few foreign-devil faces . . . and laugh: because, no matter how wild your first few days in this strangeness of language and custom may make you, it is quite impossible to dislike the cross, wet fairies, the infant Mussolinis, the sadly smiling Luise Rainers, and the old men who pat their hands over their empty bellies, groaning "No chow!"

There were a few English people staying in the hotel: but to run into one meant only that he visibly blighted like the sensitive plant, or buttoned himself up to the chin, like a very important secret service document which might be stolen unless precautions were taken. Dammit! I knew I couldn't speak Chinese. I now know that I can't speak English either.

The big, almost empty dining-room was planned foreign-style, to attract Europeans, but what it did was to drive away all the Chinese, who occupied the greater number of the bedrooms, but before breakfast crept stealthily out, and found restaurants flanked with pink, yellow, and blue dragons. The hotel's European food was excellent . . . and, of course, there was always far too much of it. It is true enough to say of China that when you eat, if you eat, you frequently eat either too little or too much. But the Chinese have made a discipline of the first, and an art of the second.

And over the radio clipped an enormous British voice:

"If you have attended properly to these lectures, you will now know what to do with an incendiary bomb when it alights on a corner of your roof."

Quite!

It was old Mr. Loo—he of the cream gown and tasselled black cap—who broke my forlorn spell. I was standing by a window, looking out, with nothing to see but grey, and black or blue-trousered people, Chinese women and men, scurrying like wet ants through universal wetness. I was fed up,

I said; some such bored nursery remark. Mr. Loo waddled over and put a hand on my shoulder.

"Everything must be *Chinese*, eh?"

His little eyes were twinkling, I stared at him: in a flash the whole absurdity of wanting a foreign nation to be a sort of giant charade, a fancy-dress entertainment for the benefit of foreigners, came and went behind those perspicacious eyes. I was ashamed, and yet happy: I hadn't really started off like that. . . Well, it was just that I felt lost, you see. I started to laugh, we both laughed. In the evening Mr. Loo gave me the jade ring, and sent me up a basket of king mandarins.

So I began to look for Hong Kong, beginning at sources ranging from a daily newspaper to its editor, a High British Official Winkle, a Chinese banker, a doctor, an Inspector of Factories; and Choomai Smerabanya.

The daily newspaper sounds obvious, like Edgar Allen Poe's letter on the mantelpiece. But a number of things happened on one day's recording.

In Shanghai, an unfortunate and courageous Chinese lady was having a difficult time, because her husband, a publisher, had quite lost his head.

Leaving that circumstance for the present, there was the case of the little *mu'tsai* who was not a *mu'tsai* because her mistress had given her one dollar.

Then there was the rather comic affair of the young English couple, their Cook-Boy, Amah, Boy Number One (all trusted servants), and 50,000 heroin pills.

There was the straight-out fact that a fleet of Chinese junks had been burned in British waters. Nothing much to be explored or unravelled there: the Japanese simply did burn Chinese junks . . . *pour encourager les autres* . . . and the fishermen, not being Channel swimmers, simply drowned, and the waters were British. But this, most simply of all, made no difference and gave no protection.

In the streets, overnight, forty people had been picked up dead of malignant smallpox, and one old refugee woman was on trial. Her first boy died of the smallpox, and then the second boy caught it, and there was the corpse, mutely demanding a coffin, and as she had no money to provide one, but was bewildered and sad, thinking about her fine sons and the good life they had had in Shanghai, she broke the law entirely. First wrapping the dead boy's body in paper, she carded it out into the street, and put it carefully away in a rubbish receptacle. . . . But the police and judges, and other people in a position to count on coffins when their time came, had no sense of irony; and there they had her in Court, rubbing her weak eyes and puckered-up face with her hands. And who was to nurse the other boy?

For if you think there were comfortable beds for these refugee people, or food, or kennels large enough for a dog to creep into, you are mistaken. But I would like to say this for the old lady; she must have been very crazy in the head when she put her boy's body into the rubbish receptacle; it was not to be expected that she could see the threatening jest she was making, any more than the police or judges saw it. Chinese people, as a rule, even if they have little else in their lives, are inclined to be particular about their coffins, which are large and very solid, with great scroll-top lids. The rich have them lacquered, and fine threads of gold trace leaf and flower along the glossy black.

The last thing in the day's paper was a telegram from New Zealand, reporting the death of Sir Truby King, who built up the Plunket and Karitane systems of infant welfare. I don't know why this should have appealed to me as Chinese news, unless it was because of another woman from Shanghai, and the waxen scrap, eyelids shut and sunken, that lay bundled up beside her in the gutter.

She kept beating her head on the pavement, wailing that eternal "*Aiyah! Aiyah!*" Somebody had printed a notice in large pencilled letters, saying she was a widow from Shanghai and destitute. The baby looked as if it had just been born, but also as if it had just died. It certainly looked very dead to me.

"Is it dead?" I asked the Sikh policeman, whose turban carried the green and yellow of a famous regiment. He shook his head, smiling faintly beneath his enormous moustache. The Sikhs are almighty handsome, nobody can deny it, but they also have the opulent vanity of cats, and, anyhow, a beard and moustache give a man an unfair advantage.

Choomai Smerabanya was a Siamese girl, stopping the night at the hotel, and sailing next day for Manila, where she was to enter a University. In Manila, poor students have to wear black, while the others wear colours of violets and grapes, mixed posies, and orchids. Choomai was plain, and plainly dressed, but she wouldn't be in black; she told me she came from the palace in Siam, and talked a lot about 'our little King.'

That was at dinner, when we moved over and shared a table in the vast oasis of chair-legs. She seemed rather tickled at being mistaken for a Chinese girl.

"But I'm not nearly as white as a Chinese," she said, in her slow, heavy, slightly guttural voice.

Afterwards we went to a cinema. Siamese people like Mickey Mouse. Choomai kept clapping her hands, exclaiming: "Oh, Mick-ee! Oh, isn't he sill-ee!"

They had good theatres in Bangkok, she said, much better than this. (The

Hong Kong theatre was a dilapidated old plaster box.) And she thought the new films got to Siam quicker than to Hong Kong. Unluckily, I had never read a good book about Siam, but I remembered a screen travelogue showing the traditional dances of Siamese princesses, and complimented Choomai on that. Choomai nearly had a fit. The upshot is this. If you see a screen travelogue of Siam, and young women with horned head-dresses and serpentine arms come out and wreathe a little, and if you accept them as Siamese princesses performing the traditional royal dances, you are doing it with your eyes wide open and your common sense tight shut.

On the way home Choomai was quietly, delicately wild, because I stopped the rickshas to find out about the bundles, and we had to walk home in the rain. The bundles were rolled up in doorways, alleys, crossings—any dark, secluded place where cars didn't pass—and at first I thought they were a Hong Kong way of putting out rubbish. But then I saw a man's head sticking out at the top of one long bundle.

That seemed likely to be a dream, because it was raining so hard, and we had passed so many bundles. But where we stopped there was a whole row of them, and a sulky little red-eyed brazier at one end of the row. The life of all, sleeping and waking, seemed to concentrate on the brazier. They were all lying so that their faces turned towards its red flameless smoulder, whose thin battle with the air made no difference to the rain and the extreme cold. They were man, woman, and child, some rolled in a strip of canvas or sacking, some naked except for blue cotton rags, and in sleep even their arms had fallen, like spokes of a smashed wheel, towards the brazier. I tried to count at first, but soon got sick of that, because in that cross-section of streets alone there were hundreds, sprawled down just as weariness had dumped them.

This was about the end of January. I remember, in Manila, the doctor who pumped my arm full of vaccines mentioned that out of the last 105 cases of smallpox reported in Hong Kong, 78 were fatal: the Hong Kong figures before the end of March were 1385 dead, with hundreds more blinded and scarred for life. I was in Canton then, and the League of Nation doctors, sent out under the International Red Cross to work with the Chinese Red Cross, had about finished their anti-epidemic precautions and drill, for which they co-opted not only students but village girls, and had also hired a sampan and poled up and down the Pearl River, vaccinating the sampan people and their swarms of children. Canton had almost every other kind of trouble, but it didn't have any epidemic.

Anyhow there were the bundles, in a short restive peace, and when the old men woke up, automatically their hands went to their bellies and they said, blinking: "No chow." Then they stretched out fingers skinny and brown as dried seaweed. The women and children did not speak. They watched the brazier, and the red light shone in the eyeballs of the lucky ones lying nearest.

Choomai forgave me for getting her velvety paws wet, and we exchanged coins before she sailed. . . . Siamese copper hole-money for my last New Zealand pennies. I thought she would be happy in Manila.

It doesn't do to be over sorry for the Chinese refugees and destitute who have to sleep out; it is probably true that when the heat comes, thousands would prefer sleeping out rather than stifling in the huge yellow plaster-and-lathe tenements. High British Official Winkle, an authority of importance, on whom I called, said that even in winter and rain they preferred to sleep out.

They can be nearer to the opium divans, he said. He was a trifle on the wry side, talking of anything Chinese, though he had a beautiful profile, and was not, in any case, so near in spirit to Mr. Hailey as the newspaper editor, who said frankly that he hated the Chinese, and had got dysentery. I thought a psycho-analyst might have found that he hated his dysentery, and had got the Chinese, and didn't know what to do with them. The Inspector and the doctor were of the opposition party. They liked the Chinese. The Inspector was all for the Chinese, but the doctor played too much tennis to go as far as that.

There is one winter street-sleepers' shelter in Hong Kong, holding several hundreds of old people. But the Chinese don't patronize it much, though they get a mattress, a couple of bags, *congee* (hot rice water), and segregation of the sexes. It's the divans, said H.B.O.W.

That brings us back to the heroin affair in the newspaper.. . English couple, faithful servants, 50,000 pills. The trouble arose because the English couple enjoyed week-ending. So soon as they were gone the faithful servants squatted down in the kitchen, and started to manufacture heroin pills, sending them off in plain sealed envelopes to small distributors and addicts. They were making the pills with a Japanese pill machine.

"Undoubtedly," said H.B.O.W., "Japanese and Korean peddlers have introduced the traffic here as in North China."

Keeping track of drug-peddlers (who often sell their goods as 'patent medicines') is an appalling task. Hong Kong knows exactly how many door-to-door hawkers' licences are issued in a year: Hong Kong also knows that for every licensed hawker there are at least ten unlicensed suavities, of both sexes, on the prowl.

Heroin, at ten cents a shot, is a little cheaper than Hong Kong opium, though that is a cheap enough drug, and likely to be, unless some submarine disturbance affects the proximity of the dreamy old Portuguese colony, Macao, whose principal industries are the manufacture of fireworks and opium. For the superiority of heroin to opium, as a physical and mental wrecker of human kind, anyone interested may refer to the notes of Russell Pasha, who after cleaning up the heroin traffic in Egypt wrote a book called *The Tenth Plague of Egypt*. Of opium divans, ninety are officially known to the police: add another naught, and you have the number usually estimated.

The opium divan is easily detected by its characteristic odour, but with heroin the chase is harder. Heroin is both injected and smoked, a special pipe having been devised; and during the last month I spent in Hong Kong not a day passed without at least one prosecution for smoking or distribution of the drug.

Sometimes (said a Hong Kong doctor) opium does very little harm to the Chinese addict who is temperate, and in rare cases it may accomplish a specific good. He was talking about the ricksha boys, among whom the percentage of pulmonary tuberculosis is high; (average life between the shafts estimated at under ten years).

"Opium stops the coughing," said the doctor, "which, in turn, stops the hmtriorrhage. Naturally that prolongs life."

In spite of the picturesque straw rain-capes and great peaked hats splashed with blue or gilded characters, sweating between the shafts and spending his spare hours on the damp pavements is hardly a healthy trade for the ricksha boy. He does not own his ricksha, and gets a small fraction of the ten cents you pay him after an easy run round the block. Behind him, untroubled and inactive and, like all sensible organizations, well in out of the rain, are the ricksha hongs, from whom he hires his painted chariot, and to whom he turns over a very substantial percentage of his day's takings.

I don't know whether in Hong Kong he has a private corner and life of his own; but in Canton, a party of students who had made investigations into ricksha conditions told me of long, bare sheds, in which the tired ricksha-puller is entitled, not to a bed of his own, but to a half-time bed. When he can pull no more, he goes to the shed, shakes his mate awake, and tumbles in, while the second man makes himself ready for more ten-cent toil and trouble. The ricksha-puller is not very often a married man. He cannot afford to marry.

Hong Kong's few surviving chair-bearers are in an odd, in-between position. Their occupation has never been legally abolished or interfered with, except that their rates of pay are fixed. They have stands of their own, and, like the ricksha coolies, squat good-humouredly beside their brightly painted wicker chairs with the tasselled canopies, waiting to catch a likely prospect's eye. Their fares are double the cost of a ricksha, and each chair-boy is paid: you can have two boys, or four, according to your sense of the grandiose. But whether because of the cost, or for some humanitarian motive, European Hong Kong frowns upon the use of the sedan chair; the peaked blue hats, the hopelessly merry faces, may wait for hours before anyone signs for the long bamboo poles on which the chair is elevated. Of course, for a wedding the red chair is indispensable, and funerals also can hardly be conducted without the use of a few chairs. But even in this prolific Chinese world, where in order to assure a sufficient number of babies there must always be a reasonable number of weddings, weddings and funerals are not enough to fill the chair-boy's rice-bowl.

I took a chair one wet night, and promptly wished I hadn't, for the dusk had deceived me: the black-trousered, black-coated, crop-haired figure which bobbed its head determinedly up and down between the front poles was not the figure of a man. It was a woman.

Foreigners may as well be advised that calling 'Put me down, put me down!' however shrilly, once you are inserted in ricksha or chair, is a waste of breath. Probably the bearer decides that you want to do him out of his ten cents, and is determined, however you shriek about it, to land you somewhere which can be reckoned as ten cents' worth. We jogged up a short, steep street, and then the chair bumped down. I got out, scarlet in the face. The chair-boy and chair-woman, who were perspiring freely in spite of the rain, entered into a brisk conversation with a swarthy Chinese.

"They want to know where you would like to go," he said civilly.

I said: "I've gone quite far enough now," and paid them off. When they had disappeared I asked the swarthy man a question or two about chair-boys, but he laughed.

"You don't take, then they starve," he said, and vanished within his house.

I walked back, past windows filled with Peiping lampshades and rolling, cavorting little Chinese horses of every colour, into the basin where from each balcony of the huge yellow tenement houses Chinese washing flapped sausage arms and legs, and between the washing peeped out the small, dark gold fruits of dwarf mandarin trees, placed in tubs, in preparation for the beginning of Chinese New Year, whose day falls this year on 18 February. Those who could not achieve a whole tree sported a branch.

In some streets camphor blew a sweet refreshing gale. Here worked the boy carvers, chipping out quite remarkable designs of pagodas, junks, trees, and fantastic gowned old men, on chests which were the beds of the two or three told off to serve as watch-boys in each small narrow factory; chests which in polished state would be much admired in their final European or American homes. Camphor is a health trade (said the Inspector). The boys in the business don't have a bad time in Hong Kong; though that mayn't be the case in other places.

'Emile Zola,' I thought, 'would have made a lot of all this'; a preparatory course of Emile Zola would be good for Hong Kong. Charles Dickens would have wept too much.

An enormous rainbow came and wrapped itself round the Peak hills and small motherless islands of Hong Kong's harbour, and I thought how Charles Dickens would have wept, like a happy mock-turtle, over the case of the *mu'tsai* who was not a *mu'tsai* because her mistrees could prove she had given her one dollar.

Mu'tsai in Hong Kong are registered, though no new registrations are allowed: in Shanghai they are unregistered, and known as *pei nu*. In either case, the traffic and the principle are the same. They are girls (sometimes very young children) who have been sold, kidnapped, mortgaged, or 'adopted,' and whose destiny is chattel-slavery, unpaid.

By far the greater number of Hong Kong *mu'tsai* are domestic servants: but *mu'tsai* and *pei nu* may also be trained as dramatic actresses or sing-song girls, mortgaged out to brothels for a period of years (sometimes paying off a debt on their parents' patch of farm), or used as rented servants, whose wages are returned to their owner. In Shanghai, the latter practice was common enough, One of the amahs, at a house where I stayed was *pei nu*, and had been acquired, with practical judgment and common sense, from a market which, after all, is not very different from the western domestic service employment agencies.

But in the west is freedom, however bare, chill, and dreary a freedom. Several years ago the Chinese Government decided that the benefits of the *mu'tsai* and *pei nu* system were too dubious to balance the disadvantages, and broadcast a statement, offering help and shelter to any girl chattels who chose to run away from their owners. Since then, thousands in Shanghai have drifted in to various welfare societies. But in Hong Kong the old system holds out, regulated by registration, and some kind of judicial attention to the complaints of ill-treated *mu'tsai.*

With the great swing of refugees from Canton and Shanghai came thousands of strangers—and with them, thousands of girl-children who were servants, not daughters of the house. Many of these orphans of the storm were left unregistered. The little girl of the one-dollar case had been beaten with a stick, and, greatly daring, had run away full tilt into the arms of the nearest policeman.

She was unregistered: but her mistress proved to the satisfaction of the Court that really she ought to have been beaten with a stick, and besides that, she had not been beaten hard. And, transcending all this, she was not a *mu'tsai*, but a paid servant, because she had certainly possessed one dollar. The little girl said it was a present, and the old lady swore it was pay. Eventually the old lady won, and they trotted out of the Court together, both scolding. . . .

Sometimes, perhaps not infrequently, there are well-treated *mu'tsai* and *pei nu*. Mistresses have been known to provide them with dowries of 100 dollars upon marriage. (There is something very terrible about the idea of spinsterhood to Chinese folk, and the *mu'tsai* and *pei nu* are allowed to marry, like other people.) A number of old ladies make a business of bringing up their 'adopted' daughters as prospective daughters-in-law; but their eyes are too sharp and their scolding old tongues too severe.

And at Chinese New Year (which has the one drawback of being the season when debtors are expected to pay back their debts) *mu'tsai* may be given presents, even a money present. But if it is a money present, it is usually taken back when the trees with the dark gold fruit are put away. Mistress will look after it.

Chinese New Year, 1938, was different from all other Chinese New Years. It is the custom to paste on each side of the door, no matter how lowly, red paper posters with proverbs of neighbourly goodwill. This year the red posters went up, but on each was a patriotic poem, calling on townspeople and villagers for nation-wide resistance against the Japanese. It was after New Year that the Chinese forces began that stiff spell of resistance and fighting back, which culminated in the Chinese victory of Taierhchwang, the first time the armies of Nippon have been conclusively defeated in open field.

Canton and Hankow and Hsuchowfu were great cities, and since they have fallen, Canton and Hankow and Hsuchowfu may be good names to the Japanese. Taierhchwang was only a little place of about seven thousand mud houses, a fantastic castle to support the weight of two great onslaughts. But in spite of all that has happened, Taierhchwang is not a good name to the Japanese.

The sun came out. It is pleasant to walk through leaves, to startle a harshly argumentative bluejay, and after him, in full sail, a butterfly with a green cravat, green and black pin-stripe trousers: Oxford, of course. Tiger and butterfly. . . .

The design of the colony is quite easy: across the harbour, reached by a ferry, are Kowloon and the New Territories. One of the red islets dotting that puckered jade (I never knew a water like Hong Kong's, that could change so marvelously from hyacinth to jade) harbours Hong Kong's Nudist Colony. I know there is a Nudist Colony, having seen the address in a directory, but really the wet's too depressing for one to bother about nudes . . . unless one could take them indoors, in settings of charm and luxury, like one original Chinese millionaire of this city, who had a hobby of building magnificent houses.

The fact is well known that the average Chinese, even if an amateur of the pleasures, thinks white people very ugly, and that in Shanghai the ordinary man has a term meaning 'red hair, big noses, blue eyes.'

But in Hong Kong, which is not truly China (though Chinese still nominally 'own' fifteen-sixteenths of the soil), whether Harlow or another started it, there is a little weakness for platinum blondes. And should you be invited to the celebrated cocktail parties of the millionaire with the magnificent houses, you may wander to an upstairs apartment where you will meet the platinum blondes, all beautiful creatures, all nudes. Of course they're in nothing so crude as the flesh; a gifted artist designed them for walls and ceiling.

The Peak, which backs Victoria city, fosters the arched yellow and white taipan style houses of well-to-do Europeans and Chinese. And once you have climbed through veil after veil of rent blue air, the clearest on earth unless one of the frequent white fogs happens to have dropped down on it, you look to east and west, seeing the island's spaces of sharp hilly green broken only by the young pines the British authorities are bringing on, and wonder why on earth the cramped, stifling basin of the tenement and industrial area doesn't smash criticism by spreading out.

But unfortunately there's a story behind that. A fine road curves around the island, a car can take you past little pleasuring bays where the great rosy mouths of the hibiscus are a wonder. When the first British garrison settled at Stanley (one of the best of these bay sites), Her Majesty's soldiers died in their tracks: bitterness arose, the Chinese being accused of poisoning the wells. Like so many old-time accusations against the Chinese, it had not one atom of truth. Stanley, and three-quarters of the swimming, sparkling Hong Kong green that tempts you, are breeding-grounds of the malarial mosquito, and so far nothing has driven out malaria and dysentery from those areas.

There has been a certain amount of expansion: Repulse Bay is a pleasure resort, its hotel a fine one, its Lido waters a shallow jade cup where a cosmopolis of sun-bathers, Chinese and European, stretches itself out on Sundays. But more Chinese homes than foreign ones are built at Repulse Bay; you would be charmed by the little pots, flowering dark crimson and pink along the walls behind which are courtyards. Among weeds and slender grass you pick up fragments of tiles, indigo and green, and finger the glaze. Even the shards are beautiful.

The Chinese own Hong Kong, but as far as building and industrial sites are concerned, much of this they rented out on leases of from seventy-five to nine hundred years, and, not inconveniently, at a tiny fraction of the present value.

There are not only the British. After the Spanish-American war had caused enough trouble in the Philippines, a Dominican order came here and acquired land dirt cheap: the Spanish Friars, as they are called, to-day are rich indeed.

Then began the infinitely long (though carefully recorded) processes of subletting, which have ended in the tenement system. There are small tenement factories, but the chief use of the tall yellow buildings (mainly built of plaster-and-lathe) is residential. Each tenement has a 20-foot frontage, and is 50 feet deep, and the average allowance is for 2000 bed-spaces. But since the war, the influx of refugees has made bed-spaces harder to get, and in some of those buildings, 4000 Chinese people huddle where space was planned for half. The technical owner or lessee of the tenement properties never comes near them, having no need to poke his nose into their darkness or light. By a simpler system, each floor has its Number One Tenant, whose job is to see that the other tenants pay up. The more he can crowd into a floor, the more his 'squeeze.'

There has been no very serious fire in Hong Kong for several years (The last one was responsible for several hundred deaths.) I have been over the modern fire station, and smart, shining and well-equipped it is, with Chinese fire-fighters under perfect drill. Moreover, even with primitive fire-fighting appliances, I saw later that Chinese brigades can be very effective. But if a real fire caught on in the basin . . . or a few of the incendiary bombs mentioned by the voice on the radio really had effect . . that yellow huddle of high walls, washing on balconies, mandarin trees, and people would be a hard proposition for the brigades.

Chinese people, including the very poor, the illiterate, and those who have something to lose by it, will co-operate with Europeans in improving conditions, if they understand why it is a good thing to do so. The last Hong Kong plague epidemic (in '27, I think) cost 4000 lives, mostly Chinese. The British then decided to stop epidemics of plague, and the Inspector told me that since '27 there has hardly been a plague death. Between the plaster walls of many dwellings and small industrial premises was space, a happy hunting-ground for the plague-bearing rat.

Hong Kong became plague-rat-minded. The system was simple and drastic. Walls were pulled down, rat nests destroyed. It is still in practice whenever necessary, and a check is kept by means of little green tins on Lamp-posts. If you open one of these, you will find several drowned rats, steeped in disinfectant. The bins are numbered, so that their area of houses can be checked. From the bins the rats go to the mortuary, and there a Chinese, who has become an expert on the subject, dissects hundreds in the course of a day; at least a million Hong Kong rats are dissected every year. He was not, by original calling, a doctor, but a butcher, and he is one of the most useful citizens in Hong Kong. Naturally, many an ancient tenant wails bitterly at the demolishing of rat-infested walls (as would happen if the same thing were tried in Old Kent Road or Chelsea). But the Chinese have become active participants in the game, which is the more interesting as they never kill mice.

Rene told me Chinese people keep cats, but keep them inside and restrain their street-wandering dispositions; otherwise they would be stolen. I don't know about that, but there are bird-shops, an indubitable passion for very large birds in ornamental cages, occasionally a serene Chinese wandering about with bird-cage and pet in hand. The only dogs I have seen are the handsome muzzled beauties of the Peak, who all look as if they came from Heaven for show-pens, and have no Chinese connections beyond a vague, dreamy-eyed old Boy to lead their lordships about.

Rene also told me about the thick walls whose tops are a mass of broken glass and spikes. You come on these climbing the Peak. A silent Sikh or Chinese gate-boy materializes out of the fountain-cool green behind, looks at you with the aloofness of the widely staring hibiscus, and squats down again, smiling to himself. Far below, you can see into a private swimming-bath whose floor of crushed turquoise mosaic shines up very clear through its pale waters.

Private . . . most beauty in Hong Kong is private, except life itself, and the passing angels of sea and sky, seen when the sun comes back. The gate-boy, glass and spikes are a legitimate defence against Rene's burglars, who *like* burgling. These gentlemen (the professionals, not the ruffian strays) are a caste.

An' even if you give them money to go away, they come back late at night with their cane-ladders, an' steal just the same. *They'd rather steal!* (Rene's voice squeaked like an excited slate-pencil.) I asked: "What about the police?" But Rene said spaciously: "*Oh, the police!*" and swept them out of the question. Apparently the correct technique, when you see a burglar with his eye on your house, is to give him a money-present, with many polite apologies and warnings, murmuring something about the superior eminence of the house next door. Rene was quite sure these burglars did not kill. That would be like asking a noted 'cellist to oblige with a mouth-organ solo.

I asked the Inspector about this, and he laughed, but said it was fairly true. A good deal of what Rene told me was founded on fact. It was true, for instance, about the tiger who ate the policeman; that was in 1913, when two Chinese officers, beautiful but dumb, successively went out to shoot the tiger with a revolver, and not unnaturally ended 'with a smile on the face of the tiger.' A few tigers, I heard, are found still in the New Territories, but Kowloon has a tiger-free certificate. If you want tigers, you must move on to Szechuan. Though Hong Kong is the home of the Very Lucky Tiger, and of that mysterious product, 'Tiger Balm.'

'Tiger Balm' is one instance of how fortunes are made in China, and is simple as the Woolworth millions, when you know how. The Haw Par brothers, who own the secret recipe, were neither very rich nor highly educated men when they started to make ten-cent pots and tins of a greenish salve, not unlike vaseline, which was sold as 'Tiger Bairn.'

The balm can be swallowed, or rubbed on the painful place, and the Chinese say, quite simply, that it will cure anything. One big factory was in Canton.

The Haw Par brothers, though multi-millionaires, are reckoned less rich than other Hong Kong millionaires, such as Sir Robert Ho Tung, whose fortune is estimated at anywhere between thirty and three hundred millions of dollars Hong Kong. (He is a great philanthropist, and in addition owns the charming little blue and green pagoda which looks at me, its pattern like a lapping-over of butterflies' wings, when I pass the hibiscus regiments on one Peak road.) Nevertheless, there is the Haw Par Mansion, opened with ceremony and floods of champagne some years ago. There is a palace in Singapore (where the brothers spend most of their time), a flock of St. John ambulances testifying to their generosity, and, in addition, Haw Boon Par, the elder brother, has said he will build near his mansion a ten-story pagoda. 'Tiger Balm' has, of course, been analysed. Many people regard it as a helpful adjunct to Couéism, but the Inspector told me that besides its very large percentage of camphor, the balm contains traces of an unknown ingredient. I know Europeans who believe in it, and was once myself treated and cured with 'Tiger Balm,' four hundred miles from anything resembling

Chinese or European civilization. It wasn't a case of serious disease, only a peculiarity; below and above the elbow, my arm came up in large pink swellings, which the Chinese soldiers said were spider-bite, though an American military attaché said they were hives. It is hard to draw personal compliments from the Chinese, but the large swellings had an extraordinary effect on my interpreter, who contemplated them a long time, and then said: "Pretty—like a peach!" This was nice, but no help; a young Chinese general modestly offered his little pot of 'Tiger Balm,' saying it was very good medicine. I wouldn't swallow the salve, but rubbed it on, and sure enough, the peaches disappeared.

Haw Par Mansion itself pays due respect to the tiger. Tigers begin with the handsome gates, continue on glass doors, form a leitmotiv in a formal garden where odd stone birds and beasts admire their shadows. Delicate as light, green mosaic shines beneath the water of the long swimming-pool. Behind the house (with an ambulance tethered in the courtyard), the rock is grottoed with tiny stairs, crannies, passages; here an elfin tiger thrusts out his ruff, a serene stork contemplates, a jolly devil slaps his belly. But the stone laughter, the light beneath the pool, are left to the chaperonage of another cross-legged, smiling boy.

Across a scramble of rocks and foaming water are very different dwellings . . . the place of men so poor they do not own a hut or a foot of arable earth. And yet they grow lettuces, and have duplicated a lost marvel of the world, the Hanging Gardens of Babylon. As an example of Chinese originality and patient courage, the Hanging Gardens of the Lettuce Growers are worth seeing. They have made cave-houses, roofing over rocks with slabs, building up chinked walls with more rocks. On tray-platforms, before the mouths of these windy houses, are the lettuces, crisp green in a soil several inches deep, and as carefully tended as if it were still in its mother fields.

Only a little below lies the factory area of Hong Kong, the basin, where for street after street the high buildings are dwelling above, factory or open shop below. Toys with bright cheap plumage, furniture, hats, camphor chests, restaurants, fish-shops where split and dried sharks show golden-brown over dangling remnants of octopus . . . a conglomeration of the cheap needs of life, and in the factories, spilled out by quick and cheap Chinese labour, the origins of all this.

China's crucifixion, China's war, was for a year or so Hong Kong's boom. In the financial year between March 1937 and March 1938, every industry is up, except the soya bean industry, which may be smashed because the bean crop, the basis of every sauce in the world, is no longer coming in from

North China; and the little pure-Chinese factory which makes oil out of sesame is also running dry. I saw the big trays of sesame drying mahogany in the sun; but supplies were sinking to a minimum.

That hardly affects Hong Kong, whose factories have increased from 541 to 731 in the period, with a shipping boom consequent upon the destructive 1937 typhoon, a rubber boom, and no strikes. Chinese factories are getting their share, in confectionery, shirts, felt hats, cigarettes, and *a big increase of educational books for Chinese people.*

Here in the rubber factory, raw sheets of Malayan rubber slide from one process to another—melted, hardened, tested, stamped, pushed by girls and youths along the road to the shoe-sole. Tennis-shoes are good business, so are tennis balls. This one factory sends a million tennis balls a year to the British Isles: and yet it has, in parts, the old uneven earthen floor.

A new sideline (of which the quiet Chinese manager, who is also the chemical expert, is rather proud) is the manufacture of gas-masks. London, in September 1938, had one inefficient type of gas-mask to distribute among her people. Hong Kong, in February 1938, had, on a small scale, four distinct types, the cost ranging from three to fourteen dollars Hong Kong, and was also prepared to manufacture masks for horses and dogs. The mould for one gas-mask type had been bought from Germany at a very high cost. Another (particularly admired by the manager) had a nozzle which could not collapse or choke, no matter how it was tested. The factory plant could be largely diverted to wartime manufacture if the need arose.

Rubber-soled canvas shoes, another move in the game. Chinese girls, swiftly, tirelessly pencilling out sections for canvas uppers; three movements, repeated hour after hour of a day beginning at 7 a.m., ending 8 p.m., with two meal-breaks. They are on piece-work, and though no permits for night work are given, they crowd around to take bundles of canvas home. Chinese girls, punching in metal eyes, stamping and testing soles, making hard rubber balls for Chinese children to play with. Football has caught on among the little boys of Hong Kong; but nothing of their tearing games is written in the vague eyes of the girls, whose hair is plaited in cones and beehives, smooth as black silk. A few wear cheap jade or silver ear-rings. Where they work near machine-belts, all must pin up their hair, and this caused protest at first. Everyone knows that a woman with her hair pinned up is a married woman; a young girl, a maiden with her marriage-chair still to be carried, rightly wears long soft hair, with a fringe cut across her forehead.

But that is all settled now, custom must not be allowed to stand in the way of remunerative work; and the pliant hands work very quickly, both here and in the electric light bulb factories, where Chinese labour can turn out a three-dollar torch with remarkably good focusing arrangements. If the dark or amber eyes have a dream, it is out of sight. The eyes are vague, the hands are swift and definite.

Hong Kong's boy glass-blowers, like so many other classes of worker, all come from the one place. Their factory has a barred window and an earthen floor, whose centre is a heaped glowing oven, very primitive, fed with wood, covered with a peak of tin. Into this the bare-footed, bare-chested little boys dip their long rods of iron, bring out the glass at incandescent heat. They blow, just the right breath, and for a moment the fierce bubble is a mandarin on a tree for Chinese New Year. Then it takes the mould-shape of a pot or jar for which it is wanted. Another bare-legged boy snicks off the bubbles as they ripen.

The Inspector asks a bright-eyed, intent face, marked by the hot shadows of the oven: "How old are you?" and the little boy (who probably knows no other English) pipes up: "Fourteen." They all say that; because child-labour is prohibited in Hong Kong, and no permits are issued for children under fourteen.

The Inspector is proud and hopeful about the conditions of these factories, which are certainly fair enough; (all the little brown faces press against the window and watch us when we depart).

I like the Inspector. He was very upset when I told him about the chair-boy who turned out to be a chair-woman, and said she was the first he had heard of in forty years.

"All right," I said, "she was the first one in forty years." And certainly a huge influx of refugees and a smallpox epidemic may combine to make conditions abnormal in the best regulated of colonies.

But, purely as a personal opinion, I don't like mass production for the Chinese. One can love beauty, I suppose, without being a fatuous admirer of the dirtily picturesque, a hand-clasper in front of every anachronism. The mass-production is still somehow wrong, and what is wrong with it is not factory conditions, hours, or pay, which can always be adjusted. But the taking of a Chinese mind just wakening from one true form of slavery, the old illiteracy, and diverting this new mind, before it has the remotest chance to test itself, to another true form of slavery, the hypnosis of mechanically performed piece-work for an industrial machine—this, however it is improved, however gilded, struck me as having more potential danger to Chinese people as a whole than the war. It is an enemy of their progress. But it is not, apparently, a danger which can be escaped. If the victory is with China, mass-production will be the basis of Chiang Kai-shek's new industrialism, or another's. If Japan wins, a thousand times more will the raw human material of China be the basis of an industrialism more ruthless, much more blind. An American arrow, which unfortunately had a tip poisoned with gold, has quivered seventy years in the side of Japan. After the war we will see what the second arrow, the same kind but stronger, can do with the heart of China.

Or what the heart of China, once aroused, could do against many arrows.

All this time, I have said nothing more of the unfortunate lady in Shanghai, whose distress was caused because her husband, a Chinese publisher, had lost his head. This was during a period when Shanghai was still badly shaken, and the pro-Japanese terrorists (usually Chinese traitors) had the upper hand over the anti-Japanese terrorists (usually Chinese patriots), who turned the tables later on.

But at present a terrorist speciality was bombing newspaper offices, and decapitating Chinese newspaper people who made too bold a stand against the Japanese. Mostly Chinese newspaper offices were bombed, though one American office got bombed five times: and first a well-known Chinese reporter, then a Chinese publisher, turned up as corpses in the French Concession, their heads missing.

The publisher's widow was in difficulties, not only for her widow's grief, but because the terrorists had given her husband the cruellest death of all. Headless, he would never be received happily in the spirit world. He would wander about, through eternity, mutilated, chilled, starving, and shunned.

She was a brave woman, and one of resource. After making every effort to get back the original head, she buried her husband, in his fine coffin, with a dummy head made of wicker and clay; and if the spirits were kind, seeing this, they would let the Chinese publisher pass quietly into their after-world, and be at least an equal when he gave them some news of the city for which he had died.

I don't think anyone took so much trouble for the reporter, nor did the decapitations stop, though afterwards it was found that the terrorists were bringing in old human heads, from the rotting fields of Chapei and other battle areas, and sticking them up in the French Concessions, where the moonlight on their drawn lips frightened Russian cabaret girls out of their wits. An ancient coolie, asked to declare the contents of his large newspaper package, showed the British police a human arm and leg. A man gave him the parcel to carry, he said; and after a glimpse at his wistful, foggy eyes and mouth, the police decided he knew nothing, and sent him home.

It was a little picture at the back of my mind, an imp, that a place like this Shanghai could perhaps use an ex-journalist for a few weeks; and that

I could make some money, and thereby afford to stay in Shanghai city, because the *shusans* and Luise Rainer types had eaten terribly into my small reserves. The obvious thing, that a city with Shanghai's depleted foreign population would mean circulation and advertising dropped to nothing, and local newspapermen reduced to occasional freelancing, never occurred to me. But I have always lived by ignoring the obvious, and so far it has proved a policy that works.

Naturally Shanghai's newspapers, Chinese and foreign, were taking their own defense measures, by which I do not mean calls on the police. The Chinese mosquito press lived up to their name, and flitted to Hong Kong; or else they shut down for a few days, suddenly opened again, and were never there when the terrorists wanted them. Months later, the Japanese were pestering the British about the harbour Hong Kong gave to Chinese papers with stinging propensities. The British, though polite, were extremely gradual in making even the motions of doing anything about it.

On the little funicular tram, whose cable slopes so steeply from the city to the Peak that the world and sky are tilted saucers, an American voice said a thing I liked. First a light voice (talking about Hong Kong) said: "One meets such nice people."

"Yes," said the American voice, quietly, "but the ones I like even better are the ones I don't meet."

Always the great hawks swing and circle over Hong Kong, and the junk-sails flutter, like red and brown leaves. 'I should like to own it for a time,' I thought, 'and to rebuild part of it, and change a few things.' It is a noble city, and there is something sad about it. That's what the Filipino customs agent said about Manila: "No, it's not beautiful; it's sad."

I saw a Chinese funeral, with the relatives in a sort of white tent, and a big rusty oven, in which would be burned all the silver and gold paper money, the cut-out paper viands, furniture, and clothing supplied for the dead man. There was a brass band in front, playing 'Ta-ra-ra-boom-de-ay,' and the vehicle in which the coffin itself was carried was massed with flowers. But the strange thing, to a foreigner, was the way in which the procession dodged up streets and down small alleys, always taking the unexpected way. This was to mislead the devils, who follow funeral processions. It is a custom observed in earnest, and one woman pedestrian was so whole-hearted about it that she was killed dodging the devil, for she ran headlong into a motor car.

Three last things call back to me from Hong Kong; the wet, cold, angry diving-boy of Kowloon, drawing blue cotton over his shivering body, while boat-women with great nets and great toothless grins swayed between him and the ship, catching the coppers flung to him from the upper deck; a junk-sail, colour of old rose, very slowly lifted by the bare feet of fishermen, who trod on the spokes of an iron wheel and raised it inch by inch, a glow against the waters. Also there was the angel in the dog-collar, without whom I would have missed my boat.

I went to the Peak, one last time, and because the moralities of Hong Kong were all against chair-boys, and the chair-boys squatted there, starving so good-humouredly and dumb, I took a chair. But it was a hot day, and the chair-boys sweated more than I thought they would, so our progress was slow, broken by halts during which they puffed dwarfish pipes. When at last we were back at the funicular, there was no funicular train due for twenty minutes, and I observed with horror that my boat was as good as lost.

There was nothing to be done by abusing the chair-boys or the funicular, so I sallied out, ran to the first car I could find, and told the two men in it that if somebody didn't drive me down to Hong Kong, top speed, I would miss my boat. The drama and pathos of the narrative quite carried me away. I had tears in my eyes.

"Hop in!" said the angel with the dog-collar, and drove downhill at a speed quite out of keeping with his calling.

As we tore, I shrieked to the angel that I was a New Zealander, and he shrieked back that he was a friend of the Anglican Archbishop of Wellington, the Right Rev. St. Barbe Holland.

"He makes good speeches," I yelled, and the angel chanted: "Not bad."

There was no time to say more. With a wild scattering of ricksha boys, we were outside the ferry. "Here!" cried the angel, and opening a zipp-fastener wallet he turned all his cent money into my hands. It was just as well; Mr. Loo had convetted my dollars Hong Kong into dollars Mex, and I had forgotten the ferry completely.

I never saw any more of the angel in the dog-collar, nor had time to ask for his name and address; though out of his cent money I had enough over to buy from a ship tout a little wooden figure of a boy on a water-buffalo, which is about as inevitable in China as an ebony elephant in Colombo. It was queer, though; the angel, since he wore a dog-collar, presumably believed in an omnipotent God. Did the omnipotent God send a friend of the Archbishop of Wellington tearing downhill, merely to see that I got off on the beginnings of that journey?

On the French boat to Shanghai, the free table wine proved almost immediately to be a lurid poison. But from the first there was a spell of gaiety over that table, which was shared by a little Welsh organizer of missions, an Englishman returning to the British section of the Shanghai Municipal Police, and a Norwegian skipper, who had been interned at Formosa for twelve days, owing to an unfortunate attempt at running a Chinese ship under Greek colours. He was not at all annoyed with the Japanese, who had been painfully polite, and almost deluged him with tea, as well as with questions. What annoyed him was that Italian and German skippers could play the flag-switching trick under the Japanese nose, and get away with it.

Presently an elderly gowned Chinese joined us, a good addition, for he spoke fluent English and had an urbane sense of humour. He seemed ready to befriend everybody, but me in particular, because his Shanghai firm, like so many Chinese businesses, had important and prosperous business connections with Australia. Nothing would persuade him that a New Zealander was more than a small and lonesome kind of Australian, like a Tasmanian.

I don't know what the All Blacks or Jean Batten would say about this; but it was Mr. Chang's story, and he stuck to it. "We Australians," he said, more than once, "must stick together."

On deck one stumbled blindly from smoking-room to conversation room, wind roaring in ears and hair, ice snatching at fingers. Yellow sea, and the game junks far on the horizon; yangtse mud spilled out, soiling the clearness of waters broken only by a few barren islands. All around us, all around the steaming rooms where the velvet refugees danced with their Argentine bears, and the delicate Chinese fingers rattled tiles at mah-jongg, was streaming, sparkling cold. We had two known spies on board. This was now the custom, applying to most big passenger boats on the Shanghai run. Everybody took it as a compliment; we laughed, excited. Chinese men came out in black felt capes, swinging to their heels, and peaked black caps of astrakhan. The English police boy, who had been in Shanghai through the worst of the fighting and the after-humiliation, was faintly bellicose. He said he would salute no Japanese sentry crossing Garden Bridge. It was a point of honour with him, deeply embedded in his mind, that British people should not salute the sentry on Garden Bridge. Before orders came through entitling the municipal police to fire on soldiers or civilians breaking the peace of the International Settlement, this young man had seen too many incidents. He was annoyed: his blue eyes turned to stone as he sat and thought about it.

He was still scowling and stony-eyed on the morning when our free-wine vessel docked at Shanghai. Down below were stout Chinese with arm-bands, and for these he had a particular scowl. I stood at his side, staring down. "Ta-tao," he said, contemptuously, speaking out loud as if he wanted them to hear.

"Ta-tao?" (It sounded like Da-dao.) "Traitor police. Chinese, in the Japanese pay."

'Traitor' is the generally accepted meaning for 'Ta-tao' in this war. But the phrase has other associations. 'Old Way,' it means, or 'Great Way'; and it goes with a five-barred flag, which was China's before the Chinese Republic arose and took to itself the red and blue flag with the pure white twelve-rayed sun.

Each bar of the old five-barred flag stands for one of the five bloods of China—Han, Manchu, Mongolian, Mohammedan, and Tibetan. And to sever these, the Five Bloods who under the Chinese Republic have said they are one, and tempt back to the Old Way, the Great Way, those discontented, grey-bearded place-seekers who have been out of office and influence ever since the Sun Yat-sen revolution of 1911, is one great aim in China of the Japanese militarists, who would be perfectly happy for the Chinese people to be governed by a certain kind of Chinese people . . . under Japanese auspices, and in Japan's chosen way. Divide and rule!

This was secretly written on the arm-bands of the brawny Chinese Ta-tao police, staring up at our vessel; in the Shanghai places where powerfully armed Chinese gangs, descendants of the old-time tongs, and all extremely anti-Japanese, were beginning to work out the first characters of their reply to the pro-Japanese terrorist gangs operating between Chapei and the French Concessions; it was written in the discontented fair face of the young English policeman, who was no diplomat, but a boy, his impulse all for shooting when his police training and instincts of decency warned him that the time had come to shoot.

I had told Mr. Chang I wanted to stay at a Chinese hotel, good but cheap. He put me into a ricksha, and directed it to the Grand Orient Hotel.

A tout, listening, said: "The police raid there every night; it is much safer at our hotel," but I preferred to trust the serene Mr. Chang, who bargained with the ricksha boy for the exact fare.

"And do not tip," he concluded, severely, "not in your posish. Later, perhaps, when you have made a thousand pounds. We Australians must stick together."

CHAPTER FOUR

Shanghai Winter-Scene

SAY IT OVER AGAIN, and in an instant it's a reality. Shanghai, the beating-up, Mei Lan-fang dancing against a curtain one great ripple of peach-blossom, the red satin quilts, Anna's little green house with the goldfish, down in the French Concessions.

Anna and Caley were the people I came to know best in Shanghai. . . . Anna, a German-born girl, who was writing for the Press and giving English, lessons, while her husband, a young Chinese official from the Berlin Military Academy, was away in Hankow on some political business; Caley, born in New Zealand, who had a job in connection with Chinese industries, and knew Shanghai inside out. These two became, in a more or less accidental way, my direction-finders in Shanghai. It's a temptation to write always, 'Anna this,' 'Caley that'; but as a matter of fact Shanghai didn't begin with Anna or Caley, it started with old Mr. Chang, who took me to the Grand Orient Hotel, and who wore a blue padded Chinese gown, but was not proud of it, because he didn't consider it sufficiently westernized. In summer, he told me, he always wore trousers and coat.

Farther south, in Kwangtung, trousers are a matter of course; but the old-fashioned gown was almost invariable winter wear in Shanghai. Even some of the western men, trying to be at least as Chinese as the Chinese, wore long blue or brown gowns, heavily padded with cotton quilting (removed and dried out once a year), or lined with the fur of tigers, leopard, wolf. I admired the gowns: politically experienced Chinese dislike them, because they made for class-distinctions . . . coolie's cotton, rich man's fur.

For the Chinese woman was the distinction between coarse black cotton trouser-suits, exquisite silken suits and gowns. But during the war, many girl students and women of the wealthier class threw themselves into the Silk Boycott, wearing plain blue cotton, cutting their sleeves short, and retaining only the ankle-slit which showed exquisitely clean white petticoats. They didn't lose by their sacrifice: it gave their dark hair, the clear flushed gold of their skins, a beauty as of walking and talking blue flowers. Only I wished the Shanghai girls wouldn't 'perm' their hair, which is too soft to take the wave, and comes out in frizzy little manes of curls. The millions of yards of blue cloth, village-spun and handwoven now in provinces still free from the war, got their exquisite gentian blues direct from small German dye-pots, which had spread all over the country.

Queer folk, the Chinese; they put up with a lot from foreigners. Remember

. . . the first day, walking from Wing On's great department stores to the Grand Hotel. An artisan was inlaying with goldleaf a huge black-lacquered glory in a coffin shop. His trails and sprays were good. He stared at me, one moment, for being a foreigner who stared so hard at his work.

"Because it is so beautiful," I explained, and he, though he didn't understand a word of English, smiled and turned to his work again.

Theatre queues of children bought very cheap, tiny mandarins. These were cut in halves, to show how juicy they were, and flies settled thick on the cut halves. Notices on lamp-posts urged people towards free vaccination. But the real troubles, at this time, were measles and dysentery, though in July and August cholera touched peak in Shanghai.

I got back to the hotel at dusk. This was good, Mr. Chang told me. The Japanese still imposed a curfew, reduced from 10.30 to 11 p.m. But for me there was a special one: I wasn't to go out alone after dark.

"Not nice for you," said Mr. Chang, vigorously shaking his head.

Just as I reached Wing On's, five men in green bolted out, carrying what looked like truncheons or batons. 'So it's right. This place is searched for criminals every night,' I thought, as the wind of their passing smote my cheek. But as it turned out, these were only Chinese postmen; I don't know why they carried truncheons.

In my room, when I stood alone, there was a scarlet satin quilt rolled up like an immense caterpillar, a galaxy of mirrors, tall frosted windows. I could see out through the bits of plain glass between frosting, or, with difficulty, by hauling open a window. On a wall hung a calendar, depicting a vigorous row of quadruplets, pink-and-white, unmistakably Chinese. 'Thanks,' I thought.

Besides these, I could amuse myself with a Chinese telephone directory and writing materials, and directly opposite my room, on a balcony, was an old-fashioned Chinese play, which so far as I could discover never stopped at all. On and on. . . .

A printed notice on the dressing-table told me I could keep a singsong girl in my room until midnight, but not after. As a matter of fact, they stayed till 2 and 3 a.m., singing in that peculiar nasal whine which is an old-style aptitude still beloved by many Chinese who would hate to be called old-style. I prefer its harsh timbre to the wide-mouthed bawling of the platinum calves who announce their blues in America, but few westerners ever acquire the singsong taste. What the great hotel would have done if I had asked for a singsong boy I don't know: I think they would have risen to the occasion.

Down in the restaurant I had turtle, because turtle being a complete stranger to the New Zealander, I wanted to *know*. When I knew, a Chinese waiter said solicitously: "This is no good for you," and steered me to the doors, past tables where enormous Chinese and girls, who had unfairly kept their figures, sat with massive tureens and dishes piled before them. Foreign music raced out of the swinging cabaret doors. The old shabby-coated key-boy, who had one immense whisker sprouting from a mole, let me into my room, and the old-fashioned play opposite my window was behaving in such a peculiar way. The curtains, painted with four ducks, a stream, and a lotus flower, were fixtures: in the small square marked off by these, scenes changed continually. People with masks, wigs, quite beautiful peach-coloured, rose, and blue costumes, were snooping round and round, bearing lighted tapers. As there was no religious in their number, I reasoned that they were looking for a burglar or spy. The audience was standing, but I could see very nicely over their heads. There was a great traffic in peanuts, popular east as west. Without warning, two of those harmless-looking actors turned and butchered the pretty girl in peach-colour: afterwards they produced her corpse; with a red cloth showing where the bloody neck should be, and everybody shouted: "Hao-a! Hao-a!"

Sleeping in the scarlet quilt delighted me, except that I didn't know if one spread it out flat, or coiled in it. Every time one wanted a bath, one gave the bath-amah a minute coin, and she, with a very pleased smile and an unwholesome cloth, went out and made the bath much greyer than before. But baths are a silly, novel idea.

Another thing about sleeping in Chinese hotels (though you must remember you can sleep in a good one for 2 ½ dollars Mex, a day) is that they are beautifully steam-heated, so when you go out and sit in an uncovered ricksha, Shanghai's winter scene sparkling like a rimed palace, immediately you take nose, throat, and bronchial afflictions. Half the foreign population of Shanghai has catarrh all winter and spring, dysentery all summer and autumn.

In the morning I was shown over Wing On's huge store, from a basement where foreign knitted clothes for the very young competed with Shanghai's own little padded winter suits, to floors where they kept the Swatow specialty of raised cork pictures, and Shanghai scenes in stone, and a great cloisonné jar was still in making, wires marking where the arrowed leaves and smooth biscuit colour would lie with the gold. It is usual for every Chinese city or town of importance to have its artistic specialty, in which it is expected to excel. Sometimes the specialty is not in cork or stone. A Soochow maidservant could get better wages, merely by saying she was a native of Soochow, because traditionally the most beautiful women come from Soochow. But Soochow was cut off; the Japanese had Soochow. . . .

The girls at the embroidery counter were a little vexed, because I mistook their beautiful cat for a tiger. All the embroidery was cheap, and I would have bought the cat-tiger but Mr. Chang pursued me, saying gently: "Later, perhaps, when you have made a thousand dollars gold. Not in your posish."

The heavily-embroidered mandarin jackets and caps of the old are going out of mode, but are still stocked; Shanghai still has many very rich old men. It is surprising how few of them the Japanese have been able to bring over to the Ta-tao form of government. But then, though Shanghai is a pleasurable city among the rich, it is also a place for going its own way, and probably unique in the strength of its subterranean organizations, among both rich and poor, old style and highly modern.

As Japanese silks are the most delicately patterned, Chinese silks are still the stateliest, encrusted with such peonies, chrysanthemums, and metallic roses as the west does not know. New petals smell good, but burning leaves smell better. . . .

In the basement I saw angel fish, with their long rosy streamers and small blue swimmers, but none so fiercely brilliant as those at Manila, where one thinks: 'God was only a less slapdash Gauguin, endowed with a better sense of design.' Also in this city, where so many gardens had been wrecked, there was an extra sale for dwarf trees in pots—pines, pensive and dreamy, white cherry blossoms, too soon scattering over their base of moss, and hyacinths.

I wanted to buy a pine for company, but was discouraged. I saw queer things to eat, fungi, stags' horns with the velvet left on (very good for a tonic, said Mr. Chang), a silvery matted substance, which I mistook for one of the seaweeds on the boat to Hong Kong, and said I had tasted. Mr. Chang laughed. I had never eaten that, it was very much too expensive. It was the birds' nests for soup, bleached like fairy bones.

When the bombardments were on this store was hit by a shell. About a hundred girl workers died. You couldn't tell it now from the inside, and the exterior shows only where wood covers up shattered bricks. So many people rushed in and out of the cabaret, so many huge dishes piled up in front of capacious men and slender silken ladies, so many thronged in and seemed happy at every show, the stranger could hardly guess: 'This is a Chinese place. The city is occupied. There's a war on, pretty much of a war.' Yet underneath, it remained essentially, calmly Chinese, already restored in vitality to what the occupying force must consider a dangerous degree.

Nine of the big Wing On cotton factories had been bombed. The remaining one carried on, and I went through it, seeing Chinese girls with masks over their mouths, working in the roar of the machinery, the white impalpable dust of cotton fluff. It was a hot, wet atmosphere to work in, pressed cotton sliding out in massive wads, machine answering machine. The machines understand one another so well, the people so badly. Some of the girls felt the hot pressure on their throats, like a hand, and had pulled off their masks; then they breathed in fluff. The others, retaining their masks, worked with expressionless faces, streaked with perspiration.

The cotton factories are supposed to be a good kind of job, and in this factory there had been some attempt to help the workers, especially in the shape of night-classes, where young girls who wanted literacy were taught to read and write, and received graduation certificates. But these classes, like the Yangtsepoo Night School Social centres, where thousands of Chinese working boys had learned their literacy, had been stopped since the occupation.

Wherever there was an upward movement to knowledge among Chinese people, now in Shanghai, now in all occupied China, a hand pressed gently down . . . gently, not hard, as it had pressed on the bombed universities, here and in Soochow and Hangchow, in broken Nanking.

When the burning and looting were on, some Chinese soldiers, retreating from Shanghai, set fire to a Japanese university in the French Concession. Although they didn't damage it much, and it could easily have been put in order again, the Japanese now said that in retaliation they would take over the Chinese University of Chiao Tung, and use it for themselves.

It was a pity about Chiao Tung; the university was in use as a huge refugee camp, harbouring about two thousand refugee women and children, and the reason why it seemed such a nuisance that the Japanese insisted on grabbing it was because this was one of the few refugee camps where the children had an open place to play. The grounds were plain enough, but there were a few real trees, real grass; among these the urchins, bare-legged and having a picnic time better than any in their lives, were growing sturdy.

If Chinese poor people aren't actually the cleanest poor people on earth, it is no fault of theirs; they have such an inordinate passion for laundry work, and wherever they are, out it comes. The entire stone block of Chiao Tung University, that stately pile, was covered, roof, balconies, windows, with little refugee unmentionables. Somewhere in the offing hung tattered Red Cross and Salvation Army banners, also a French flag and a large Rising Sun. The French (in whose Concession the property stood) had sensibly taken it over, the social relief societies were administrators, and the Japanese military, with their Sun, were encamped in an annexe block, so that the women and children should know they were there on sufferance.

But Rising Sun, Red Cross and Salvation Army flags, tricolour of France, all looked sick beside the real flag, which was Chinese washing.

This was the best refugee camp in Shanghai but one, run in an empty college by the Chinese National Welfare people, nurses and young men. They were all young, all very courteous, these organizers. Their camp showed what Chinese children can be. These, mostly peasant children, ran in the sunshine and played with the drops of a fountain; through the gold of their skins showed the clear red. They were graduated by age, the little ones taught just enough to distract their starling minds. The older refugee girls took advantage of many new needs in Shanghai, created by fads, or by the destruction of stored goods. There was a fad for crochetted gloves; their hands crochetted dainty gloves. Flower-gardens were mainly ruin; so their hands made exquisite artificial flower-sprays.

Upstairs, the nurses showed me their plain, small bedrooms, not as good as those of the refugees. I often wonder what is happening to them . . . running children, knitting girls, courteous young assistants.

If you don't adopt a Chinese name in China, you will probably have a nickname. For that matter, Chinese people all seem to have nicknames among themselves. I asked a Chinese teacher to tell me some and they weren't very bad—he himself was called 'The Long,' a certain pastor was variously known as 'The Shrewd' and 'The Oily,' while a shortish fat man was 'The Japanese.'

But there are four hundred names, real names, out of which the foreigner may decently select the name he wants on his indispensable visiting-card, without which he is socially extinct. His card bears this, with something vaguely resembling his Christian name bringing up the rear, and at one side a graphic and ostentatious description of his important business and place of origin.

Countries also have their characters. Australia's means 'The New World of Gold,' but though there is a character for New Zealand, I could never get anything out of its meaning, except that it somewhat resembles a character meaning 'Silk Button.' A button, of course, is impressive as token of scholarly rank—if that's any consolation.

My name and origin, with a lovely full stop, the printer's own idea, plump between surname and first name, were romanized as Wei Iri. Wei is a common name, but not so popular as Wong or Wang, which name means 'King.' In China there are several million Wongs and Wangs, and in Kwangtung province, a whole village community named Wong (or Wang) was supporting as many strays of the name as original inhabitants. The reason for all these Wangs and Wongs is that in the old days China had many kingdoms and many kings; each king usually had many wives and concubines; the ladies knew their duty, and, anyhow, there seems to be no danger of Wongs and Wangs dying out.

The people, the great plunging, sweeping mass in blue cotton or black trousers, the people-mass who lie prone and yet bear the world on sore shoulders, was expressively known as 'The Old Hundred Names.'

I was tired, getting back to Wing On's; tired so that I could have sat down and wept. Instead, I sat in the downstairs tearoom, drinking hard brown foreign tea, bushman's kind, which steeps the mind in insulated stupor.

I had been into several Shanghai newspaper offices, with the obvious result. Their circulation was nuts, their advertising was nuts, the idea of their taking on a stranger was nuts, the war was nuts, in fact, we were all nuts together. The only rich newspaper concern was pro-Japanese, and had a secretary-bird. Platinum. I left him a brief, blasting message, but really, when there's a perfectly good secretary-bird, what's the use?

The much-bombed American office was amusing. The editor there was making preparations for a flight to Hankow. While I waited, he had a long conversation with a telephone-crackle about the 'plane. So I went into a kind of mediumistic trance, and, when at last shown into his presence, forgot to ask if I might do a little bright topical freelancing. Instead, I said: "May I come with you in the aeroplane to Hankow?"

His pleasant enough American mouth fell open, and hung there: before it could close again, I shot in several bait-reasons why he should take me to Hankow, but they didn't go down. Presently he got his jaws together again, and then opened them (but not too much), saying in a choked way: "Young lady, I am going on very important business to Hankow. This office has already been bombed *five times*."

He proceeded to retail the story I already knew so well, sympathizing with himself as he went along: as I listened, nothing seemed unlikelier than that I should ever go to Hankow.

Fallada, Fallada, there thou art hanging! I sat, steeped in dark brown tea, while the lift clanged up and down, and hundreds of gowned Chinese rushed for cabaret, leg-show, restaurant. Anyhow, why *does* one go to Hankow?

A small blob of foam, rainbow for an instant, fritters off the side of a rock. It was restless, you see, with the near-cosmic restlessness of man, frittering and rubbing off the side of the cosmic stillness of things. And one cannot see what does not move, and keeps always in the shadow. But always the argument runs: 'I shall see. . . . I shall *discern*. . .'

There was a foreign man in the tea-room, drunk all by himself, neither lonely nor merry, just turned nasty about it: He saw me and thought I was a missionary, for he began to swear at me as such, not loud, but with tongue-scouring words which made me feel, 'Any moment, that *pakeha* is going to be very damned sick.'

He was sick behind his eyes and in the lines of his weak, slack mouth; and he wanted to get out of that by wishing his weakness and failure on to the Chinese. The waiter kept passing, and the sick *pakeha* said: "Goo'. Chinesh all goo'. 'Syou misshionriesh!"

He curled his tongue again, using the words our wharfies use, or our timber-loaders and workers where a wheel won't pull up out of the muck; but because he was so sick and cheaply drunk, he made the words sound all wrong, though in their right place they sound all right.

The waiter came past with a tray, and the *pakeha* pawed at him, saying: "'Sallri John, ya'rallri. S'misshionriesh." The waiter, impassive, took the hands off and put them aside, having no use for them, and then went on with his own work. I can see now it might have been doing the *pakeha* a good turn to hit him very hard in the face, but at the time I felt done myself, and couldn't be bothered.

I squeezed into a lift, which shot up sky-high, letting me out on the roof-garden. There it was better. After a short while of air, of feeling my way about in the new place and the dusk, it was almost lovely. Young trees were planted, not in leaf yet, but looking as if they wore dark coats done up with small pink buttons. This seemed a crowded industrial area; and yet, once you were high enough, you could see into a clay section where the broken black tiles of huts were rounded like hands, like the breasts of doves. There were lovers on this roof-garden. At least, I hoped they were lovers. They looked like lovers. The girls in the leg-show kicked up from dusty brown and gold costumes, sunflower colours. While I stayed still, the slight freeze and mist of air about me, my mind said: 'Now it's all right.'

It was next day that I first met Caley. I wasn't looking for him, didn't even remember that I had heard of him, and a little about his job in Shanghai. . . . I was looking, in fact, for a Miss Smith, supposed to have some information about refugees. But the Chinese boy, who guided me to Miss Smith's department, made everything very confusing by calling her 'Mees Mess.' He said: "Mees Mess has, gone," and I was about to leave, bewildered, when he mentioned Caley's full name, and said that he was working upstairs.

Instantly I had a vague memory, far away, then clear. There was a house, so small it looked like a duck's egg dropped among reeds. I hadn't met Caley, but in this house I met somebody related to him. One of his in-laws had gone to school with me. In after life she was named Eupheme, but we called her Effie, and her father, whose camera stood up on legs under a black cloth, took photographs of us all, sitting on the balcony: mine was awful, of course.

Effie-Eupheme was with one with the house like a duck's egg. She had told me about Caley.

So I met Caley, who was sitting in an office, the walls festooned with vivid woodcuts and linocuts, showing what awfulness can happen to Chinese workers if they don't mind their eye with machinery. There were Chinese with their arms cut off by machine belts; Chinese girls being dragged backwards by the hair torn from their bleeding scalps; Chinese surveying lopped legs, Chinese falling into vats of boiling fluid, Chinese disembowelled, Chinese starting enormous conflagrations, Chinese in every way getting the worst of machine-battles beside which the Sino-Japanese war looked like a zephyr.

These demonstrations (really an excellent way of showing the raw recruit among machinery what may happen to him if he doesn't look out) were the work of intensely interested Chinese artisans themselves. But as a point of honour, they had depicted themselves undergoing every excruciating torture with countenance showing neither distress nor surprise. The result was quaint, and would have taken the wind out of the sails of any Japanese who tried to get tough in here.

After taking in the scenic effects, I said "How d'you do?" to Caley, who occupied a fat respectable-looking red leather chair.

Caley knew Shanghai; he had been there over ten years, and besides speaking Mandarin he knew the rough local dialect, almost a patois, but full of idiom without which Shanghai was not Shanghai. He had studied and learnt provincial dialects also, so that it was he who could talk to the old peasant soldier in the secret amputation hospital, whose Honan dialect was so rough and countrified not a Chinese in the wards could twist his tongue to it.

But Caley didn't think he spoke Chinese: his teacher still came every day, and besides giving him a lesson, the old man talked gossip pretty freely now. Besides this he had been into every village within explorable reach, and knew not only the surface look of the place, but the kinds of games the children played, the names of the agricultural implements and those used by the labourers, the customs of the women; if there was an alternative name he usually knew that as well.

I don't mean, by a long chalk, that he was omniscient, omnipotent . . . in fact, at the moment, he was bottled up so that he couldn't get at his villages; and even in normal times, like every foreigner who tries to learn anything about China, instead of drawing grand bird's-eye conclusions, he was learning piecemeal, by a way of pebble and dropped leaf and syllable.

Caley wouldn't have put it like that, because he had a horror of anything savouring of the romantic or dramatic, and it nearly assassinated him when somebody put on a Chinese gown (and didn't change it often enough), or picked up a Chinese opium-pipe and blew out a few puffs, and thought that this, in some obscure manner, was a shattering compliment to the Chinese. He knew the Chinese don't shatter quite so easily; which was one of the few things that comforted him, when a stark tidiness began to succeed the first disorders of the occupation, and the twenty-two new Japanese censors sat installed neatly enough in Shanghai post offices, opening all correspondence, not excluding foreign correspondence.

He rather thought at times that I was working up the romantic and dramatic street, and I didn't know how to contradict, couldn't come back with any politically purposeful repartee. So I either orated or stumbled, as usual, but without clarity. Caley naturally damned the sentimental with the romantic and the dramatic, but he couldn't keep down his abrupt compassion for the very poor . . . for individual faces suddenly looking up, under the foot that presses and kneads the very poor. He was annoyed with me, I remember, for criticizing the harsh voices of the singsong girls.

"Most of them have been kidnapped, or were flood or famine children, mortgaged out to the brothels when they were eleven," he said. "That voice is as artificial in them as it would be in you. They're what they have to be."

That was sense, and I felt ashamed. He had a dwarf cherry-blossom tree in his flat, and it had come into flower, some of the petals already lying like pale shells around its patient roots.

"Fool thing!" he said. "What's the use of it, anyhow?"

But he kept it. Soo Yang, his boy, had been a famine kid, sold and brought Sown to the city and tormented in one of the big industrial works until Caley pulled him out. He said he did that because Soo Yang's little brother had been eaten by a wolf.

"After all," he said, "there's something in having a boy whose little brother was eaten by a wolf."

To look at Soo Yang, you would never think, however, that he took this episode very seriously. He was not a sad Chinese boy; he was a quietly joyous Chinese boy, in a blue-lined gown, with sparkling brown eyes, self-possession, and a good hand for making dog-in-a-blanket.

Soo Yang had besides a habit of under-statement. Caley lent him to me sometimes, complete with two rickshas, and we bowled away to Jessfield Park, where, under the glistening rinds of snow, small daffodils were coming out . . . those and crocuses, and dark bushes, but little else, for the gardens had been so neglected during the bombardments that almost everything but the inevitable Chinese rock-effects, and small round-roofed summer-houses, had failed the season. We fed peanuts to the monkeys, birds, and marsupials, and I tried to draw Soo Yang out, but he wasn't much interested, except to tell me that while the bombardments were on, every animal and bird in the Jessfield Park assortment found a kind home, except the bear. Nobody would take the bear, they were afraid it would bite.

So we went to see the bear, which proved to be a small-sized brown, harmless article, with unkempt nails and a long tongue curling for honey, but no wish to bite either gods or men. I was a bit worried, in retrospect, to think of this bear sitting completely alone during the bombardments, wondering why nobody came to take it away: but it had worn well, it was a Chinese bear.

The white people were as good as the Chinese about finding homes for animals during the bombardments. While thousands of houseless people were starving in the streets, dazed kids wandering about lost, food for the kidnapping gangs, Shanghai had excellent refugee homes for pets, with veterinary surgeons in attendance. These were still going strong, as not all the owners had returned from Hong Kong and Singapore.

Five months after the cease-fire in Shanghai, people, attracted by queer moaning sounds, found a Chinese girl in one of the wrecked houses of the devastated area, quite near to where people were going and coming. She was dazed, had been dazed and a living skeleton for months . . . crawling a little way to some dirty source of water, then crawling back to hide. She was still alive when she was taken out of the hut; I don't know what happened to her afterwards.

Behind Jessfield Park (now the only outlet for Shanghai, when Shanghai wanted to walk on paths and grass) there was more barbed wire, a railway station cut off, and Japanese soldiers pacing up and down, the bright sentry bayonets in their hands. They looked bored to death, but their red tabs showed bright as cocks' combs on their dun uniforms. Soo Yang gave me an example of his powers of under-statement. He turned, with a sparkling-eyed smile, and shook his head a little.

"Don't *like* the Japanese," he said, almost in a whisper; "they always make too much *trouble* . . . too much *noise*."

Meeting Caley was good in most ways, but troublesome in one. As soon as he introduced me to Miss Su and Miss Chen (young welfare workers and friends of his), the two slim, black-mittened Chinese girls flew off the handle to Caley about my living at the Grand Orient Hotel.

62

They were not younger than myself, so both, probably, were married: Miss Su had a family living at Soochow, of whom she could get no news, and Miss Chen, the elder of the two, was a Peiping girl, and had had a little summer house up the river completely destroyed while the fighting was on. And they had narrow hands in black woollen mittens, and quiet voices and ways (though their eyes could flash). Miss Chen was taking me to a Chinese concert in aid of the refugees, while, next day if it was fine, Miss Su was introducing me to some of the places where the kidnapped children are housed.

Of course, they didn't say a word to me; but to Caley they became dramatic, especially Miss Chen, who was coming to pick me up for the concert.

"I cannot go there!" she cried, trembling, "I cannot!"

Westernized young Chinese who want to be very respectable look uncomfortable, and smooth their knees, and say that the Grand Orient is too 'noisy, as indeed it is. What they really mean is that there are too many singsong girls; though there is not the slightest compulsion on anyone to have a singsong girl, and the Chinese habit of never interfering is strictly adhered to. I went to the hotel, in the first place, because old Mr. Chang took me there, and he was a friend. And I liked the boys and even the bath-amah, certainly the scarlet silk coverlet and the sprawling Chinese quadruplets on the calendar in my room; also I liked wandering about in the big place, wondering why this was eaten, and that was worn, and what the party whose chopsticks splashed so quick in the red dish mounded before them were really saying, or thinking about.

But Miss Chen couldn't be expected to know that, so she trembled and cried: "I cannot!"

Caley evidently told her: "Yes, you can," and she took his word for it; for she took that fence like a thoroughbred, arriving in my bedroom at the appointed hour.

She gave me a rather flat little smile, sat down, and said: "This is a new experience for me, āā? I have never before been inside such a place."

I took that on the surface, and told her about the leg-show, the bowing trees of the roof-garden, the dwarf pines downstairs, and about Mandarin jackets for the old men being out of fashion. By that time we were fanned smoothly through cool black darkness, in rickshas along the Bund, and saying "*Mei-yu! Mei-yu-la!*" to cross, tired little girls who tried to hang on, begging for cents.

The concert hall was all dark; suddenly I found tears running down my face. I had been in refugee camps all day, and didn't care in the least to weep over them; they were not a matter for tears. Miss Chen was a thin, dark silhouette beside me, cut off by her own private thoughts, thinking wearily, perhaps, about the little summer house up the river, where it used to be cool and pleasant. The Chinese part of the programme was almost all classical music, very difficult for a foreigner to understand, though it has a beauty and a strangeness, now massive, now wild. The thin flutes and moon-guitars I could decipher; there was a wooden instrument which simply pecked, like a woodpecker, and another which gurgled a sacred sound, through what looked like a flotilla of silvery-white balloons.

They were playing 'The Rain Prayer,' a song and a music so old that it was woven now into Buddhist religion, and the people took it as a prayer for peace. I closed my eyelids: yes, that could overcome the strangeness, and press down for ever into the brain. I didn't understand 'The Rain Prayer,' but it understood me. To be possessed of things is more sacred than to possess them.

The rain fell on the dry, tired soil which was all these people leaning forward in the audience, Chinese and foreign people side by side in darkness, the unborn safe again, blind, only dimly sentient, in their earth. Certainly we wanted rain . . . rain and peace.

The Buddhists took a good part (far larger than I was able to estimate) in coping with Shanghai's refugee problems: it wasn't only a case of dancing round bonfires burning papers, or of passing, as sometimes I saw a coarse-gowned Buddhist monk pass, along the slushy ways of the French Concession, his hands fondling a string of twisted and weather-worn beads like a rosary.

There weren't many temples in Shanghai . . . years before, the Chinese Government had suppressed temples throughout the land . . . but the Temple of the Jade Buddha, to which Caley's friend, Jim, took me, was quite famous. Although the red lacquered house of the Buddha and his attendants, and the companion house of the four great gilded Guardians continued in their original purposes, the side-buildings and temple courtyards had been given over to refugee women and children, who were having a good time. The small boys were playing a game like battledore and shuttlecock, their darts tailed with cheap bright-coloured feathers hitting the air: but everybody broke off, first to be photographed by Jim, whom they knew and whose camera they obviously adored, and then to fall into line, carrying rice-bowls, for their *chi fan*.

Chi fan was hot rice soup with vegetables, and maybe an ancient, slightly decadent chicken, like a Georgian poet of the English school, doing her leggy bit beneath the steaming greens.

We went into the Buddha's red-lacquered houses, passing the round, blue prayer-mats, the great temple gong, and a coffer in which alms could be left, if the passer-by wished it so. But no sign came from the slender young priests, whose long red wands of incense, tipped with spark and scented ash, bowed always towards that great gilded figure, whose eyes slept, dreamed, and smiled in wide wakefulness. . . .

O thou Jewel! I liked this Buddha anew, because I heard for the first time the story of the blue snails, which, like an incrustation of aquamarine stalactites, formed the giant crown on his head.

Once, when the Buddha was meditating, so hot grilled the sun that it *almost* disturbed his meditations. But the chill-blooded snails, watching and adoring from their cool damp places, realized that this must not be; so across the heated road they trailed the little wetness of their bodies, and climbing anxiously to the Buddha's crown, made him a living headgear, under which he might meditate until the vast golden limbs of his dream no longer moved, until no thing animate or inanimate asked for his meditation's being to encompass it.

After this the Buddha honoured the blue snail-children, wearing them for his crown rather than jewels or gold.

On the reverse side of the great altar, Kwan-yin, Lady of Mercies, was shown standing on the scaled golden head of a huge fish, which was bearing her at top speed to an island of her desire. In the background tilted her little barque, which had sunk, and probably faithless disciples, now thigh-deep in the waves, showed in the admiration of their faces a veneration for Kwan-yin.

Chinese Kwan-yin and Japanese Kwannon, the two eastern Mercies, are not the same: yet look at their mouths, and you will notice one haunting resemblance. Both these women smile: it is a smile tender, everlasting, and wise. Then think how few of the immortal women of history or mythology are given to smiling. The Mona Lisa . . . call hers a smile? Yet the blood rains thick as locusts between Kwan-yin and Kwannon.

Anyhow, I have small use for the female principle segregated from life. It could help, and it won't; it knows nothing, cares nothing, except to be pitiable and bear children. For the rest, it is all talk.

If people in China want to give to their dead, even the very poor man, who has nothing but a few copper cash, can buy and burn some silver and gold ghost-money, which is just as good as wealth.

Many of the soldiers who fought out in the old rotting battlefields carried more up-to-date ghost money for their personal use in the next world. I still have a silver cardboard dollar, a good big handsome dollar like a crown piece, which stands to some dead Chinese soldier's account; and also a note for 1000 dollars, drawn on the Bank of the Other World. A few cents, or, for a very large equivalent, a few dollars Mex., would set a man up handsomely with a bank account when he got to the land of the spirits.

In the Temple of the Jade Buddha, the Buddha's companions were represented by strange gilded figures, man-high, towering on the two long lacquered benches which flanked the altar. The most interesting companion was the war god Kwan-yu, who is the paragon of Chinese democracy, having started off in life as a beancurd seller. (Personally I don't like beancurd, which has an odd, burnt taste, but it is a Chinese staple of life, like rice or noodles, and was keeping thousands of refugees alive.)

Kwan-yu was too enterprising to stay long in his simple occupation; he started out anew as a young fighter, defending the oppressed of his village, worked his way up to be a famous general, and at last an invulnerable and legendary leader, against whose shining mail of laughter all swords would crash in vain. And after his legend-death, the village people of China (who, after all, make the Chinese world) loved him the more: they sang songs about him, weaving him into the folklore of the race until Kwan-yu shone as brightly as a star. So the young beancurd seller and warrior became a god, and a companion of Buddha, and may be known in temples by his deeply slanting eyes.

These eyes (strangely believed by foreigners to be characteristic of all Chinese people, but actually a rarity except in certain parts of the north, and accounted a striking feature even there) are called 'the eyes of Kwan-yu,' and when a boy is born having such eyes, it is known that he will be a good warrior.

Anna's husband, who came from the north, where his father had been a leader in peasant revolt, had the eyes of Kwan-yu, and though I never met him while I was in Shanghai (he was always away in Hankow), at a Hankow reception of the Fourteen Federated Culture Societies, where there must have been hundreds of Chinese people present, I knew him the instant I saw the eyes of Kwan-yu looking at me across the table.

Anna gave me another example of Chinese democracy, having to do with examinations and buttons. The money dynasty, with which great families like the Soongs and the Kungs have commonly been associated (and the loosely knit fabric of industrialism and capitalism that has sprung up in coastal cities to give vent to it), is, after all, a new thing in China, a thing hardly yet tried in the depths of the nation.

Before money had the greatest prestige or power in China, scholarship had yet a greater prestige: it was worked by a system of examinations and buttons, and any poor boy who could somehow achieve the means of literacy and ram his bent for scholarship down the neck of his village ancestors (see *The Wallet of Kai Lung*) could settle down to serious thought of buttons. The fact was, according to Anna, that by passing examination after examination, a young Chinese man could *even* graduate as a possible son-in-law of the Emperor, with the moral right to a Princess for his bride. Only the examinations of candidates were not so pure-minded or so indiscreet as this may imply; and the Emperor of China (while there was an Emperor of China) was unlikely to be seriously afflicted by sons-in-law from the ranks. In the last instance, young candidates for examination were closely scrutinized for their good looks, which was only fair to the Princess. Some generations ago a paternal in-law of Anna's had very nearly achieved the honour, "But he did not quite pass," she related. "He was not, alas, beautiful enough!"

Meeting Anna was the direct result of Caley, and the indirect result of Miss Su and Miss Chen.

Miss Su, as promised, took me to the places where the kidnapped children were kept, when they ran away of their own accord, or when, after they had been used in the brothels, they became diseased and were turned loose. In either case, they were never more than young girls, and some were children. The Salvation Army had worked in here, and had a Door of Hope place, where children could stay for a few days until arrangements were made for them.

It was kind, but I could not bear the fuss they made over one fat little girl, who had had the brains and energy to scream in the streets when she was being carried away, and so escaped without moral hurt; while in the corner sat meekly enough the others, who had not cried out. One of them had caught smallpox, and then they turned her loose. She was sixteen. There was a little girl in mauve cotton trousers and jackets, with hair cut short, who sat still and said nothing. I asked what her story was, and Miss Su translated: she went out to pray at a shrine, and she missed her way back. That was five years ago.

The big Salvation Army home for the very small kidnapped children was pretty good. . . . I never saw so many rocking-horses and harmoniums before in my life, and in a classroom grave infants bowed and sang an exact Chinese equivalent of:

'Good morning to you,

Good morning to you,
Good morning, dear teacher, good morning to you.'

But that wasn't polite enough for Chinese kids, so after they had bowed and warbled to the teacher, they bowed and warbled to one another. And I liked their little gravity, and the rocking-horses. They were all sleeping foreign-style in foreign beds, I can't imagine why. Still, I liked the place, except for the booklet that told how the very young prostitutes in another home repented first of the sins other people had committed against them, and were then forgiven.

But you can't get away from the fact that general attention, cleanliness, and food are important, and all these were dispensed; whereas the last-visited home, which was purely Chinese, was about the worst yet. It was entered by a high gate, up a narrow alley, and the girls weren't allowed to go out, in case they should get kidnapped again. This might have been preferable.

Hands scaly and red with skin disease, as if they had been badly scalded; everywhere eyes narrowed and weak under the swollen pink eyelids which are soon shutters over blindness, the blindness of trachoma. But, mind you, those eyes and hands worked. The girls were employed doing a very fine type of embroidery which was sold at a cheap rate to big department stores, and thus not altogether wasted . . . except to the girls. They got paid, all right. Miss Su, the younger one of the two welfare workers, and the most fiery, became quite excited and annoyed over their rate of pay, which was usually about a dollar a year.

"It is not right, not right at all," she said. "This old man in charge knows nothing. Those two old women have no business here. There is no place for them to go. But what we need is more young people."

The old women were two widows, very aged, one an idiot and the other partially paralyzed. They lay on their sides on the floor of a room, just looking up, helpless and elephantine. Among the girls with the pink eyes and scalded hands you could look back and see several who would normally be lovely; and out of the dust, clay, and asphalt of the alley pierced one or two spears of green, living green.

'I will be an anarchist,' I thought, 'I prefer that to being a Communist, though Communists are usually better people.'

We went to one or two other places, including some factories where the Japanese dormitory system had been introduced. Some say the British introduced it first.

"That is not good at all," said Miss Su's level little voice. "It means that for twenty-four hours in the day, the girl worker is at her employer's command."

The Japanese were commandeering Chinese female labour for the same sort of factory system on the other side of the creek—but leaving the Japanese and the system out of it, I suddenly had a mad idea that everything would be improved, everything would be almost sane, if instead of the girls' dormitory walls being a dirty white which immediately became grey, they were splashed with colours, hard defiant colours—none of your pale stuff, but paint pots flung splash in the face of the system.

I didn't in the least want to leave the Grand Orient, but Miss Su and Miss Chen were equally determined that I should leave, and because of them Caley was bothered about it. At last I said I'd go.

Miss Chen rang me up, saying: "You are not under any obligation to stay; you will do as we say because it is right, āā?"

Momentarily I could have assassinated Miss Chen: she was Chinese, and fine, and self-controlled, doing ten times more good in the world than I had the slightest impulse to do: and she had lost her little summer house up the river, where she used to relax and have her idea of a good time. But she knew no more about my obligations to angel fish, bath-amahs, leg-shows, row, life, than she did of conditions on Jamaica sugar plantations.

I went downstairs, very nearly in tears, and tried to buy a dwarf pine, but Mr. Chang interpolated: "Not in your posish!" and I was fobbed off with a white hyacinth, which still had its hair in curl-papers.

I never found out if Mr. Chang had any politics. Certainly he wasn't worried about mine. His only anxiety was that we Australians should stick together . . . which meant that he was very civil . . . and that I should make a thousand pounds, or, as an occasional alternative, five thousand dollars gold.

"You are still a young woman. I have said to myself, I would like that young woman to do well. So perhaps, before you leave China, you will make five thousand dollars gold. Then, perhaps, you will buy me a big dinner." Laugh.

A very ordinary old Chinese man in a blue gown. I have always had a weakness for the gentle. Old Mr. Chang was only that—the gentle.

Anna's little house in the French Concession . . . the faithful amah; Anna's baby, Daybreak; a book called *The English —.Are They Human?*; reading the unfortunate news in the dailies by the warmth of the long-nosed German stove; settling down, after a few days of cringing before eggs in the soup, to a glorious mixture of Chinese chow and foreign-style cooking, whichever strikes us at the moment. When we are hungry, and there is nothing of solidarity to eat, we go out, through blue bubbles of cold, to the Russian cafés. We go to a Chinese talkie, which is bad, or, rather, about as good as a Wild West of ten years ago. But then, all the good Chinese talkie companies have been driven out of Shanghai. Butterfly Wu's *Two Sisters*, the story of a singsong girl, had been screened abroad. The last one, *March of Youth*, had to be very good, because the Japanese were so near. So it was good, flashing glimpses of the famous Eighth Route Army . . . *chi lai!* But now the companies have decamped to Hong Kong and Hankow, suffering, *en route*, only one serious, loss. Butterfly Wu, China's most striking screen star, is now otherwise engaged. Butterfly is going to have a baby.

On the walls of Anna's house, quick,cherry-blossom paintings, the work of a famous woman revolutionary artist, whose husband was one of the Seventy-two Martyrs of Canton . . . slain a little before Dr. Sun Yat-sen's revolution arrived. Two goldfish sail round in the dim oblong dream of their underwater existence: you must understand no Chinese home is quite complete without a goldfish for a focus, a radiant point of contemplation.

Those fine characters, black brushed heavily on white, are the work of a revolutionary poet. Her little room is half-way up the stairs. I am sleeping in the real bedroom, under another red quilt. Anna and her husband met in Berlin, where he was a student at the military academy, and she at a university. To have married in Germany would have created too many difficulties, so in their own time they ran away to London, were married there, and found their way to China.

In the old days, which are not really so old, Anna's husband's father was a parent-lord of his village. It had thick flat-topped walls, and he would walk around them at dawn, hitting the yellow clay with his old man's stick, telling the people to get up, when it pleased him to. But it is too cold in the winter there, a great deal too cold; in Shanghai are German stoves and braziers, but in the north there is nothing to do, except put on more and more padded clothes, like a stuffed animal, and look at one another, and pay calls of ceremony. Too cold, too cold. . . .

I think she is very beautiful, blonde, with hair cut and curled like shells round her ears, and a clear-cut Nordic profile . . . Hitler's one and only true Aryan. Only the trouble is, Anna simply can't stand Hitler. She is two things at once, the clear-cut, slightly arrogant German of East Prussia, and the temperamental progressive, who has by circumstance become the Chinese radical.

When she tells me, "My family were peasants," I think automatically of our isolated little New Zealand shacks, the poorest of the poor trying to stamp out a living with a hard die from a hard soil, nothing around but miles of scrub and shiftless, silvery grass, the rain sucked down into a wry mouth of salt.

Then she shows me pictures of a couple of houses like mansions, one in Poland, one in East Prussia; and herself slowly growing up.

"Our peasants," she says, "despise our aristocracy." But then a Chinese boy goes past in the alley, making an awful noise with a huge bunch of keys, which he jingles from his metal rods. It is all right for him to sing without ceasing, 'I mend keys, I mend keys,' but why should he make such a hideous key-noise into the bargain?

"He does it because he is a Chinese," says Anna, "because he is so *happy*." She is very German, very Chinese.

Anna has her doubts of the English, and it's a hard time for both of us. Unfortunately, Hitler has just got away with the *anschluss*. Unfortunately, Mr. Anthony Eden has just been forced into resigning, and Mr. Chamberlain is steaming placidly ahead into waters all dotted with little Fascist flags. Anna rather cottons to the *anschluss*, because she is a German, and Austria a German-speaking country. But she can't cotton to the way it has come about; Hitler and force, suborned votes, *coup d'état*, the old dark weapons never shining unless there's blood on them, rape where her sentimentalism directs there should be nothing but the most affectionate embrace. *The English—Are They Human?* To stop me from any possible criticism of the *anschluss* . . . a subject I should never dream of raising unaided, as I am much too hypocritical . . . she wages war on Chamberlain.

"It's *all* Chamberlain's fault," she says, looking at me over the top of the newspaper, as if I had personally created an individual quite strange to me, who has never, as a matter of fact, set foot on New Zealand soil.

Anna with the blonde shells of hair over her ears, wearing the green Chinese gown a Chinese tailor made her for seven dollars Mex.; Anna with her grey-blue eyes lit up, telling me how one writer speaks Chinese in her books, but in practice converses with her Chinese escorts by calling vigorously, "Lai, lai, lai," beckoning all the time; Anna coming down the stairs, saying: "This is the day that makes me happier than my birthday. It is International Women's Day."

We celebrate International Women's Day (I am afraid I had scarcely heard of that) in a Russian café, with two other girls, a Russian, who is not a White Russian, and another German. They all have medical or legal degrees. I like their lit-up eyes and ciphered faces. They were here in '27, and through the great bombardments that had smouldered away before I reached Shanghai, and before them I feel ignorant and childish.

She made me cry once, not on purpose. This was after the white hyacinth had settled down in the room upstairs, and I was used to writing there, and the younger amah, not the old servant, had learned two words of English, 'Hullo-yes!' which she always used, on any occasion, as greeting, repartee, occasional comment, or farewell. She was quite young, fat and pink-faced, and if Anna moved away she would go back to her master and be rented out again to somebody else, for she was that kind of amah, *pei nu*. I was sorry for her and tried to be very friendly, so immediately she thought I was insane, and I couldn't stop her from feeling my clothes all over, top to bottom, and fingering the paper when I wanted to write.

'Hullo-yes!' Are the English too human? I think so.

Anna was a good hand at taking photographs, and had one of those cameras which can be set to take photographer as well as scene. The camera had wandered beautifully up and down her Europe, up and down her childhood, with its clear profiles and lit candles. Then there was a little photograph of her husband and herself, before they were married; they had knapsacks on their backs, and were entering the Black Forest. Shadows elongated between the creamy and sooty trunks of silver birch trees, but I could not see the faces of the two young people, because they were turned aside . . . those two beautiful children, entering the woods of the world. I handed back the album, with a compliment, and Anna certainly did not know why I was crying.

Well, well: and the Ta-tao General died at about 10 p.m., not at dawn. He just stepped out of his car, and there was no time for his bodyguard to argue, for a gun cracked, making a blue mark between the surprised eyebrows. Those who had disliked the Ta-tao General never got caught. They ran away, and got lost in the Shanghai maze of small alleys which have high iron gates like garden gates.

"This is all very pleasant," I said, and Anna laughed.

"You wouldn't have said that a month ago."

It began then, it has continued ever since: when last I saw Shanghai, Shanghai had just celebrated the anniversary of the Japanese incident by blowing up the Yokohama Specie Bank. It was extremely unwise of the pro-Japanese terrorist gangs, in the first place, to decapitate newspaper publishers, bomb their offices, and leave smelly heads about at disconcerting places in the Concession. It stood to reason that once the overwhelmingly Chinese population had recovered the breath shaken out of it by bombardment and retreat, and the old and new organizations had taken up the interrupted threads of their discourse, the Japanese and, above all, the Ta-taos, would get so much the worst of it.

CHAPTER FIVE

Dark Places

WINTER LAY BETWEEN freeze and thaw. In a single night, I remember, the snow came down in big flakes as I lay wrapped in the scarlet quilt. The gutters of the short alley, where a few months ago the blood of wounded men had poured out, were flowering white; white the spikes and scallops of the black-tiled Chinese houses, whose iron gates were opened after so much banging and clatter; white the garden, three doors away, where robed Buddhist monks made twig and paper bonfires, and danced around that red streaming hair of flames, waving their arms and chanting wildly.

The second night, while the delicate crinkled flakes fell like silver ferns, losing their shapes as they piled up, fifty Chinese refugees died in the snow, quietly as the flakes.

The spring rains were bad, but it was hardly yet spring, and snow is such a rarity in Shanghai that Daybreak, sent out in his little padded winter suit to play with the beautiful stuff, sat down surprised, splodging the whiteness with his bucket and spade, not knowing what to do except grin at us over his shoulder. Most little Chinese boys are sewn into their winter suits, warm and padded. But Anna wouldn't have that, and Daybreak, whose Chinese name was Li Ming, was always bathed and immaculately changed at night, to lie in the firelight, chuckling and murmuring, until his amah, the old peasant, arrived to spread out the blankets—on which she slept at his feet.

After that Anna and I went to bed, because there was nowhere much else to go. The German stove was in that room; in Anna's or mine it was really too cold to write.

"Why," Anna once demanded of me, "has the great, the subtle, the inventive, the ingenious Chinese nation never invented a decent working *stove*, a comfortable *stove?*"

At the time, I couldn't think of any reason why the Chinese nation hadn't invented a stove, but later it came to me that since, centuries ago, they had cut down almost all the fuel wood in China, and old women now made thrifty livings picking up cinders and bits of coal from railway tracks, for richer people to use them in braziers, the Chinese nation had seen at once that to invent great flamboyant stoves would be purposeless, because they had no logs to keep stoves going.

Not fifty yards down the road was a big refugee camp of the matting type, its roof-mats now sagging with silver; the refugees can't have liked the trickles inside. When I went out, a straggle-haired woman knelt in the slush, right on the centre of the pavement, beating her head and wailing: "Aiyah!" Men, women, and dogs, shivering in their cosy pelts, hurried past her. Really, if one listens long, life no longer seems worth living! I had lost all my Hong Kong confidence, and no longer felt I could give dollars away, so I got back as quickly as possible, unleashing Eruish, who, with a joyous, tearing rush, knocked down Amah Number Two ('Hullo-yes!'), just as the fat girl was bringing mop and pail down the stairs.

I hoped Anna hadn't put too many eggs in the soup. That, more than anything in politics or race, tended to divide us.

"This is a completely Chinese house; you will find everything very plain," she told me when I arrived.

As a matter of fact the cooking had reached a compromise between China and Germany. At one meal we ate noodles and vegetables, completely Chinese: at some other time, Amah Number One took care of the baby, and we went around to buy sausage at a German shop, where Anna knew the scarlet and liver-coloured varieties from A to Z, and was friendly with the fine young German butcher who sold his sausage by the slice. The Chinese have a minute sausage, made of red scraps and fatty bits, but I never heard that foreigners eat it. Sausages I like; but to come upon raw eggs looking up at you like drowned suns from the soup is what I can't bear.

As often as not, we stopped at one of the small White Russian cafés of the Concession, and ate what must be the best chocolate cakes in the world. They're not even expensive: but no other race (Shanghai has the lot) knows so well how to produce saltish coffee and these cakes, and conspire over them, as the White Russians do, the tall, stately girls with plaits braided like coronets round their heads, the saintly-looking old men with silken beards.

The girls are rather uppish. Anna naturally doesn't like them much, for the White Russian minority (which is the second largest in shanghai, and has its own regiment and regimental band) harboured so many pro-Japanese spies and traitors when the five months' bitter fighting was on, out at Chapei, out in the devastated ghostly streets I have seen, out behind rotting sandbags of the race-course. Besides, the mentality of White Russian girls doesn't appeal to her.

"They will beg," she says, "they will lie, spy, cheat, swindle, steal, prostitute themselves, in fact, they will do anything at all you can think of; but they will not work. The Russian in that film *Tovarich* was supposed to be funny, but he was perfectly correct. Works! Don't mention it, even as a joke!"

Caley has already told me this, and a bit more; but the old White Russian men are more tiresome than the tall, beautiful girls, whose looks give them a just place in Shanghai's unborn but stirring spring.

Just a few yards away the blue and gilded domes of the Russian Cathedral float like a not unattractive pipe-dream above the matting roofs of refugee camps, continually raided by Japanese soldiers and Ta-tao police, who are looking, poor dears, for conspiracies and guns. They never have any luck.

Every Sunday, lines of respectable-looking old White Russian beggars form up near the cathedral doors, begging not from their fellow-countrymen, but from curious passers-by. If you say: "There's a Russian gentleman, why don't you ask him for a few cents?" they draw themselves up, and remind you that this is impossible, as they do not belong to the Orthodox Church. This makes it more difficult for everybody; unpleasantly drunken White Russian men beg outside the butcherly shop-cafés where Anna and I buy cheese and raw salmon, or raw red caviare, whose salty little red bubbles are quite cheap.

In the bleak trees interlacing the roads of the French Concession are great nests, out of which caw, claw, and tumble the uncouth rooks. The Concession is noted for its, flower-shops, though the Chinese have no idea about conventional flower arrangement. They will make you gilded baskets, with small liver-purple lilies sticking out like pokers all the way round, all the same height. Otherwise you do better to stick to a hyacinth in a pot.

I'm beginning to feel at home, can tell a ricksha boy 'Avenue So-and-So, Rue Joffre,' without ending up somewhere along Soochow Creek, that locked water into whose upper reaches a rain-swell brought so many sightless bodies tumbling less than two months ago . . . the bodies, especially, of young Chinese girls. Soochow was dished, like Nanking and the other cities.

The spring, which is such a good time for hyacinths in pots, is a bad time for refugees, because with the rains come measles and, smallpox. Every morning, the bodies of refugee children were found placed neatly, almost primly, outside tenement refugee camps, whose inmates had not ventured into the street daylight for weeks. But when the children died, in semi-darkness, their parents or some other weary old pair of black trousers carried them outside, and then they were collected by the corpse-wagon.

I once ran into the corpse-wagon, which was stationary outside a building, and open at the back. A piece of canvas was dragged over almost all its contents, so that I might have passed it by without knowing what it was, but the body of one little boy lay face downwards on top, wearing a padded winter suit like Daybreak's, only very much torn and untidy, and in colour a faded pink. I suppose in the beginning it had been red, which is China's good-luck colour for children, and almost always used for the suits of the important boys. For a moment I thought the baby in the corpse-wagon was nothing but a large doll, but then something about his very stillness made me sure.

Soochow Creek at this point (where sampans and boats lie locked as if they could never be poled apart again, some fluttering the Rising Sun) is a good long way from the French Concession, which is considered the safest part of Shanghai. The Concession seems to contain every kind of human being, except English, American, or French, the only ones whose languages I can speak. The traffic police are big Chinese, and stand glued to little stands; certainly they don't speak French or English. I mention this to show how wise and yet how difficult it is to get one's bearings.

Caley, my real guide and moral support in Shanghai, seemed to be the only person who might answer that need. Caley was staying on in Shanghai, because that was his job for the present, and the Chinese working people with whom he had been associated for the past ten years hadn't stopped needing assistance and supervision with the fall of the city.

But he had got a restless idea into his head that working in Shanghai was the same thing as working for the Japanese. All this meant was that he had a need to be in direct contact with free China, and to use his own abilities more fully than his diffidence he had let him use them up to the present time. With his friend Jim, who had a couple of other bloods in his veins besides the predominating Chinese, he stuck around quietly in his flat after working hours, or on Sundays they slung their cameras, and went off to the devastated areas or the few villages still accessible.

"We're devoting our lives to photography now," said Caley, "aren't we, Jim?"

They had some good shots of the dead soldiers lying out in the devastated areas. The front streets had been cleaned up by Chinese coolies working under Japanese supervision, also the ground floors of most of the wrecked and eyeless houses left standing. Personally conducted tours of the battle areas had started almost as soon as the shooting stopped, and the Japanese were well in on the racket.

It was certainly a racket. I know, for I made the tour from the Grand Hotel on the first afternoon of my stay in Shanghai, and it cost me thirteen dollars. The car had a red spot on the windscreen, and the driver, who spoke excellent English, said: "You will be able to go a long way, and the sentries will not stop this car." But if I had gone in a car without a red spot, and chanced the sentries, it would have cost me six dollars only, and as the Japanese sentries at that time were seldom very rude to foreigners (this was before the long, sad line of slapped American and British faces started lining up on Garden Bridge), I don't know that the red spot was worth seven dollars extra.

The devastated areas extended far past the factories (which were a mass of sheer ruin) to smallish cotton patches, and the huts of peasants. The Chinese could not get used to the idea that they were not allowed to go back to these little places of their own, now the big smoke appeared to be over.

Indelibly it is Chinese custom, once some big excitement has passed, for those who have gone into other places to pick up their ragged bundles, replace them on their sticks, and, calling to heel such family remnants as they have left, to start back home again.

The Chinese tried to do this regularly every night: you couldn't call their agitation a riot, it was too weaponless, too determined to reason this matter out, rather than to fight the Japanese soldiers and the more officious Ta-tao police. But there was usually the same soft black surging forward of the unarmed, the same upcry of voices, and, like stones, the same sharp commandments and blows beating them back.

This endeavour to get back home accounted for a good many of the beatings-up in Shanghai; others happened at the barbed-wire entanglements, where peasants who *were* allowed to go backwards and forwards, bringing in some of their produce to the city markets, got into arguments with the soldiers and Ta-taos.

There were rows of barbed wire, where the peasants were supposed to pass four in line. That was why one man was shot, while I was in Shanghai. He fell out of line for a moment, lost his head, and stumbled forward as unwanted fifth man, and a Japanese soldier plugged him through the breast.

And another stopped to pick up a piece of wire which was lying on the ground, because a Chinese can make almost-something out of almost-nothing, and whenever he sees such a thing as a piece of rope or wire lying loose, the affectionate thought pops into his mind: 'Now, *this* will just about do for *that!*' Half the time, *this* will do for nothing at all, and the probability is that his piece of wire, when he got it, would not have been good enough even for a mouse-trap: but he got plugged for it, and the plain daylight murder, seen by plenty of foreigners in Shanghai, was labelled 'For Looting.'

Because of this fuss at the barricades, and equally because of a Japanese order against replanting cotton or letting the junk-fishermen go out in safety, there was a shortage of almost everything at the Chinese markets, which I walked through, thinking how far the Chinese can make one pig go per person, by cutting it up in small knuckly portions for sweet and sour pork, and throwing away none of the more bloody bits. Also, of course, the Chinese use sow-meat, and almost everything hanging from the butchers' hooks seemed recently to have been a mother. But because of the fresh fish shortage, Shanghai was falling back on salted fish: because the peasants could no longer maintain free contact between country-side and markets, there weren't many vegetables.

On my first trip out through the devastated areas, the rotting cotton plants, limp in patches of water, some with their bolls still showing white, were the one thing that really moved me. The rest, the endlessly repeated phantasmagoric streets with their wooden and paper bowels gushing out, their fronts ripped off, chairs and tables still standing or lying at the queer angles the bombardments had thrown them, should have been sufficiently effective; but it looked silly, you know. There was so much of it, and no possible sense to it, and though these houses had been alive once, with the currents of humanity dammed up or free among them, there was nothing to connect that recent past with the present. Total effect, silly.

The red spot guide pointed out the Doom Battalion's factory, where the men hung on, and a Chinese girl named Yang Hui-ming ran across to them, under machine-gun fire, carrying a Chinese National Flag. Yes, that was brave: and the kiddie's broken blue motor car, pulled up in front of the grandstand at the race-course, where behind rotting sandbags Chinese divisions had held out for five long months, should surely have been touching. If only it hadn't all seemed so dead!

My little guide and I got out, and walked about the race-course, among pits and dead men's sandbags. Some Japanese people had come also, and appeared to be dignitaries, for they were behaving towards one another with elaboration; they were well-dressed, warm people.

I tried to glare at them, but couldn't get over the feeling that we were all puppets, acting in a dead man's farce, where silent dead men had booked all the seats.

The guide picked up a wooden ball (which I have kept ever since as a souvenir) and gave it to me, saying politely: "Look, a bullet!" I wondered why he thought I would think it was a bullet, but was too polite to ask him. He was only trying to give me thirteen dollars' worth. At another place, he stopped the car and said: "Would you like to get out and pray?" but this was so unexpected that I felt sure I had misunderstood.

"Well," he said, "many people come to pray here," and I saw the neat, small oblongs of ground, marked with white sticks for dead Japanese soldiers. If the soldier were a private, he got a little white stick, but to a lieutenant was allowed quite a dominating stick, and from each plot pointed a small, dark tree.

It was a neat conception, and better than the teeming burial of the Chinese soldiers in the back streets, so many of them lying face downward in pools of water and mud. But none of it lived until the cotton patches came into sight, and there, with the white fluff clinging on water-logged stems marked out for decay, something was trying so hard to grow.

I might have said to the guide: "Stop, I will pray here, if you like," but there was no point in unsettling his thoughts, and we slid on through one area which was unbombed, and kept for Japanese people. Kimonoed women walked there, their shoulders broad because of the babies carried on their backs; they stopped one another, and talked, and a tiny doll had a jet fringe above such laughing eyes. It was odd to see how the Japanese boys had taken to roller-skating, and were cutting merry figures in these streets so close to dangerous or silent streets. One of them carried a miniature bayonet.

Meanwhile, the peasants now corning to market carried their produce on their backs, or, at best, pushed it in wheelbarrows. In the days before the war it had come by boat down Soochow Creek, or quite handsomely by lorry along the roads; to-day every member of the family was pressed into service. Once they had passed the barbed wire entanglements they no longer cared about time, and plumped down where they were, their heads lolling back against brick walls; tired fairies, the barefoot girl-children, carrying bundles of thorny twigs which they thought they could sell for firewood; elderly women with bound feet, who expected to sell old vases, clocks, household goods of Heaven knows what trivial antiquity; old men, whose produce was wilted and bruised. There was a faint jollity among them, and behind them shone the neat green rows of vegetables planted by the children of a comparatively good matting refugee camp, one where there was not only space to move around outside, but a patch for planting things. I asked a ten-year-old boy, all ribs, what they had planted, and he said importantly: "Wild vegetables." I am convinced they were any sort of non-poisonous green weed, but nevertheless they were at least growing, and could be eaten or sold.

The refugee camp, inside, was held up and divided by bamboo poles. Each little space was separated off by matting, and cross-sectioned by more bamboo poles, covered with matting which acted as floor and ceiling. The whole effect was a system of ship's berths, upper and lower, arranged in a giant dormitory which might accommodate several hundreds, and between the berths squeezed narrow earth-floored corridors, on which the refugees and their camp officials came or went. In each matting berth lived a refugee

79

family; so many of the black-trousered peasant women, lying back with their jackets open over their brown breasts, were suckling children born to this estate.

But here, where the people could get outside for a breath of air, and even grow wild vegetables, the matting camps seemed not so bad. It was the city camps I minded, especially one other, after this same style, but much more constricted, and a tenement camp in a rotting, lightless old building, where the pale children looked up, as if fungus should suddenly be presented with eyes and little crying mouths; They did not merely cry, they shrieked when strangers came down the dark ladders, because they lay all .the time in the dark, and the outside world was a dim dream to them, holding voices and movements of which their senses were afraid.

And there, too, women lay with their jackets open over their breasts, and gave suck to infants for whom Life itself said in the rustling voice of a serpent: "Death."

But it wasn't all like that: I must remember more clearly. i remember, then, the thin rods of glass, almost as fine as strands of a cobweb, laid out red-hot across the soil of an alley where a miniature glass factory had established itself next door to one camp. The optimistic factory had started with no capital, next-to-no labour . . . a bare roof, a bare floor, an improvised oven, some interested boys and some glass. It was now turning out glass pipes and pots, and its boys were getting paid, though a Trade Union official's hair would probably turn white in a single night at the thought of what they were getting paid. At the end of the same alley, a Chinese urchin with a promising belly (considering the times) staggered out clutching a fowl to his breast, uttered two English words, "All right!" and sat down in the mud.

I went out again to the devastated areas in Caley's car, which didn't cost me thirteen dollars. It was a fine day, and there were big red earthenware jars of soya bean lying about. We came to a place where an entire though miniature village, clay-walled, black-tiled, had died twice over . . . once swallowed whole by the Chinese factory areas, which had swept around it without disturbing it, and once killed for keeps, when the Japanese arrived.

It had missed the bombardments, and had, I suppose, little to loot, for it stood almost intact . . . quite still, quite uninhabited, quite dead. We went through a courtyard whose communal well showed a glossy dark mirror, foul with the slime of years, perhaps, but clear when into its lifeless waters looked down two living faces.

We went past that into a temple. Blue and red paint peeled from the noses of door-post images. The toppled gods were all clay. Caley said this must be a temple for the very poor, the sweepers and cleaners, or at least some of the gods would have been painted wood. But village women had made Kwan-yin a neat trouser suit of beaded apricot satin and put beads and silver leaves in her hair. Before her lay toppled a tree about a foot high, sweetened up with bells and pink roses. I stood this on its feet again, and its child branches touched the childish suit of apricot satin. The temple was hung with scarlet cotton bags, containing the paper prayers of women who wish to bear children. There were also thin red wands and coils of incense. One of the red cotton prayer-bags I took away, thinking Kwan-yin and the woman who put it there would not have much use for it now.

There was windy, white-cockerel sunshine, tail-feathers streaking about in the mud, for this was nearly the end of winter in Shanghai, and the days, except when splashed sloppy with mud and rain, were blue-clear, taking in their arms new branches of cherry trees.

They livened up the red tabs and dun forage cap of the Japanese soldier, who stood watching us climb into the car, wondering why the car had stopped there, and were we having the cheek to loot in those ruins, and anyhow, what there was to loot. His fingers looked as if the streak of his bayonet had frozen to their skin; most of his face was divided between cap and leather beak. I asked Caley why one never saw a Japanese soldier without a beak, and he said it was because the Japanese have a horror of germs. But Percy, the Chinese chauffeur, leaned over and cracked his joke, saying that Japanese soldiers always want to bite the Chinese so much, they have to wear beaks to stop themselves.

As a matter of fact, we *were* doing a little looting. We drove next to a school, a big, wrecked place for Chinese boys. It had been bombed, so one side was down in a slide of bricks, and the inside was a proper mess. The smashed desks, the sheer filthiness of the floors, the children's exercise books torn and scrabbled over, struck me as being a waste of time and sense. As usual, the drunken looters had been too busy having fun to get what might really have been some use to them.

I had plenty of time to take a look round, because Caley was going through one room, looking for something, and it was a while before he collected it all. The first time they got back to this school, after the sack, they found the boys' mascot, which was a little monkey, tied up by its neck and starved to death. In the spilling coarse green plumes of grass were hidden pits and gashes.

"Look round," called Caley. "Maybe you'll find a few bullets there, or a shell."

But I had my wooden bullet, which was good enough for me, so I came back and took a look at Caley's collection. It was all anti-Japanese propaganda. I couldn't read the Chinese, but some of the cartoons were hot stuff.

I asked: "What will they do if they stop the car?" (The Red Tabs had the right to stop any car in this area, foreign or Chinese.)

Caley said: "They won't do anything to us, but they'll shoot percy." Percy was sitting outside, smoking and reading what looked like the Chinese equivalent of a penny novelette.

"That's no good," I said, "I'd a lot sooner they shot you than Percy. Percy's all right."

"The odds are they won't stop the car," said Caley, coming out to stand in the windy sunlight, with the lines of two wars furrowed almost in a V-shape across his forehead. Percy told us there was nobody coming, and we got the bundles, done up neatly enough in sacking, into the back of the car, where I sat unnecessarily close, like a hen covering her chickens, or some old Cavalier dame smuggling a refugee beneath her petticoats. But the Red Tabs took no notice, and Percy drove us to a place where the bundles went through a green gate, up a garden path, and that was the end of them. And there were white spring flowers against a wall.

Mei Lan-fang dances his performance, 'The Song of Madness,' in aid of the refugees.

He is part of China, the Peiping man with the exquisite art of female impersonation, the fine-drawn face. He went to U.S.S.R., and Moscow was crazy over him: he went to U.S.A., and an American university made him a Doctor. Nothing has impaired his popularity with the Chinese, but so far as we can count, there are only six foreigners in the audience, and Anna is scandalized. In time, she is also scandalized by some Chinese, who spit in little puddles all round us.

"They will have *New Life!*" she whispers, in tense sarcasm, "they will not *spit!*

Not spitting is a definite item of Chiang Kai-shek's New Life programme: but one which unfortunately has not taken full hold as yet.

Mei Lan-fang is considered a daring innovator, because he has concealed the noisy orchestra behind curtains. His trophies, little baskets of azaleas and sticking-out liver-purple lilies, sit in rows at the sides of the stage, while the audience becomes one vast litter of peanuts, small grubby mandarins, ices. Into the first scene roll two scarlet-clad tumblers and a young pink-turbanned actor, who performs a sword dance, crossing and uncrossing his bent Legs over the swords with considerable speed and grace. When this seems to pall, he leaps up on tables and chairs, still with knees bent, continuing to dance long after a mere human being would have been out of breath. In the next play, silken flags show the strength of the armies commanded by beautiful generals, whose costumes are amazingly fine. When a general carries a whip tasselled with wool, he is riding at top speed; a blue cloth shows that he has arrived at the walls of a city, and to enter a door he has only to make the motion of turning the handle. Nothing so crude as a real city, horse, or door is requisite. The important man in this play is not a general, but a civic official, wearing silver-bordered robes, who sings in a lady-like voice so weak that continually he is refreshed with cups of tea . . . real cups of real tea.

"Hao-a! Hao-a!" cry the Chinese.

Over the yellow silk curtain, the great branch of cherry-blossom; as a stage backdrop, a second cloth, showing one bough of wistaria, a stork's wide wings, black rook-like birds dropping down softly on their nests; Mei Lan-fang's beautiful simplicity of costume . . . pale green, with silver leaves of willows, white and black in a bamboo pattern, and peach-colour for his triumph scene.

Long, entirely straight black tresses fall to his garment's hem. Pink and white pointed face, arched brows, hands hidden in white square sleeves of finest material. The sleeves are a part of the dance. His dumb amah wears purple and white. She is dumb on the programme, which does not prevent her from singing louder than her young mistress, the beauty whose husband must be murdered to satisfy the lust of an evil viceroy, and who, taking the dumb amah's advice, feigns madness to get out of an entanglement which could bring only financial profits at best.

Mei Lan-fang, going mad, weeping quietly, stoops down and pulls one tress over his face. It is extraordinary how this dishevelment alters him. He opens his mouth, and out flies a little catlike "Aaa!" His sleeves fall back, showing those *hands* I have wanted to see all the evening . . . little, clawlike in narrowness, but strong and expressive to the last degree. Even in the presence of the Emperor, he begins to fondle the wicked Viceroy's silken beard. He tweaks: imagine the Viceroy's embarrassment!

The Chinese, who think that with this climax the best is over, rush for the exits. As we soon discover, all the ricksha boys have doubled their charges on the strength of a Mei Lan-fang performance.

Old songs in Mandarin, old songs with haunting airs, are known to every Shanghai coolie. The Chinese have written 103 war-songs since the beginning of their conflicts with Japan, and if we put on a record shouting "Chi-lai! Chi-lai! Chi-lai!" (the famous Manchurian marching-song, now a Chinese 'Marseillaise') we are liable to have a ring from the police, asking us to change the record. The Japanese are sensitive about the song, which has become most popular. Others are lovely . . . the old, slow fisherman's song, the lapping about of a race in songs of its occupations, its mythology, its lines of growth.

Almost, every night, lying in the red padded quilt, I dreamed about New Zealand, dreams so sharp and vivid that when I woke up, it seemed the black-tiled houses that were a fairy-tale. People walked . . . an old sailor who was anxious for me to write his life-story, Elsie at the bay, a poet who never could stand me, but who in the dream was walking on our hills, and his words were like Christmas stars, so wise and kind and fair. I was restless for these dreams, and turned for them from the early shadow of sleep, like a drug addict for his drugs.

About this time I got my marching-orders. At first there was the offer of a job in Shanghai, writing straight-out propaganda for circulation in America's Middle West. After a look at the straight-out propaganda, I refused the job . . . foolishly, perhaps, in the long run.

"If you do anything more to the mind of the Middle West, it's going to turn anthropoid."

"But contributions and circulation of this stuff have trebled since we started," objected the quiet man with the silver-grey hair, who was doing the talking. He was not of the Middle West, he was from England, and wading knee-deep in the blood of people he cared about; for his particular job was documenting the Nanking atrocities, so fortunately witnessed by Fitch and an American camera-man . . . whose white-hot indignation eventually went for little in this world, our accustomed soft-boiled world.

To the quiet man with the silver-grey hair, I was the smallest of small fry, and didn't deserve another chance after turning down the first: but eventually I persuaded him that I could write better, if allowed to write in my own way, and the end of it was a month's roving commission in Canton, where I was to write articles, human interest stuff, for a Chinese paper.

The editor of the Chinese paper, Dr. Wen Yuan-ning, is down on the P.E.N. Club circular as China's delegate and representative. I was a member of the New Zealand branch. Like other publications not dulcet enough to suit the Japanese administration, Dr. Wen's several papers had moved their headquarters to Hong Kong. Theoretically, the little *Far Easten Mirror*, for which I now wrote articles, came out in Hankow; the Japanese were being so rude to the Hong Kong British about the anti-Japanese publications anchored tight in Hong Kong, and the Hong Kong British, in their gradual, courteous way, were stalling the Japanese on the one hand, and on the other hand telling the Chinese that really they mustn't. So the Chinese sometimes compromised by bringing out anti-Japanese publications in Hong Kong, and saying they came out in Hankow.

Anyhow (as I had very few dollars Mex. remaining to me) I got 500 dollars Mex. for the assignment, including travelling and hotel expenses whilst in Hong Kong. Of my five hundred, 'Hullo-Yes!' immediately stole fifty, for which I couldn't find it in my heart to blame her.

Before I came to Shanghai, Anna and Caley used to go out every Sunday to the Chinese village at the Great Western Road entrance, now almost the only Chinese village where you could walk free, once you got to it, though you had to negotiate some barbed wire first.

Now I came too, though Caley wasn't so sure about that.

"A man's got his own little group that he's built up around him," he said.

And they weren't there, but they looked at me with shining, half-ghostly eyes . . . the veterans, Chinese and foreign. I hadn't anything much to say to them. For this reason, I felt glad I was going to Canton, which was a free Chinese city.

It was all right when the weight of their experience stopped being collective, and politics weren't walking all over us; when we, instead, were walking out past the Chinese gates of the Zacchewei Road and the Great Western Road, where the first flakes of spring had fallen in such wide and glistening snow on the extended cherry trees. There was a filthy little cesspool of a creek, so jammed up with boats you couldn't see how their dwellers would ever get anywhere again. The boat-dwellers were nearly all spotlessly clean, smiling up from the usual flap of washing; all the children looked to be in good repair. Men sold pastry-twists, anything from six inches to a couple of feet long, pink sticky rounds of candy pierced through by a stick, and Chinese jelly-sweets.

You saw the family auctions against the walls, sometimes with a vase whose smooth crimson looked like Sung, if you didn't know any better. In the village market were stalls selling sweetmeats, pork pies, old books, mechanical odds and ends, pink rice-cakes, pastries, beancurd, and tools: as a sideshow there was a booth with Siamese twins pickled in a jar. They were real Siamese twins, but they looked pretty old and decayed by this time.

Then came a bridge, so nearly broken you could never tell if you would fall in or not, and a strong ammoniac reek from ploughed fields . . . the first ploughed fields of Shanghai.

Huts stood, sunken in mud-ruts to their knees, lowly beside the peak and spire of a Roman Catholic cathedral. The cathedral owned the green, bushy garden, its few trees in ghostly bloom. And looking across fields where

Chinese grave-mounds ate up the space of the living to feed the dead, I could see a plantation of slender young pine, a stone shrine put up to the memory of some Chinese. Over a clutch of peasant cottages the tiles made all one roof, one sunken and humble roof; and out of walls, which were little but earth and dried grass worked together, I could hear voices whispering. There were babies in the sun; a Chow dog barked his head off, imitated by a puppy so fat it could barely stagger, and there was no other animal in sight except, on a grave-mound, the largest black billygoat I ever saw.

In the days before the trouble you walked out to little hills, and there were the wild azaleas, many-coloured. On holidays it was very common for Chinese to make up excursions, and go out to see the azaleas. But now the azaleas were not for Shanghai.

Anna and I are alone in the crowd by the western market gates. A young French policeman, mounted and gallant, didn't want us to go into the crowd. There is some sort of trouble, right up at the gates, but with so many Chinese in front, around, behind, it's difficult to see. A surge backward, the soft resistless surge of flesh that is frightened. Now we can see the whips rising and falling; there are two Japanese on guard at the gates, and they are moving into the crowd, beating it over its head. The French policeman is visible, prancing.

Anna's laugh cuts the air, hard as the whip.

"Our beautiful white skins!" she says, "he's afraid for our beautiful white skins!"

Nothing happens to our beautiful white skins. But the same week is an unlucky one for poor Dr. Birt, who has the misfortune to be mistaken for an Englishman by two Japanese. In reality, he is a German, nobody more inoffensive; but before he can open his mouth to explain, he is on the ground, being kicked by the large boots of little men.

"Dirty English pig! Dirty English pig!"

The matter is serious for Dr. Birt, who suffers serious danger to the sight of one eye: but the Japanese, after all, apologize.

They didn't, so far as I know, apologize in the Remedios case, which has always struck me, irreverently, as being very funny. In the first place, Mr. Remedios (a British subject this time) was sitting in his car, when two drunken soldiers came along, pulled him out, kicked him—and one of them, who had evidently left off the indispensable leather beak, also bit him.

The newspapers gave full publicity to all this, but in a few hours the Japanese published this denial. No Japanese soldier could have forgotten himself so far as to bite. It must have been a Japanese civilian.

Little cups of hot rice-wine at the Sun Ya restaurant, to celebrate my going to Canton: the little cups are filled from a silver kettle.

We are not precisely gay. I want to go to Canton . . . isn't that a free Chinese city, half the way to Hankow? . . . but can't help feeling that maybe I should have stayed in Shanghai, and written myself blind, deaf, and dumb for the Middle West.

The man with silver-grey hair is going to England soon. Anna still wants to go to Hanko; Edgar Snow says; "Perhaps I will see you on the way to Hankow."

Caley says, in a voice of subdued passion; "I expect I'll rot here." Working under the occupation is tramping on his nerves. All I can do is to feel bad-tempered as well, and wish people would have some more rice wine.

Chinese laughter comes over the walls of the cubicle. The Sun Ya restaurants are marked off in cubicles, and not really Shanghai style, but Cantonese importations. Cantonese are the people who like to eat and drink.

From the boat in the yellow water, bound once again for Hong Kong, you can look back at Shanghai, thinking (as perhaps the foreigner always thinks): 'Well, hit and miss. Hit here, miss there.'

A little silver-locked English girl in a blue frock and panama hat was climbing up steps into a British man-o'-war. She stopped, waving and waving her hanky at a Japanese gunboat, which had just turned downstream, and from the boat's side waving sailor-figures answered her back. I guessed they had given her such a good time, that they would so much enjoy giving her, or anyone else, a good time. Never with men, the accursed quarrel: with abstractions, with instruments, with the obstinacies of minds fighting against their own free, dangerous current. I wondered if she would now cry into her hanky. But she made a brave little picture, waving away.

Downstairs, a young English stewardess was doing some ironing. This old boat was a P. and 0., making her last voyage, and Shanghai her stopping-place after a round of Japanese ports, which the stewardess, apparently, had both loved and hated.

"It's all so *un-necessary!*" she exploded. "Some of those houses—just hovels, and how they can let the sailors . . ."

A little sadly, after more conversation, she added: "I wish now I hadn't seen it."

But an older stewardess came in, and asked the young one, had she got the bronze vase with the irises? And my little stewardess gushed: "Oh, *yes*, wasn't it luck to find it again, when she nearly gave up the idea?"

And I thought, moving off: 'A winter in a quiet English township, with a lot of Georgian houses and practically no boys, ought to make that trip to

Japan seem quite iridescent, little one.'

We sat at long tables, almost completely isolated. On one side sat Colour, a long line of Hindus, Parsecs, and Chinese, and opposite, grouped at the top, languished the Raj, comprising an English boy with a moustache, a seasick commercial traveller, and me. Various European nationalities straggled along after us—a silent Italian, a very jolly Swiss aviation mechanic (who claimed to know more about Madame Chiang Kai-shek's reasons for resigning the National Aviation Commission than any but Madame Chiang Kai-shek's dearest intimates would have known), and a German, cross. The loneliest atom was a small round Chinese, overflowed from our opposites, and seated, perforce, at the very end of our thin red line. To speak to him at all one had to shriek across a gulf of several empty chairs; my heart nearly broke for him until I discovered that he was Ta-tao, and insisted that the New Soul of China was only to be discovered in Tientsin.

The principle of sitting us all opposite was horrible, and we ate into our plates and avoided one another's eyes. Only the Swiss, who talked all the time in a loud, mechanical voice about inside information which he could not possibly have extracted, and would not have spilled so publicly if he had, was ever in a good temper.

Nobody ever weeps for the white people. Is it because the white people have such reservoirs within themselves? Or do we look as if the tears would bounce off? Certainly there's our damned proselytizing, imperializing, interfering streak. But that has passed its meridian. The Mohammedans also proselytize.

Anyhow, I don't like the look of it. It looks as if the white people might soon be weeping for the white people.

On the whole, it was an unsuccessful trip, though if I had known that the ship was making her last voyage I'd have tried to like it better. Old ships have their feelings, their failures, like ourselves.

There at the journey's end were the Hong Kong refugees again—the little boys begin to show shaven summer pates, marked with the scars of ringworm, the street Chinese gloriously happy in any battered, dilapidated remnant of a sun helmet.

It was funny about the refugee swing. Sometimes, simultaneously, refugees were flowing to and from Canton, into and out of Shanghai. Up and down China. Up and down China. Some from Peiping to Yunnanfu, the capital of the red and green province which is farthest south. Scale it on the map, then remember, their feet were bare, or wearing at best canvas shoes or string sandals. Many of the women from the north had bound feet. In the northern interior, nearly all women over thirty are thus, because, though the Chinese Government made this custom illegal thirty or more years ago, it took the country people several years to catch up with the idea. Later I saw villages where little girls still had their feet bound. Such markings, in such dust.

I met Jim Bertram, who wrote *Crisis in China* (the first book out concerning the Sian incident), and who had been five months in the north with the Eighth Route Army, accompanying the forces of a Chinese General named Ho Lung.

He was another New Zealander, a Rhodes scholar. But he didn't look like Oxford now, having just come down; he cracked pretty good Chinese with the waiters, and took me to Macao, the Portuguese colony, a place four hours' sail away, which dreamed. It was a silver-grey day, all mist, and the junks lying flat against the water, and at the end of the trip Macao's houses were colour-washed pink, green, and blue, with Chinese girls under rimmed parasols walking in the wet streets, and big Chinese policemen wearing the colours of Portugal, red and green. It had to be Chinese, though Portuguese, for it is the great opium-font, feeding China with opium through Hong Kong, and by other routes.

But the day lay so windless, nobody was going to worry about opium, and we drove through narrower cobbled streets than any I had seen as yet to a spacious forgotten palace, which condescended also to be a hotel-restaurant, and sold us purple *vinto teinte*. This wine of the place is cheap, but when you drink a little you feel lost, in a dreamy way; we went on to the villa of a man who had come to Macao when he was eighteen, and stayed there ever since. It wasn't built like a Chinese house, but pointed up in several one-story green peaks from the flat of grass, and anemones lay there, purple and scarlet, on the listless air.

Down below, re-ached only by a curving road which made the harbour look far away, spat the red crackling fireworks of some religious procession. The aristocracy of Macao is Portuguese and Roman Catholic, and the Macanese as a whole adore religious processions, so fireworks form a tiny industry. An English poet, Will Empson, was here in the green villa. To me it seemed we had all arrived, without knowing why we arrived or what would happen next, though I daresay this was the *vinto teinte* (of which I had some more), and the others had intentions more clear-cut.

Once the poet Camoens landed on Macao, and one of his sonnets is engraved on the stone of his grotto, translated into French and German. But better than Camoens' grotto (with the little pots of red geraniums making a double sentry-row down before it) I liked something on the one remaining wall of the cathedral, built for Macao by persecuted Japanese Christians.

It appeared the Japanese Christians could be persecuted, like anyone else, and a band of them, sick and tired of their persecutions, eventually turned up in Macao, where they were well received and at once put to work. Fortunately, they were skilled masons, and having raised and carved the cathedral (whose crumbling facade shows the queerest Japanese-looking virgins and saints you can expect to meet), they did better. . . Right at the top, they carved the masons' tools, the ropes, the chisels, with which this good work had been built. A typhoon blew away all the cathedral except this fragment.

Past the shut eyes of a convent one goes down a sloping path, beyond a small locked chapel, and into a green garden of the dead. It is well kept, yet wildness has it at the heart; even the pale roses, shedding their petals, are more distraught than English roses should be.

And yet this soil is very English, being the Protestant cemetery where young men of the East India Company were buried, in years longer ago by mood than by time. Some relative of the Churchill family was buried here. But while they went looking for that grave, over wet grass, I found a way between Hannahs and Abigails and their young husbands, and discovered a well, over which a dark bough and white roses leaned, and the clear water was a mirror, far down.

I looked, but if there was anything blew across the mirror, I have forgotten now what it was.

The man who owned the green villa and the anemones told me, courteous as Portuguese or Chinese: "You have always a house on Macao," and we were off, talking all the way back about opium to a Chinese gentleman, who insisted there was plenty being smoked below, that very minute. I wanted to go below, and see, and try, but they said quickly: "No, you must not do that."

Dr. Wen Yuan-ping, a slender youthful man who had graduated at Cambridge, in his office was ceaselessly, impossibly busy, and could not be talked to at all. When we went for lunch, he talked not of the war, but of modern poets . . . T. S. Eliot, Rilke, Walter de la Mare. I wanted to bring in the war, and Canton. But he was pleased at having received a letter from Walter de la Mare, and to interpolate seemed a little rude, or anxious, like Mr. P. Soo, coming over on the boat. "If, please? . . ." As soon as dinner was over, he was ceaselessly, impossibly busy again, doing ten men's work, and for the time I did not see him any more.

A friend, who had tried to get me a seat on a munitions truck, told me the Kowloon—Canton express would not be bombed. The day train had been bombed and machine-gunned that week, killing twenty-three passengers.

"But if the train *is* bombed," he added, "hop out and lie in a good big ditch."

'Well,' I thought, rather depressed, alone again and crossing the waters by ferry-boat, which was necessary to connect with the Kowloon—Canton express, 'Life in China seems to be rather like that. But it has movement.'

CHAPTER SIX

The Shadow of the First Pagoda

THIS WAS A DAY getting on in March, the day of the Festival of Ching-ming, which is known in English as the Sweeping of Tombs.

It is the day when the ancestral dead are properly attended to and fed, and every filial son makes an effort to get back to his *hsien* for the occasion. But if he cannot, there is a second opportunity on 9 August. The festival then is not quite the same; it begins with the lighting of pink candles at about seven o'clock in the evening, and little gold and silver boats, canoe-shaped, are burned in the streets, and the sacredness of the occasion continues, at least technically, until the morning, though most people are asleep long before then. But on one day or another, all except the most unfortunate dead receive their due, and although the Cantonese is the Gascon of China, in many ways the most up-to-date and progressive of Chinese peoples, and the first to urge contact between East and West, still in 1938's wartime year the day of Ching-ming was treated seriously as ever, and not only by the villagers.

Wen Tsung-yao, the President of the Legislative Yuan of the Reformed (or Japanese) Government in Peiping, was a Cantonese man; and so was Dr. Chen Chin-tao, who accepted another good post. Now the people in President Wang's native village in Toishan had obtained permission to seek and break open the grave of his father, the unfortunate Wen Chingk'uei, who slept on Tiger Head Mountain, and the ancestral graves of Dr. Chen were also destroyed. It was difficult for the ancestors, but it was war.

Three people, Aysgarde, Paul, and I, were walking along the narrow grass and stone borders which keep rice planters from spilling into their glassy patchwork of pond and plot. This part of Canton, Lingnan side, was meant for rice planting, sugar cane, and, bordering its paved roads, an outcrop of orange trees.

As it was full spring, you never got the combined whiff of orange blossoms and fertilizer out of your nostrils. The oranges reputedly kept old 'Lamp-Chimney,' who started as a very poor bandit and ended as Canton's orange king, happy though a millionaire in his feudal-style castle, where he did as he liked and foreigners were not received. 'Lamp-Chimney' reputedly got his nickname in the days when he was such a hard-up bandit that he did not even possess a revolver; and once, hard pressed by a policeman, he threatened the man with an old-style, slender-necked lamp-chimney, which in the darkness was mistaken for a revolver; so everything worked out very satisfactorily, and he escaped.

It was a good thing, for when he had made a little as a bandit, he invested in oranges, and instead of gambling the profits away, or smoking opium, he soon had a piece of land rented, and planted orange trees. That started his career. He was now a politician of importance, noted for having refused a really handsome bribe a few months before, when the Japanese were making one of several attempts to buy their way into Canton.

His were the stone roads of Lingnan, and the big roofed-over market town, where I spoke to people who frankly said their town looked so important and prosperous because a big man in politics had been born there. His was the scent of young orange blossoms, always with us when we walked, floating now across the rice-fields, where the grain seemed to be at several stages of its life, without order or consequence. Here the young green floated, tender as a mirage, its points just above the glittering water. Here a man and a woman were laboriously putting in every plant with their fingers, and an old water-buffalo rolled his thick girth, leather, mud, and hair, puddling the pond softer between them.

Paul said that in the Boxer rebellion the water-buffaloes had been trained to lead troops, the front ones having red flags tied to their horns. He looked almost desperately serious when he made jokes, and sometimes after you had decided to laugh, and laughed, you found out that he had been quite in earnest.

Not that Paul was deliberately making things difficult. He was simply a queer young man.

Aysgarde was different: there was nothing you couldn't understand about her, though at times she said and thought things far queerer, more fantastic, than Paul or I ever did. But that was because she was slightly shell-shocked, after the first five months' heavy bombing in Canton, and for some reason which now seems quite idiotic, we were both pretending that she was not. She was dark and slim, and wore a white beret.

The shape of Canton's First Pagoda cut into the nearer horizon, clear rose. At the angles of every rice-plot were tied bunches of red-papered fire-crackers. I don't know whether this was to bring good luck to the rice-plots (some of which were so tiny you simply couldn't understand how a man, a woman, and a water-buffalo could put in a life's time and energy cultivating them), or whether the crackers were additional to the grave-decorations for Ching-ming.

In nearly all the villages there were soldiers billeted, and the main temples had been converted to meeting-houses or officers' quarters; but each village had a thick gate of clay or stone, raised up like part of a castle wall. In niches of these sat the painted clay figures I knew only as 'the gate gods.'

Often in their battered, wise faces and bright robes there was something beautiful, and nearly always they were man and woman: I do not remember ever passing through a Kwangtung village gate without seeing, before these clay figures, the soft red spark and smoulder of incense.

This was a very fine day. It seemed, ever since I came to Canton, nothing could go wrong with the weather, and I had almost forgotten that in Shanghai I had a cold all the time. We all felt good; Aysgarde was having one of her bright times, clear and happy, stung fresh as the grass itself in this stinging air of spring.

That was one moment. Then she was stumbling a little on the mud path, and crying, turning back, with her fists in her eyes, to talk at a kneeling man. He was a peasant, and his big, rather harsh face was momentarily open-mouthed with surprise, but quickly closed up again. He had a box of matches, several of which, burnt out, lay on the grass: he was finishing off the biggest slug I have ever seen. Aysgarde kept trying to tell him what she thought, out of a mouth shaking as her knees shook.

The peasant looked up at her, but then he looked at the slug again, and continued to finish it off with lighted matches out of his box. It wouldn't have been so bad if the slug hadn't bled red blood. But its big knot of flesh bled like a pig, there was quite a lot of red on the grass, it looked neither animal, vegetable, nor mineral, and so for a second the damned thing looked human, while Aysgarde kept sobbing: "If *that's* what you're like . . . if *that's* what you do . . ."

Paul put her out of the way. He was perfectly white with rage, because he couldn't bear a word of criticism about the Chinese, and didn't see that Aysgarde wasn't criticizing the Chinese, so much as criticizing the effects of five months' heavy bombing on her own nervous system; and slugs; and a big mutt of a peasant—any nation's peasant.

I wanted to put my foot on the slug and squash it dead, but Paul and the peasant together were too strong a psychological combination for me; I felt it was their slug and they'd better do what they liked, about it. Aysgarde and I went first down the wet path, and I tried to remind her: "Don't you remember? We used to go out with tins of salt after dark, and put it on the snails, because they ate the lettuces. And they used to *sizzle* . . . don't you remember?"

Aysgarde and I came from the same place, and her father's garden was much the same kind as my father's, so though we had never sizzled snails jointly after dark, I felt sure she must have done it, just as we did. She did remember, and started to laugh in a choky way, wiping her nose on her sleeve, and Paul came along, still quite white, declaiming: "It's the man's own field. Now he'll only think foreigners are all mad."

It was just one of the things that happen. In about five minutes, Paul was trying to explain reasonably to Aysgarde, and then to make her happy again.

They were married only a couple of weeks before the heavy bombing started, the first terroristic phase, during which, the Governor of Kwangtung Province, General. Wu Te-chen, told me, the civilian casualties numbered something between 2000 and 3000. But because Aysgarde was dark and attractive, newlywed and brilliantly entertaining whenever she liked, nobody, least of all Aysgarde, was going to admit that the bombing had played merry hell with her nerves.

The Kwangtung country-side, its way of setting out its fields and roads, is softer than the yellow plains of the northern interior, where the clay-baked houses take on the colour of their acres; also the variability of its villages is greater. South in red and green Yunnan, road-gangs totalling nearly half a million Chinese coolies were said to be working, finishing Yunnan's part of the new road connecting up with Burma, which was to be used if anything happened to the Kowloon–Canton railway. It was a munitions road, of course, and the British part had already been completed,

Kwangtung, which with its sister province of Kwangsi, was supposed to be better organized for village resistance than any other part of China, was green and rose. Spring was shaken out all at once in the delicate pearl-pink masses of blossom on the camels'-foot trees, in the rosy leaves of lychee trees growing thick on Lingnan side, in the darker burning of cotton trees, whose arms reached heavy with crimson against the blue tiles of the Sun Yat-sen. Memorial Hall and University.

For a while the American University of Lingnan felt rather small, because the Japanese refused to bomb it, while the Sun Yat-sen University, being Chinese, had a campus full of holes. But the Japanese dropped Lingnan a little one, just before crossed I the Pearl River to stay with Aysgarde and Paul: and before the full story of Canton was ended, Lingnan had as much bomb trouble as anyone was looking for.

And now the land smiled, like a green child who has done her embroidery and patchwork exquisitely well. There was the rice pattern, green, water-glass, lighter green, or flamingo when sunset lay on the watery seed-plots. The villages grew up as they pleased. In one small area, you'd find a village of palm-thatch, a golden brown-fringed oddity from the tropics; an old stone village, vines growing through and over the walls of its courtyards, dark until lamp-flames were threaded from hut to hut, like blue and golden beads on a black thread; a village of rambling bricks; a village completely covered overhead, dwelling in perpetual dusk, tired ricksha coolies sprawling in its big tea-shop, young girls hand-spinning and weaving the blue cotton cloth popularized throughout China, tiny cordial shops where red-paper temple crackers were sold over the same counter as writing materials and ancient salted fish.

War had marked all Kwangtung villages with outstanding characters, for better or for worse. During the first intensive bombing phase, village lamps were commandeered as a safety measure. (There were too many cases of spies signalling and sending up flares to the 'planes.) Many of the poorest dwellings never saw wartime lamplight again, as the people living there could not afford another lamp. Blackness whispered and stirred as you passed such dwellings, blackness uncannily human, but its shapes unseen. Always shadow, till you came on the high-roofed, lantern-lit places, where the tired ricksha coolies, having drunk their wraith-like tea, sprawled out in sleep. Rickshas were scarce and dear on Lingnan side, this being so nearly country that not much in copper cash and cent money could be made.

There were soldiers of the Fourth Route Army, peppered through all the villages, wearing their cotton imitation of khaki: round-faced, friendly soldiers who let us pass by their drill and manoeuvres without any more challenge than their grins.

'There's no earthly reason,' I thought, 'why we shouldn't be Japanese-paid spies and traitors: there's no earthly reason why one of these soldiers shouldn't take it into his head to ask why we are always about the villages, singly or three at a time, wandering around, asking questions, sticking our noses into even the water-buffalo's business, when nobody else does that. No other foreign face ever seems to shove its whiteness and peering look through the thick gateways where the incense smoulders in front of two figures of clay: and, indeed, sometimes the wild village children, especially the little girls with flying black plaits, do rather mock us, crying: "Foreign devils have foreign money!" or "How much foreign devil money have you got!" '

But their mothers always quiet them at once, and as for the soldiers, they go on drilling, or grinding their brains between the millstones of lectures. Their sweet bugles break our dawns, haling back our spirits to our bodies. A hospital, sheltering crippled veterans of the 1932 war with the Japanese, stands five minutes' walk from Lingnan Taihok, and those patients who can walk, leaning on their crutches, come out to buy peanuts and flabby candy-sticks at a little booth. The fixed look of men shut in. . . .

It's true, Paul was very nearly shot, for a spy once, but that had nothing to do with the soldiers. A frightened young Chinese policeman, who didn't know Paul by sight, being new in the place, heard Paul coming across the campus, and in the darkness concluded he had better stick his revolver into the stranger's ribs. Paul said the worst part of it was the way the revolver wobbled up and down: he felt quite sure it would go off. But then the chief policeman came along, and after a look gruffly told the young fellow it would be unreasonable to shoot Paul as a spy.

There was the mark of war on the old temples. I forget how many years ago the Republic ordered its great demolition of temples in China. Canton still has some famous ones, but in the villages most of the old places are useful as meeting-houses and instruction halls; though you will always pass a joss-house of two, perhaps set high up over the village, on a hill.

On the outer walls, bold anti-Japanese slogans, drawn with the quick, pointed integrity of Chinese work, ancient or very modern, show how enthusiastic student propagandists are helping the mild-looking young soldiers to fight this war. And in the first months, thousands of those soldiers, who looked so mild, were marshalled into crack regiments, marched off to places odd to them, whose people spoke a dialect at least as different from Cantonese as German is from Dutch. At Shanghai, Nanking, Tientsin, Soochow, and places farther still, the first died, the pick of the youthful aviators being killed very soon.

But always the remnant, and the new soldiers coming on, look out in a friendly mild way from under their peaked caps, accepting both the fierce young students and stray foreigners. And the students bring them comforts, slogans, patriotic oratory and songs, delivered both by youths and charming slender girls. They are eagerly taking part in the great campaign against illiteracy, which is of first importance in this strange, loosely-knit, oftentimes tragic and splendid mobilization, a mobilization against more enemies than the Japanese.

In Kwangsi, the women wear uniform and drill, and photographs of them look fierce, but when one asks if they really fight like the men, it is extremely hard to get a straight answer. The usual answer is: 'Our girl soldiers are not yet sufficiently expert with machine-guns, but in the last resort; they are prepared to fight.'

In the heart of green, we are quite lost to the road villages, at which there are things for sale, . . . big peaked hats which the coolies will brush with the words 'Lingnan Taihok' for ten cents extra, Chow puppies, Chienmen cigarettes, limp vegetables, peanuts, and sweets.

But the villages across the fields, sunken down among the narrow pavings and rice-plots, sell nothing, though sometimes a Cantonese woman may offer cups of tea. Everybody but the rice-workers seems to be sitting or standing out under the great banyan trees. Everybody, in order of importance, means children; enormous grey swayback-model pigs, whose pregnancy is guaranteed to produce at least fifteen piglets within the next twelve hours; raggle-taggle white poultry; Chow dogs, whose slinking and growling means nothing much; and women, whose black jackets and trousers, in the end, direct and manage the activities of the rest. The young men are usually away working, and the old ones keep out of sight.

In the last village, whose deplorable muddy patches are strangely repaired with bricks (there are even bricks built into a few of the tumbledown walls), not a living soul is in sight, with the exception of some striding, gasconading cocks, and a great coop under which ducklings fuzz together.

Paul says: "Chinese ducks may be dirty, but, anyhow, a Chinese duck speaks more Chinese than an English duck speaks English."

That makes Aysgarde laugh: Paul is very anxious for her to forget he has scolded her, but he knows that with a little sundew like Aysgarde, it won't go out of mind unless everything is cleared up.

"You see," he says gently, "it was *his* field."

Aysgarde has gold dots in her eyes again; it is quite all right, the shadow of the five months' bombing has rolled back from her mind and nerves as swiftly as it came.

This is the First Pagoda. It is falling to pieces, because of the villagers' depredations. Here is where they come to get the bricks for their muddy places, or to patch up tumbledown walls. It had four arched entrances, but the gaps made by bricks stolen from the foundations almost make two more: really it is more dangerous to go inside than to stand underneath a bomber at fair height. One day a villager will steal five bricks too many, and the sky will come down on his material world.

Its head is a wild turban, bound with bushes at the height of a hundred feet, and out of the bushes fly black birds with silver-white dots on their underwings; my God, out fly the tossed handfuls of black and white birds! This wild verbena stuff, yellow and pink flower-heads with a rough scent when bruised to make a bed, grows all round it. I suppose it is a common weed, grows anywhere; but to-day I've never seen anything more marvellous, the flowering weed, the pagoda's wreath of birds.

Inside, the original structure has gone without a trace. There are some engraved characters, and Paul says they read that the pagoda was last repaired over two hundred years ago. Sitting on the bill, his back towards us, is an old man with a silvery stick, like a crook, between his legs. I think he is another form of the First Pagoda, but Paul says he is a villager come to steal bricks, and will sit there and swear inside, hoping we will be gone before sunset.

Aysgarde and Paul curl up on a stone ledge crumbled only at two places (if they really shouted, it might bring the pagoda down), but I won't stay, because they want me to discuss, with serious eyes and much in earnest, whether Aysgarde ought to get upset and cry every day. She does cry every day, we are always discussing it in earnest, and I Love Aysgarde and wish she wouldn't, but can't you see? To-day I don't care if any one of us remains alive another moment, I don't care if we have never been born, I only want to sink into the green jewel's heart, and think about the pagoda. So I go away to the bed of crushed verbena, and almost immediately a snake slithers out, a three-cornered grey fellow with a flat head. I don't know if he's poisonous, or one of the kind preserved and eaten as a delicacy. Anyhow we give one another a look—pass and countersign—and he slides off. Over me, sloping away from me, a shaft of deep blue, the shadow of the pagoda.

That is the important thing, the shadow. It sleeps over village and rice-field, always deep and strong, stronger than the substance. It seems that while this lasts, China has no choice but to last. Inside the pagoda there is lovely old rose and grey dog-toothed stuff, but I don't mind about dog-toothed stuff. In eternity, all minds are equal, though they mayn't meet: the shadow of the pagoda is its mind. It darkens the glittering rice-ponds, the sugar-cane standing so high and green that nobody sees the water-canals between the stalks, and pearl-white junk-sails move by magic, without a stream, without a tide, quietly up and down a green land's deepest green.

There is a woman walking on a stone pavement, quite far away, on the other side of a long flushed rice-pond. Her shadow moves in the water, crossing a pavement of rosy cloud. She is a peasant and wears black trousers and an amulet, and perhaps she doesn't know how lovely her shadow is.

The sugar-cane wasn't harvested this year, because four of the five big sugar-mills have been bombed (I'm not supposed to know that); and though the fifth mill is working twenty-four hour shifts, to bring in the cane isn't worth the peasants' while. But the village children, hanging about the booths where peanuts and candy are sold, always have a length of green sugar-cane in hand or mouth.

'I make,' say the great hands, 'I make and I break.'

'I listen,' says the great ear, 'I listen and I hear.'

'I watch,' says the great eye, 'I watch and I have seen.'

'I smile,' says the great mouth, 'I smile, yet fear me, because one day, in this place, I shall speak.'

That is the spirit of the pagoda talking . . . but he is only an old man with a silvery stick between his knees, getting cold because the clouds are turning grey.

There were small soft fires blowing about like hair of salamanders, on the great grave-mounds which eat up so much of China's small-patched earth. The peasants had put red joss-papers between the main cone and top flap of soil, which gives the mounds their cotton-spool look, and had brought rice for the dead, meat of ducklings and chicken, eggs, with portions of favourite dishes, and paper money, both silver and gold. Some burned little boats, and others the paper likenesses of dresses and such necessaries. For at the Sweeping of the Tombs, a piercing hunger is at the vitals of the ancestral dead.

CHAPTER SEVEN

Big Hands beating on a Roof

THE PEOPLE WHO MADE these gifts were not a dainty, flower-like people, a people whose minds ran either to butterfly poems or to bombing aeroplanes. They were, above all, a peasant people, their faces seamy and harsh, their clothing all of a type, and ugly as a rule, their hands more earth-coloured than yellow, which came of grubbing like their water-buffaloes in mud, with rice and sugar-cane as their chief crops in these districts. Planting still deeper ponds with water-lilies, for edible lily-roots was also of importance, and one usually saw a few women stooped over, wet as the millions of frogs who chorused day and night from the ponds. Soil-possession seemed to matter to them above everything else; yet out of the tiniest plots imaginable, somehow they all thought it right to reserve huge mounds for the dead, and to feed these mounds, out of their bitter wartime necessity, at least twice a year.

This feeling towards the soil and the dead did not stop with the poor peasant: in Canton, and in Cantonese districts, to each man his own *hsien*, which, after his family, has his deepest ties of feeling. One could see among the Lingnan grave-mounds the graves of peasants who had become rich: they were made in big collar-shapes of concrete and marble, very handsome, sometimes marked with characters to point out the virtues of the deceased. Also it was not uncommon to find among the huge twisting roots and century-thick leaves of trees around some village the concrete entrance of a very large, up-to-date and even ostentatious dug-out. Certainly no poor man built dug-outs like these.

March, until after the Chinese victory at Taierhchwang, was a soft time for Canton in matter of air raids, because the Japanese were engaged in what Governor Wu Te-chen called the third phase of aerial bombing . . . bombing the main roads and highways. Occasionally some harmless old sheep of a village got bombed and machine-gunned; (after the first phase there were seldom any visible defence 'planes in Canton, and though the anti-aircraft guns rattled away so importantly, really all they did was to drop remarkable quantities of shrapnel in everybody's backyards). For three weeks, while I was there, bombing casualties were few and purely sporadic, though we had at least two air raids and probably more signals every day. In the last week, the bombers were annoyed, changed their tactics, killed 180 civilians, besides bringing back the old fuss and nervousness.

You couldn't, without a knowledge of the language, get much information as to what the peasants thought about this state of war, except that the old men of the villages, whose politics were all bound up in pre-Republican ideas, drew in their heads and horns like snails, and simply ignored the wartime activities carried or thrust into normal village life by eager young parties of students.

The students didn't look much like the peasants. A fashion for suéde lumber-jackets with zipp fasteners had caught on among the boys, who wore their hair fairly long in front, and short behind, and whose eyes sparkled as they talked of anti-epidemic measures, impromptu propaganda plays, patriotic songs and oratory, and the village courses which small parties usually took on for about a month, simultaneously sharing in village work and activities, and doing their best to inoculate the villagers, all ages and both sexes, with anti-Japanese mass resistance ideas. They did very well with most people except the old men, who, as a rule, sat back and wouldn't have anything to do with it; but the married women, who might have been expected to show an equal conservatism, did the other thing . . . they brought their kids along, listened, and joined up.

The young, from staggering four-year-olds just big enough to be fitted out in a cream shirt and pants (China's Boy Scouts are Creamshirts), took to it *en masse*. Besides the lumber-jacket brigades there was an almost equal number of Cantonese girl students. They all wore short-sleeved blue cotton gowns, slit half-way up one leg, showing spotless white petticoat underneath. They didn't go in for trimmings or jewellery, and their soft hair was straight around their narrow, sensitive faces; they used little make-up, and didn't frizz their hair, but it was a point of principle with them, as modern women, to cut it off, never shingled, but the style of a long western bob. To them short hair or long hair are almost political insignia.

The present air-raids, which meant a shrill screaming of sirens every morning, followed by anti-aircraft guns yapping, and after a few minutes two or three silvery-shining Japanese moths beating it back to their air-base, were taken seriously by nobody, and in a way rather fun, because they brought us out of the cool houses, roofed with blue or water-green shining tiles, into fresh air.

After squinting upwards, in the vain hope that a Chinese 'plane might appear and stage a dog-fight, we had time to realize that this was another Lingnan morning of spring, and those mornings were so beautiful. Over the cream or brick walls, under the glistening Chinese eaves, tumbled great sweet-smelling masses, wistaria, jasmine, honeysuckle. Then you couldn't take your eyes off the pink-pearl blossom of the camels' foot trees, and all the way from rose to blood-red, hibiscus opened their mysterious faces between them, though only the bees knew what the golden mouths said.

There weren't any fences; rough shallow seas of grass just sloped into one another, and the green of one roof, or the dark blue of another, struck through eyes to heart. The roofs were wholly of Chinese inspiration, and a lot of the Lingnan Taihok buildings and houses had been built by Chinese architects, pupils of Murphy's.

Murphy was the young American architect who hit the idea of combining the best features of old-style Chinese buildings, especially roofs, windows, and arches and gates, with the best features, both artistic and hygienic, of western ones. His mind, and after his, the Chinese pupils' minds, were behind the building of the beautiful Civic Centre Buildings in Shanghai (wiped out by Japanese bombs, 1932; built again; very badly damaged by Japanese bombs, 1938); and for the many Government and university buildings in Nanking (wiped out in 1938).

There were a lot more Murphy-type buildings in different Chinese cities, and the style varied widely . . . for instance, the indigo tiles and many-arched gateways of the Wuhan University, a few miles over the Yangtse River from Hankow, was as near as they could get to the design of a very famous ancient building in Peiping.

Those at Lingnan were partly Murphy, partly Chinese, and bastard in construction. They looked Chinese outside (you can't imagine the glistening of those water-green tiles, with the slender dog-figures, like greyhounds, cocking up above them, and the camels' foot flowers on the grass beneath), but within they were cream-washed and cool, with deep alcoved stairs, like a Californian's idea of what a Mexican house would look like inside, if the Mexican had any sense.

Lingnan Taihok started off very modestly, by the way, in mud huts instead of Murphy buildings; the first Americans who came over had to build a mud road down to the wharf (Lingnan *matoa*) with their own hands. When they were buying land for the university, they had much grave-mound trouble, most of which they settled by paying the outraged relatives off at three dollars Mex. per grave. But there was one big grave-mound, right where they wanted to build something important, that couldn't be settled until they got a little political influence (Chinese) to go along and have a talk with the grave-mound.

Later on they got their bombs; but now it was all so sunny, and when the Japanese dropped a bomb, or the Chinese some more anti-aircraft shrapnel, the villagers collected it and sold it at ten cents a catty for souvenirs. At the beginning of the war it was worth twenty cents a catty, which shows how uneconomic competition knocks the bottom out of every trade. Part of the uneconomic competition was living next to us, in the shape of a preternaturally grave American kid named Jackie, who used to buy up the stuff at cut rates and sell it in collections to anyone who had the brow of a souvenir-hunter. Jackie was also interested in orchids.

Air-raid signals make long spiral 'Yee-ows!' twisting and turning in the clean air. We'd got past the stage where, as soon as one sounded, every strong man had to cry, 'Where the hell are my braces?' and, giving a lead to the women and children, rush to the Science basement. Things were now almost pleasant, and very punctual, as the Japanese fixed things so that anyone breakfasting between the hours of 8.30-9.30 a.m. could be sure of a couple of alarms, a couple of dull, soft thuds (bombs dropped in the distance), and then the quick-clapping guns, whose big puffs of smoke, too low, fade out in the sky.

Aysgarde was always the first out in the garden, looking up ; these raids never made her nervous in the least. Then her voice would trail away. "Come inside, there's nothing to see."

Three alarms before breakfast. Outside, only the drifting camels' foot colour-washed between grass and tiles. There are big butterflies, striped peppermint, and wasps get drunk on the cider of a tree with white flowers.

Air alarms, nobody cares . . . Paul went off to school, riding a bicycle with the extreme yet quiet force which he seems to impart to everything he does; Aysgarde outside to pick nasturtiums; I to the study upstairs. The anti-aircraft claps came over the margin of time like big hands beating the roof. After this had kept up a while, I called down: "That's near, isn't it?"

"About eight miles."

Aysgarde went on picking short stems. I thought: 'They ought to know their air-raids, they were married in one,' but five minutes later Paul put his head round the door, to say the 'planes had unloaded a lot of bombs down the road. Nobody was killed, but the bombs had made big holes this time, so the population was turning out to see.

I went in a ricksha, for if there's one beast I can't bear it is a bicycle, and Paul and Aysgarde rode bicycles.

Aysgarde hung back, close to me, so that we could talk across. She seemed not to care much for all this, she wanted to talk about things that had happened long ago, and what made her cry so regularly, at least once every day. She couldn't think what it was, an illness, or some sort of psychological wrong track, or whether she could or couldn't stop it. She kept talking of this, and yet behind her eyes, which started to fill, and at once lost their gold dots as she talked, the subject was dull, tame, uninteresting. She wanted to leave it alone. She was as happy as a chained animal set free when *it* left *her* alone.

She had ten times the sparkle of the normal person, but it was just, somehow, that during the first months she had got caught. Now she went on, and you couldn't help, and she knew it, and after the first half-dozen times you both knew it, so implacably that it was like watching somebody draw the dripping red razor very slowly across a throat half-cut. And she didn't want to. You wanted to call out: 'Stop doing that!' but neither was that any use nor sense. If ever a girl wanted to struggle out of one body and into another I didn't understand then, but now I do.

Paul wheeled back to listen, and Aysgarde said: "This'll be a godsend for Jackie." Jackie's real opportunity was due in the fall, when his father was taking him back to U.S.A., where bombs were still luxuries. Jackie was going to be a big man among the other kids.

We passed the little boys selling sugar-cane, the mothers whose babies flopped heads and hands out of shawls; a gate let us into a barred roadway, and there were the bomb-holes, beauts. There were six holes. Two bombs had smashed a wooden barracks, one scoring a direct hit, so only matchwood remained. One hole gaped among trees, the others in sunlight.

"Five hundred pound stuff," said Paul, who was talking to some very hot, very happy Chinese soldiers. I had a feeling we ought to stand the soldiers a drink, but the place was dry as a wooden god, there was nothing to buy except peanuts or green sugar-cane with the flies thrown in. The soldiers, who numbered 100, plus an officer, had just left their quarters when the 'planes came over. They had no time to make for proper cover, so they threw themselves flat in the road where it parts the trees. The 'planes then unloaded, but were off quick; the anti-aircraft guns must have been near their tails, or they would scarcely have missed an opportunity like 100 soldiers. That was a narrow clay road, yet the only casualty was a man with a scratched arm.

It is always good to lie down flat when a bomb comes if you can't make better cover in bushes or a ditch. The fragments from an aerial bomb usually strike breast-high.

"Very, very frightened!" said one soldier, with a grin. The reason why they were all so pleased with themselves was not only that they had escaped being blown up, but because they had just had their morning rice, and for some reason they thought this was funny, as also the fact that the Japanese had failed to hit the cook. Paul had got hold of the officer, who called himself a name something like 'contendent,' and seemed shy, but happy enough to talk, smiling and mopping his face as the sweat broiled out by a very hot sun streaked his cheeks.

Perhaps, he said, the Japanese thought they were smashing munition dumps. Nothing in there but a few old boxes and sacks, and his hundred men. Now they wouldn't get any more rice all day, and would have to sleep on the ground that night; but he grinned, and these hardships didn't seem to worry them. We had a look inside the second smashed building, which was a job; but the bombs hadn't touched the small cookhouse, which stood among some more trees.

The officer wore two medals on his tunic, and on his hip was the beautifully engraved hilt of a knife or short sword, we didn't know which, because he was shy and did not want to show his sword.

His English was superbly bad, but that was what he said when I tried to talk to him in Cantonese: "Very, very bad."

I didn't think it deserved 'very' twice over, but the officer liked the word. When a khaki-uniformed kid not older than fourteen passed us, goggling with round eyes, he grinned again, and remarked: "Very little soldier." He had fought at Shanghai and Nanking, but he liked it here better, because his own village was in Kwangtung. We talked patriotism, sympathy, and the more disagreeable features of bombing: but whatever the officer got his medals for, it was not for patriotic oratory.

"Japanese very silly," he said. "Very cruel," and grinned as if be thought maybe he was sounding a little severe.

His men, among scrubby pines, were carrying blankets and bits of wood about. Paul and I discussed the contendent, coming back, and agreed that whatever a contendent was, in rank, he was all right.

When we got back, we found that Jackie had been ahead of us and effected a minor corner in shrapnel; but he gave me a free piece, and I still have it. That was for knocking him back. He wanted to know, did I come to China to see some real life?

It was partly true, and I guessed it came from his mother, so I had to knock him back.

I told him, What did he think we all did in God's extra country, anyhow? Sat around with our knees drawn up, like premature mummies? And anyone worth a grain of sand saw plenty of life without going off his doorstep.

Jackie thought about this, squinted, took it seriously, and then got me the bit of shrapnel.

"Of course," he said politely, "if you wanted a real good collection, I could get it for you."

But I didn't shell out, and Jackie later slipped me two orchids from his father's collection; (his father was out).

"Anyhow," said Aysgarde, beginning to cry without sound or fury, the tears slipping down her cheeks, "I know it isn't because of an appendix. I knew a woman in Paris who was simply poisoned for two years, and all the time it was her appendix. But it can't be mine, because the thing's out."

CHAPTER EIGHT

People of the Pearl

TO GET FROM LINGNAN MATOA to Canton city, you cross the Pearl River by launch or sampan. If the tide of the extremely yellow Pearl is right, going by sampan is a much easier and pleasanter way to travel, and profusely though the sampan people sweat, by the way scores of them yell for your blood the moment you hesitate on the little wharf, you know that they want you. There's no sentiment about that except what you, as a foreigner, will create from your own side.

Once you get into one of the little hooded boats, valanced with gaily-patterned calico (rather like old-fashioned knickers), spotlessly clean, and very comfortable where the customer is concerned, you're safe. Everybody stops yelling, as if a tap had been turned off, and among the mouthing faces and clawing old hands, you never see one that looks resentful. You've patronized one of them. That, like one person marking the right ticket when a Chinese *pakapoo* bank is drawn, seems to be enough for them. The sampan people are better off than the ricksha boys, being, in a small way, capitalists; about 150 dollars Mex. should set you up nicely as a sampan capitalist on the Pearl River, and I can think of worse ways of earning a living.

Whether you like or loathe Canton's ricksha, sampan, and beggar population depends, I think, on the human rather than the political outlook. The beggars outside the Oi Kwan, Canton's new skyscraper hotel, the boys dropped between the shafts, the women who know a launch has just left for Lingnan wharf, and consequently you've got to take a sampan, don't understand why they shouldn't yell all they please. Some of the beggars will grab hold; they are nearly all able-bodied men, but have a sore on the heel. You must be made to look at their sore on the heel. A smiling woman is pulling at you, beckoning you to see how trachoma has gummed and reddened her baby's eyes. They must live, they must shout to live, they can't afford to look around and think 'Fifty of us, all yelling at once,' or think that every foreigner is not stinking with wealth. Rich or respectable Chinese know how to handle this; they walk through, never rudely, but in a kind of dream. Shouters part for them, as the Red Sea a little unfairly parted for the Children of Israel.

On the other hand, there was the wild little girl who guided me miles back across the rice-fields, her pigtails flying. She wouldn't take anything but two cents, and she was scared of those. When she had them, she ran away like a rabbit.

On Canton side, the hundreds of sampans, hundreds and hundreds of sampans clicking like long, curled lines of wooden sabots, lie ready to pole between Canton and a score of green places, all except Shameen on the far side. Where the great moored border lies, seeming locked together, many thousands of Chinese people, mostly women and children, live out dexterously formalized lives. Often the sampan women have coolie husbands, who join them after dark. Their iron kettles and frying-pans, favourite cooking utensils, slap lids up and down over bubbling contents, meat-soups, and green. No butcher wastes the scraggy inner bits of meat, giblets, bags of blood tied in the natural skin-fat.

Often the little awninged sampans have painted inner roofs, gilded or done up with cheap pictures; a long cushioned seat where the customer reclines, an uncushioned plank for the boy or girl whose behind rises up in the air every time he puts his infant vigour into the long pole's push.

There is no seat for the adult pole-wielder. The poles, very long, and flat as oars, have no rowlocks. They are tied to sticks at level of the wrist. Downstream it is easy, except for the up-and-down of the little sun-browned behind . . . flop, flop. Children who look no older than seven work at this.

An island, flaky pink with blossom, humps in the middle of the river, which never runs less yellow, but is broad and calm. You can live in a world of sampans, poling to and fro, quite cut off from all the other worlds. There is even a sampan post office, high upstream. Pearl River, with the yellow smile curling broader on its mouth, flows round Shameen, and out to the regions where the great booms have been sunken to block the Japanese ships from approaching Canton, out past the Bocca Tigris forts, where there was a conspiracy a few months ago, and one or two junior officers, wounded by silver bullets, were going to turn machine-guns on their own shipping.

But that was all very silly and unfortunate, and nothing happened except that a few men got themselves beheaded or shot That is always unfortunate: in the early days, when spies were much more numerous, or at least bolder, the Cantonese used to tie them together, big bundles of men, and drive them through the city in lorries and trucks flaming-lettered with their iniquities. Then, of course, at some suitable spot they were shot.

Paul and Aysgarde were on the Kowloon—Canton train one night, when they saw a man with his hands tied behind him, bundled roughly through the compartments. There were a lot more, dressed up as beggars, but carrying under their rags a very large sum of dollars Hong Kong. This was part of a rather picturesque conspiracy, during which the Mayor of Canton, Mr. Tseng Yangfu, and the more recently imported provincial Governor, General Wu Te-chen, were both to have been abolished. So safe was the conspiracy considered, that the Japanese news agency published the first news that the Mayor had been critically wounded and the Governor imprisoned by his own officials; but it was all very premature, resulting only in an unexpected Japanese donation to Chinese war-funds, as the bribe-money was kept.

Lovely when you weren't in any hurry, the sampans were Hell's delight when your system was poisoned with the western electro-bug of speed. It wasn't even their slowness . . . left to itself, your other western bug, your conscience, would have pointed out the sweating of the sampan-puller, the vehemence with which the little boy's behind flapped up and flopped down. It was that you could . . . not . . . make them understand . . . you were in a HURRY!

Foreign devil emits roars. The old man, old girl, little boy, little thin-as-a-lathe plait-tossing girl are anxious to oblige.

"Lingnan matoa! Lingnan matoa!"

Nods, smiles, but nothing happens. Tide takes us nearer the squatting sampans on the other side. Your sampan exchanges confidences with the other sampans. The foreigner inside does not believe that he is going in the right direction for Lingnan. The poor, exhausted, crumpled foreigner, limp as a deflated balloon, thinks he is going the wrong way, and will never find himself at home again. Aiyah! He is probably ill in his head. Foreigners are always sick, from taking too much wine and never opening their bowels. This one roars like a man with toothache. The girl-child here (dragged forward, hiding her face between her hands) can read and write from a little book. Aiyah! Bad, perhaps, for the brain.

But when finally they unloaded me, two hours later for an appointment that ought to have been important, if appointments in China are really important and not a dream, their smiles and gestures took in the blue-tiled waiting shed, the beautiful horned sweep of roofs behind, and, sure as ever, the lily-pond where a fat old woman waded with petticoats rolled up, grubbing stem and root. White Cloud Mountain was looking very clear, and Thousand Pines Mountain, and pinkening in small ruffles behind them, the shameless Pearl.

There! said the sampan-people's dark eyes, a trifle rueful but not reproachful. There! Foolish foreigner, was it not Lingnan matoa, *all the time?*

"Serve you right," said Paul, pedalling up on his cycle like a damned soul condemned to some very excruciating torture, "taking a sampan against the tide. Can't you *look* at the tide?"

I looked at the tide, but it seemed always the same to me . . . just yellow, and rippling, and as if I wouldn't want to fall in there because of what I might swallow.

Further facts about sampan-people: the flower-boats and flower-tax (polite for small floating brothels and Government tax on their prostitutes) have been abolished, though where the sampans are tethered round Shameen, there are always young girls and women laughing up from the boats, French marines trying to flirt with them.

"The French," say some, "like to go away with women. The English like to get drunk." I take it this is a compliment to the French. What the Chinese like is left unsaid.

The friendliness of Chinese people is illustrated by the way sampan-pullers, seeing a launch or larger motor craft scurrying by, utter loud cries of instruction and camaraderie, and fling a rope round a stick, clinging to their sister-ships, who hardly ever turn these lift-bummers adrift. Some of the most magnificent carved and tough-hided old wooden vessels of this world's backwaters floated far out on the Pearl River while I was in Canton, though at least half these craft had been sunk to make the booms farther down. It is not likely that many are alive now: I hope their great sides flared up with the Viking death they deserved. They were ships.

Canton, skeleton leaves painted with bright legend pictures by the monks and sold in the Sun Yat-sen Memorial Hall, where the executive of the Kuomintang used to meet, and the portrait of Dr. Sun Yat-sen looked down from its half-smashed frame. That was quite funny, like an Angels of Mons miracle, but it was true. I saw it with my eyes, and besides, any person who was in Canton at the time could tell you. The great hall got several small bombs through its domed roof, and a splinter shore away an almost exact half of the frame round the Sun Yat-sen portrait, which still had much spiritual mastery in this hall and in Canton. The Chinese had filled in the broken frame with putty.

Dr. Sun Yat-sen was painted foreign-style, but he was Chinese in that he looked imperturbable. At the meetings held in this hall (which was reserved exclusively for its political purpose) an empty chair was always kept in the place of honour for Sun Yat-sen. Generalissimo Chiang Kai-shek's dictatorship was proclaimed this month, and very well received by all, including the Chinese Communists, with whom his Central Government troops had waged bloody warfare from the 1927 *coup d'état*, when the capital was moved from Hankow to Nanking, until Japanese troubles began to create so much thunder, left and right, that the players had no option but to take an interest.

Against the dark blue tiles of the Memorial building, dark red of that spring's cotton-flowers. Canton is burned down, it is done with, the Chinese city first seen by Marco Polo, the city which sent the first Chinese student to a foreign university, the city where Dr. Sun Yat-sen studied and practised medicine 'in order to obtain that social position' which would allow him to work for the Chinese revolution of 1911, for the hardly born Chinese Republic, begrudged from its birth by old men like the Anfu clique, discredited and displaced, whose long grey beards, like cobwebs, brush the council tables of the Japanese, and like cobwebs are brushed aside.

Canton is called 'The City of Rams'; nobody seems to know why, but spring and the pride of living are tossed upon its horns. One famous traveller (I think it was Sir Frederick Treves) annoyed the Cantonese very much by calling it also 'The Nightmare City of Canton.' But nearly all the medley of cobbled, labyrinthine streets which might have won it that name have been modernized during the past ten years, though old warrens like Blackwood Street still hang on, muddy cross-sections of small factory life.

And there was a lovely street, oh, a sentimentally lovely street! which sold nothing but fans. Some, of course, were plain turkey-feather fans, but others showed glow of amber, cerise, and blue. Only I could never get a ricksha boy to stop there, because if you can't speak the dialect fairly well, and have once given a ricksha-puller the right destination, he thinks if you try to stop him midway that you're annoyed about something and will do him out of his full fare. The more you try to stop him, the more annoyed he believes you are, and so, flinging the blue rags of cotton from his shanks, he cries "Shameen!" and hurtles with great exhausting bounds towards the place where you can't do less than pay him his full fare.

And wild though you feel at missing the fans which shine like soft jewels, the ricksha-coolie is by that time dripping with sweat from head to foot, and everybody looks at you accusingly, even the police stationed on the foot-bridges over which you pass to the island of Shameen; so cursing yourself for a fool, you fumble in your purse, and then hurry past the police and the small side-booths selling books, magazines, and incense to the island of Shameen itself.

The flanked rows of barbed wire behind you are to keep off the Chinese, in case there happens to be a major air-raid over the station, and a crowd tries to rush the foot-bridges. There is always this possibility, as the main station was a first-class bombing target, and once I saw what happens when the 'planes came over myself. But if the British keep off the frightened Chinese, so do the other nations whose consulates are built on Shameen, especially the French, who are normally so affable to the pretty girls round by their wharf in the sampan boats. Shameen still had its useful wartime

112

aspect from the Chinese point of view, as its proximity to the most crowded part of Canton undoubtedly helped to check bombers. The British Consul, Mr. Blunt, was a perfect old fire-and-pepper-eater about his rights, and if a Japanese 'plane so much as breathed in the vicinity of Shameen kept sending notes protesting against flights over neutral territory.

Shameen is founded on a sandbank and a quarrel. The name means 'sandbank,' and when the Chinese Government of the day gave the consulates (the British Consulate, in the first place) this once-contemptible little hump in the middle of a tidal estuary, they had no intention of being polite.

The former British Consulate had been a big, handsome building surrounded with lawns, palm trees, and other ornamental foliage (used in these wartime days as the headquarters of the provincial Government of Kwangtung, and of the Governor, General Wu Te-chen, who, incidentally, told me all this). In the 'high and far-off times,' when the British Consulate stood in Canton city itself, there were continual rows. It may not be international courtesy to call them rows, but they were just plain rows, arising mostly from the fact that a number of old-style Cantonese dignitaries were not sure it was good to have this British diplomatic headquarters in their midst.

The offer of Shameen was a little politer than saying, 'Here are your shoes, walk off!' and everybody waited to see how the British would take the situation.

But the British, with remarkable sang-froid, left the situation tying where it was, took Shameen, and made it something—an island of lawns and shady, sweet-perfumed camphor trees, rose gardens where opulent English roses dawdle away their time, handsome buildings of brick and stone. The whole looks very shady, deep-set, and hard to disturb. All the other consulates fly their flags there, so that you can pass along broad asphalt and see a flag-day in which almost everything is represented, except perhaps the twelve-rayed pure white sun on a background of red and blue. Hindoos walk here, with their turbanned heads and sparkling eyes, and Chinese amahs see to the well-being of little white girls, one of whom has climbed to the third bough of a tree, and sings: "Aih'm a *bird!* . . . aih'm a *bird!* . . ." in a sweet elfin voice which slips through the crack between quarrel, sandbank, camphor trees, stately implacable portentousness, and is a fairy, all by itself. The notice which a few years ago said over one of the green gardens 'Dogs and Chinese not admitted' has been taken down, and belongs to the past, which is just as dead or as vital as the inheritors of the past wish it to be.

But at least this is Shameen, 1938, not Shameen, 1927: politically there is a difference, and structurally the place is an achievement, green where so many people stood in crying need of green. The big foreign banks are nearly all on Shameen, as stately and stony as the rest. But the ugly yellow arm of the Pearl, clinging round Shameen, seems to me hungry yet, hungry for some ungiven understanding or acceptance. Whether that hunger lies only on Canton side is more than I care to say. And on both sides, after due attention to pride, there is a choice.

Whatever Canton city may have been in its pre-modernized times (apart froth the green spots where Murphy and his disciples had been allowed to take a hand), it was too rampant with life, too arrogant with large grey western buildings, for anyone to have called it pretty now.

Instead, it was interesting. The pavements rounded off in little stalls, with many goods, such as maps and painted skeleton leaves, pinned up on the walls. I liked the war-maps, which optimistically showed the Russians as red-clad figures advancing over the northern border, while Japanese troops were horrible white figures. They were also depicted by *fei chis* ('planes), slaughtered peasants, villages in ruins, and a good many other palpable atrocities.

For a nation with so large a percentage of illiteracy (though this was probably less in vigorous cities like Canton), the people seemed to have versatile and dramatic ways of telling one another, on paper, exactly what they wanted to convey.

The most important new hotel, the Oi Kwan, was glistening-white all over when its massive stories and tower were reared. Almost immediately it had to go into wartime grey, which vexed the Cantonese, who were proud of their Oi Kwan. I stayed there when first I came to Canton; but just as in Shanghai I had immediately taken a fancy to the frosted windows, old-style play, leg-show, and bowing roof-garden trees of the Grand Orient, where there was always something to see and usually far too much to hear, I was unhappy at the Oi Kwan. Cantonese friends were a little annoyed about that.

"It is the best we have," they said.

I couldn't help it; though looking down at night on the crouching cotton backs of hundreds of orange-sellers, each with his chimney long-necked as a stork beside the dark gold of his oranges, might have induced happiness. I can't think of a sound reason for disliking the tall Oi Kwan, except that I was inwardly sore about leaving Shanghai, and somehow always cross with the girl at the cash desk.

I stood and looked like vinegar, she sat and looked like jam; and now it seems not only far away, it seems ridiculous to have disliked a building of at least ten stories for such a reason. For the Cantonese people were proud of it in its days of glistening whiteness, and had a good many of their best parties there.

The Oi Kwan went up in smoke even before the rest of the city. 'It can be seen blazing,' went a foreign correspondent's dispatch, written, of course, on Shameen. And I read it safer still, in an English house.

I remember one day Paul got excited about an old sampan man's daughter, a child of about ten. She was quite pretty in that blackbird way, you know, but looked rundown and weak, from the evident cause of a huge abscess, inflaming and devouring one ear. On this her father had plastered a grey bag like putty, and fixed it up with an amulet.

Paul was not the type who could normally bear any interference with the Chinese, because he approved of them too much, and the slightest criticism made him feel: 'Here's some more hostile criticism!' But that afternoon, the girl's frail look and the red spreading up her ear must have bothered him, for he tried (talking in Cantonese), first to get the old sampan man to send the girl to a hospital, then to let her trot along up the road with us and see a good doctor, just here on Lingnan side. Finally, when the old man shook his head, and said the girl had already seen a doctor, and it had cost much money, but done no good at all, Paul pulled out money, and tried bribery and corruption. But either the bribe wasn't heavy enough, or the old man had a genuine superstitious fear of hospitals, and by now thought Paul mad, like the rest of the foreigners, for he dumped us out at Lingnan *matoa* as quickly as he could, and the listless figure of the girl with a pain in her ear was quickly pulled away from our sight.

"Anyhow," said Paul, quickly recovering his natural position, as we strolled up through the cool-treed twilight, "the old chap had been quite generous. He'd already spent a lot of money on the girl's ear."

He went on, with a sigh, to think of university housekeeping expenses, as you might call them: Lingnan Taihok looked so beautiful, because it was comparatively easy to induce wealthy philanthropists to give fine buildings, like the hospital, which would commemorate their names. But talking to them about Upkeep was another proposition, in which no amount of salt was good for the average bird's tail.

A further trouble was that American philanthropists were reacting in much the same way. America, for some reason known only to the Americans (who should have been coining money hand over fist on the munitions they were selling to Japan alone—that is, if Japan paid for them), was now having a private slump, and its contributions to the university, which was primarily a U.S.A. brain-child, had fallen to a fraction.

Meanwhile the tall bushy heads of sugar-cane stood up higher than ever. There was a rice shortage, in spite of the Provincial Government's efforts to cultivate in the people a love for red (unhusked) rice, and pleasure-loving Canton city was under something close to a self-inflicted Volstead Act, for the people no longer liked to use up rice in making rice wine, and even when they already had it in stock, some patriotic impulse made them dislike selling the bottles for restaurant dinners and parties.

It was a patriotism somewhat akin to that which, in the early stages of the war, had made parties of young students, mostly New Lifers, tear down streets, buttoning up the coats and other garments of astonished old men, who seldom really needed to be buttoned up. In Japan, an identical patriotic swoop was sending the youngsters into ballrooms, where they shouted, and swished with sticks, even with swords when they could get any swords, at the legs of dancers who were disgracing themselves dancing foreign jazz.

CHAPTER NINE

Some Important People

GOVERNOR WU TE-CHEN told me about the rice shortage; that, and the difficulties the blockade was causing to junk fishermen. Fishing is an important industry of Kwangtung province, whose other main industries are ... were ... the export of raw materials, wool, silk, ivory, and embroidered goods, china, and teakwood. The camphor trees are not native, though so many camphor chests are carved here, as well as heavy blackwood furniture, adorned with marble cloud-pictures, which gives Blackwood Street its name.

In spite of Kwangtung's thousands of rice-plots, at least a million tons of rice was usually imported each year, for every Cantonese, even the poor coolie you see in the streets, likes to eat well. He likes to eat white rice.

Governor Wu talked to me in an upstairs room of the Provincial Government building, a grey place surrounded by mists in which the heads of palms and other trees were faintly lashed by wind outside the windows. The Governor, who was also Chairman Wu or General Wu, sat at the head of the table; I at one side, with a cup of tea in front of me; and at the foot, wearing a Cantonese expression faintly bland and ironic, the Governor's secretary, Mr. Edward Bing-shuey Lee, who had written several books in English about Chinese affairs.

In spite of looking bland and ironic, Mr. Lee made himself very obliging in Canton, and helped me in several ways. Governor Wu Te-chen had been abroad for a short while to Europe, and was supposed to speak English, but not very well; where his English was thought to have broken down, or a small oration was slipped into the conversation, Mr. Lee looked blander and more ironic than ever, and took over, with perfect command of all the polysyllables. But I thought, as a matter of fact, Governor Wu Te-chen understands English and speaks it as well as he pleases, and the way he watches his secretary to see if any slip is made is quite fascinating by-play.

The Governor was one of Sun Yat-sen's revolutionary generals. I don't know how much fighting he saw, but after the establishment of the Republic he was transferred to be a garrison commander. He was a wartime Mayor of Shanghai, and made a singularly dignified speech when in 1932 he was forced to hand over that city to the Japanese. But after they went, he, who had seen the new Civic Centre destroyed, saw it rebuilt again. Then, once more, he saw it destroyed.

"That is six years of my life gone," he said, without any appearance of sentiment or insincerity.

He was transferred almost immediately to be wartime Governor of Kwangtung. He was a Cantonese, his own *hsien* was in the province, and he looked it, having the broad forehead and face, at once sensitive and slightly aggressive, which mark out the Cantonese. He did not look to be a man of more than fifty years at most.

It is true that Governor Wu Te-chen had already several black eyes from his friends and enemies in Canton. They said to begin with, that it was a good thing he was transferred so quickly to Kwangtung from Shanghai, because no Mayor of Shanghai would ever be able to pay off the heavy debt accumulated on that second dose of magnificent Civic Centre buildings

They said that he was an implacable Rightist, who had used a thick stick on young students and other Shanghai people involved, or said to be involved, in the troubles of 1927.

They said the real patriot of Canton was its Mayor, Mr. Tseng, who was indeed the fiery Mayor to declare (when the Japanese, after air-raids, started telephoning Cantonese go-downs to find out if they had done any damage to their own stored goods): "Let the Japanese come down and look at their go-downs, if they want to see what has happened!" and who showed every sign of being ready to eat the Japanese like spitted larks, if they did happen to arrive.

About Wu Te-chen, nothing was dramatic except circumstances which repeatedly flared up like torchlight, but showed in him nothing beyond enigma.

In the last days, when Japanese troops were forcing their way through from Bias Bay, and a cry came out of a jumble of local ineptitude that the city must be defended, but its proper defenders, all the best Cantonese Generals and picked regiments, were many hundreds of miles to the north, begging Chiang Kai-shek for their freedom, Wu Te-chen was openly accused in the foreign Press of not being very satisfactory as a General, nor as a wartime Governor.

But afterwards, when more famous Chinese names, like the name of Wang Ching-wei, were disgraced and driven out, because the owners had first disgraced and driven themselves out, his position has remained doubtful rather than disgraceful.

Since the war started, last 12 August Japanese air-raids over the province have passed one thousand (said the Governor). You can divide this bombing into three parts—first into the heart of the city, which was the terroristic phase, and killed a great many civilians. The second period, they bombed the railway tracks and bridges, and trains when they could catch one, and did heavy damage, but our railway repair kits are very good indeed. As soon as they had flown away, our railway-gangs came out and repaired the breaks.

The third period was over the highways, and they have bombed the hangars all the time.

There are many aerodromes in this province. People are getting air-minded now. We give them an air-raid course. At first, they used to go outside and take a look up to see what was happening, but when a few hundreds got killed, they thought better. We are training a great many women in first-aid in the interior, and there are also many hospitals administered by foreign doctors.

The coast of this province is blockaded by Japanese warships: Japan didn't declare war, so, of course, she has no right to blockade, but . . . ask the third Powers.

During the blockade activities, we have had two periods. The first period was one of threatening the junk fishermen: the Japanese ships tortured them, sunk, burned, and machine-gunned hundreds of their boats. That was to frighten them.

Now, the second period, they try to bribe the fishermen by means of offering much higher prices for their fish than the shore markets can afford, and then by selling them heroin. That traffic has also gone into the interior. Then they try to obtain secrets. But a very careful watch is kept round the coast, and the fishermen are patriotic: we have organized them with a Government subsidy, and let them settle on reclaimed lands.

Mr. Lee here took up the threads with a patriotic oration, ending up: "China is too big for Japan to swallow."

"Yes," added the Governor. "During the Manchurian incidents, the Foreign Minister of Japan said: 'If Japan swallows Manchuria, she will swallow a bomb.' Only Manchuria! Now in Kwangtung, the villagers have been armed, more or less, for half a century. The Government will reorganize them and give them better training to defend their homes, especially guerilla training."

"Do you think it likely Kwangtung may be invaded?"

"Oh, well!" he stood up, politely, "it is not at all *unlikely*."

I was told, if I needed anything at all in Canton, to ask for it; practically a city for the taking. But I was always too shy to ask for anything, except that once, being in doubt, I rang up the Governor's secretary, Mr. Lee, and questioned him; and after that, Mr. Lee came several times to Lingnan side, and reclining with his head on Aysgarde's cushions talked to us of this and that.

His was not the only Chinese head to sink into those restful cushions. There was a Mr. Tseng, who had a note for me, and who turned out to be part proprietor, editor, and chief-of-staff on one of the several underground newspapers in Tientsin, which city was doing remarkably well in secret papers, considering the recency of its occupation and the uncomfortable feeling experienced by the Japanese on discovery of anything of this nature. The Chinese discomfort on discovery is, of course, much greater; which may have been why Mr. Tseng had one of the only two Chinese faces I ever saw that looked slightly nervous.

When he talked of the old days, riding ponies with Chinese and foreign friends up in the north-west, then he could smile. But he had to talk also of his paper, because it was largely to obtain a permanent dwelling-place for this that he had risked being asked a lot of questions, getting in and out of Tientsin.

His idea, and that of his friends, was that perhaps some foreigner at Tientsin might be a friend, and known as such to other foreigners outside, and might, on his return, risk giving an anchorage to the mimeographing machine on which his paper, which had already a circulation of over three hundred copies, was run off.

At the present time the machine and all supplies, such as paper and ink, had to be carried about from place to place after nightfall, which was a nuisance, though they had been lucky and never run into any trouble. The circulation was put on by a simple man-to-man process of 'sounding' the subscriber. They never worried about printing on the same kind of paper, and never bought a good deal of paper twice at the same shop. Sometimes ordinary tissue paper was used, and on that the type came out good and clear. . . .

Shoemaker's cartoons, and pointed stuff collected from the foreign exchanges, side by side with local news picked up as subscribers were picked up, from Chinese mouth to Chinese mouth. He had a good number of his papers . . . there were ways of getting these out, just as there were ways of getting the international news in . . . and I tried to get him to leave me one of these, but he would do everything except that. Thinking it over, he was right. A souvenir is hardly worth the risk of a bunch of lives.

Unlike the Japanese, the Chinese are not fond of death as an abstract proposition. Since the war some of their propaganda, based largely on western propaganda, exclaims heroically: 'We will die for, this!' 'We will die for that!'

120

So they do, the soldiers fighting and dying with superb courage, the civilians taking an important part.

But they have no death-concentration, no fascinating death-idea, as have the Japanese. Read the little poems of great Chinese poets, translated by Arthur Waley (which is about the only way you can get them), and I don't think you will find a single one in praise of death.

Read the works of Lafcadio Hearn, including lovers' farewell letters, and you strike another psychology altogether.

What the Chinese apparently likes is to live, to have a reasonably good time, if possible. He is a harvester, accepting summer. There are many beautiful poems written by old poets, expressing the autumnal mood, but the richness of these is the richness of bodily eyes spending the last of their sight on a meridian passed from them; hands grown thin as shells, stretched lovingly out to draw upon the last lakes of sunlight.

Chinese people can suffer the evil things of the world . . . famine, deprivation, torture . . . none better. But they do not make a special personal policy of dwelling on them, like the ancient Roman or Japanese *Samurai*, who gets a certain kick out of his own disembowelment. Having to dwell so frequently on distasteful possibilities was probably the little instrument of torture which had stretched Mr. Tseng's eyes and mouth, and made him restless, even among the cushions.

Moreover, nothing could be done for him, as we knew no friendly foreigners in Tientsin. But he was proud of his three hundred odd subscribers and risky mimeographed sheet, and would wander along looking for some friend in some Place else.

There is a slender white stick (I have forgotten the name of the game) and over it you slide rings, coloured red, green, yellow, purple, and so on. I have to slide my rings quickly, because I have my railway pass; I'm going to Hankow.

Munition trucks were hopeless . . . those are so badly needed for men and munitions that many thousands of pounds' worth of medical supplies can't even start off for Changsha. And the mobile medical units, China's new and extremely clever way of swinging her Red Cross workers from front to front as they are needed, are all dressed up, irritated, agitated, but not infrequently with no truck to go.

I haven't made any more dollars, have spent quite as many as I expected to in Canton, but I throw a ring and it sticks: free train pass to Hankow. There is a sleeper to pay for and fourteen dollars for a travelling visa. To get the travelling visa you go to a Chinese official department, and answer questions on a form.

'State reason for wishing to travel.'

I wrote: 'Travel and health,' and the big official who took and read over the form grinned, but he took my fourteen dollars and stamped my passport with the visa. It looked untidy beside the little unused chrysanthemum one on the next page.

"The rest," stated Mr. Edward Bing-shuey Lee, "is up to you."

He was a nice young man; it was he who got me the railway pass. My visa notice strictly forbade any visit to military or prohibited areas.

"But that is what I want," I explained.

Mr. Lee waved his hands.

"Everything," he said, "in time."

Ring on stick. . . . Aysgarde, coming down the white cool Mexican stairs in her Manilan frock. She has been to a Chinese woman doctor, who has given her a bottle of medicine, and says she'll be quite all right. It wasn't anything serious, it was the bombing, and a slight physical disorder.

I do look better? she kept saying.

We all said, Of course you do. And she was like a child who has recently been blind, or badly crocked an ankle . . . putting out her hand to touch the banisters, withdrawing it, walking down in a straight line. Watch me!

Paul said something funny, but true, one night. He said, wrestling with a collar and stud: "Oh, well, I guess most women are permanently shell-shocked."

I guess we are. But I don't think for a moment that most men quite understand what it implies, what it might lead up to, without any premeditation or sociological homework. Just tearing a world up like a piece of dirty paper, setting a match to it, and saying, There: now I hope you like it, as it's been a long time you've kept on asking for it.

Aysgarde's Manilan dress of apricot satin, dark rosy stuff with a transparent net bodice, and standing up from the shoulders in stiff wings, came steadily down the stairs: it made hex cheeks redden, her dark eyes bright, and she said: "Do I look all right?"

We all liked it, especially Mr. Pseng, the tired young man from Tientsin, who was over for supper that night, and who stopped looking dead-beat among the cushions, sat up, and heated the kettle for us to have some more rice wine.

Paul had been showing us his treasures . . . an old-style Cantonese silk painting with lute-players and stick-pinned women on a background of faded chrysanthemum pink and gold, a green bottle he got for twenty cents, with 'Water of Heaven' charactered on its rounded base, a lively rampageous painting of Mongolian horses, and Kwan-yin, cream porcelain cooler than ivory, with mercy given or withheld by those exquisite little six-fingered hands.

For the moment, Aysgarde in her Manilan dress looked more lovely than any of those.

Rings on sticks. . . . In the Temple of the Three Buddhas, which is sacred and possesses a tooth of the Buddha, before the altars is the slight swing and rattle of hundreds of prayers in bronze, carefully carved out. At the altar's reverse, Kwan-yin and her gilded fish are missing, but there is a convex mirror, a great mirror reflecting all things from its many facets of mother-of-pearl. A priest is giving a scholar instruction, the old voice thins upward, like a thinning streak of incense, and although I want to watch the mirror, it seems insolent to stay. O broken mirror of mankind . . . And the mirror has also a deep significance in the Shinto creed of Japan.

Strange! As a rule it is only the lesser despots among the gods who quarrel, those and the barbarian gods who must always be proving what man-god tools and fools they are, by filling up their drinking-vessels and great sprawled bellies with blood.

Still, sheep-foolish, serpent-wise, we have allowed these world quarrels, we have even deliberately fostered them. So now we can take what price is offering in the blood-markets, and walk on, as I walk through the white blown blossoms of almond-pale sunlight, along the road by the Pearl River, where the children play with cheap pink and white wind-toys, little sails whirring round wildly in a slight breeze, and the wicker lanterns are still tied up on trees and lamp-posts, reminding the City of Rams of its Dr. Sun Yat-sen.

The most important living man in China to-day is, of course, its military dictator and leader, Generalissimo Chiang Kai-shek, to whom goes the principal credit for the historic wartime unification of the Chinese people, and for a stubbornly determined yet acute leadership of the nation against terrible odds. Without Chiang Kai-shek, national and Republican China might have disintegrated: but without China's dead leader, Dr.Sun Yat-sen, that Republican China might have taken much longer to evolve. In the span of years covering the young Republic's lifetime, no man, living or dead, is more deeply venerated than Sun Yat-sen; not only because to him, the Founder, is chiefly owing the State's political existence, but because his book, *The People's Principles*, became adopted as a kind of spiritual constitution, a foundation on which Chiang Kai-shek and others have been enabled to build. The Chinese Communist Party and armies, whose intense loyalty in the civilian-and-soldier mass resistance has been such an important factor in the war, have expressed themselves in harmony with the principles of Sun Yat-sen.

After the years of waiting, the crucial period of struggle and the establishment of the Republic, Dr. Sun Yat-sen remained the Founder, but not the President. The Presidency went to Yuan Shih-kai, the wealthy and powerful northerner strong in Chinese political circles long before the Manchu dynasty fell. But Sun Yat-sen's was the more lasting power, the inspiration of a people; Sun Yat-sen's, the chair left empty at executive meetings in the great Canton Memorial Hall; Sun Yat-sen's, the three bows with which the little Kwangtung village communities opened their patriotic programmes.

Some foreigners decry Sun Yat-sen. Yet a man so well hated by the enemies of his country (the Japanese have even changed the name of a Tsingtao street called after him) must have given China an abiding cause for love: and especially in Canton, the scene of his youthful study and service, few things have more real life than this dead leader's name and prestige.

This river-road, these children playing with whirring toys, the villages, the lanterns, all seem to me like a ball of bright ribbon, unwinding from the hand of Dr. Sun Yat-sen. In China, the superficial melts away swiftly, no matter how great its fame of the moment.

Sun Yat-sen stayed, still stays. On the night of his birthday, in a little Kwangtung village where everybody except the very old men joined in to celebrate the village graduation as a National Health Centre, we all bowed three times to him, after singing the Chinese National Anthem. Then we bowed three times more, and after that the smart drilling began, the young women, married and unmarried, going through their anti-epidemic and first-aid work, the young men physically perfect, as well as practised, in their weapon-fighting, the Boxer's slender rigid shadow thrusting here and there in those changeless movements which, according to legend, not only conquer any adversary, but make the Boxer invulnerable. And when it was all over, the tiny Crearnshirt staggered to his feet, his hands in his eyes, and his trousers fell down, and as his smiling mother hurried to pick him up, there was such a great hearty, kindly village laugh. Then, with two young Chinese students, I was walking back seven miles along the narrow paved roads to Lingnan, frogs chorusing, orange blossom and fertilizer blurred with a half-sleep, and in front of us bobbing always the great wicker lanterns, the beautiful rosy lanterns.

In Shanghai it is differen : when Caley took me to the secret amputation hospital (secret, because wounded Chinese soldiers weren't so popular with the Japanese), every ward was strung with little rows of National flags, and ornamented with great oval photographs of Generalissimo Chiang Kai-shek. Every wounded soldier, ranging in age from a seventy-year-old peasant to a fourteen-year-old Boy Scout, whose leg and arm were torn off, one day as he was running his ambulance into a hot spot near Chapei, had the Generalissimo's photograph on a medallion. The same were sold by the thousand whenever Chinese schoolgirls decided to hold another patriotic day. But as far north as Hankow, soldiers from Shanshi were selling photographs of mass meetings in the interior, and on the great banners swayed by uniformed patriots (a good many women among the men) the rather sad face of the author of *The People's Principles* was crudely painted, and looked down.

Canton Hospital, grey-painted. A little more Sun Yat-sen, a memory, in a model of the original college, showing the room where he slept. Downstairs, rooms full of gravely merry young doctors zipp-fastened into lumber-jackets, concentrating on little maps covered with pins (they love maps covered with pins!), which explain where every mobile medical unit, whether X-ray, surgical, or anti-epidemic, is located.

Everyone and everything is to be self-contained. Even a cook travels with the units, only six simple drugs are included in the fifty-pound kits made up at Changsha, they will all carry their kits in an emergency, and really, if they can only grab trucks. . . .

They can already congratulate themselves on having broken down (with the co-operation and supervision of the League of Nations' International Red Cross doctors, the only thing the League has moved itself to do for China) any local possibilities of the smallpox epidemic still frightening Hong Kong. Also it is true the Japanese can no longer bomb their mobile units as the Red Cross hospitals were bombed.

A young doctor, Cambridge graduate, tells with sparkling eyes of the pleasant retreat he had just found for himself on a hill-side, while Japanese bombers attacked his truck.

"And this boy came running down, all in white, dazzling white! So I called: 'My dear boy, won't you please go away?' But this boy . . ."

The little mangy animals of the experimental rooms, and a dog's long-drawn howl. There are three of us, the medical superintendent, a Cantonese doctor's very dainty wife, whose hands and throat are sparkling with pigeon's blood rubies, and myself. In the bacteriological research room, a young man with a switchback seems very eager over a new process of staining slides: alcohol and fat come into it, he says it's far quicker than any of the methods now in practice. Door after door locked: that is because of the bombing.

Dr. Wong opens the door of the dissecting room: "Are you brave enough?"

Mrs. Yik gives a little cry: "No, I will go round the other way."

The man on the dissecting table is a big fellow, almost gigantic, stark, with a little blood fringing his crushed skull. Even in death, his body has a fierce look, as if it could hardly stop fighting. But one hand, slightly limp, falls against the edge. Dr. Wong opens the lid of a tub. Other, darker old corpses come swimming up, like pitiful brown mermen in the alcohol.

"There isn't anything in death."

"No, nothing at all."

We rejoin Mrs. Yik, going down past good little wards, very full of visitors.

"The families, of course, never stop visiting the patients. If we tried to regulate the hours, they would say: 'Now you're acting like a foreign devil.'"

Dr. Wong thinks perhaps this was rude, and add: "They're only joking, of course."

We all have tea at the Oi Kwan. Mrs. Yik pretends to be impressed by travel: "You would go by India? No, it would be impossible for one of our women to do that."

But from the red sparkle of her rubies, her delicate little hands, dark hair under a fashionable hat, above all from her smile, I know Mrs. Yik has no complaints on the score of India. She is happy where she is.

A messenger from the hospital summons us all back; the ambulances are growling out, like great beasts, from a basement garage. The second lot of bombs comes down as we stand in the basement: the beams and sandbags, building the place up so that the patients can use it for their bomb-shelter if necessary, are shaking and trembling. News comes through very quickly. They are bombing Western Village, three miles away, and already thirty dead people have been pulled out of flames and rubble. The number of other casualties is not known. I would like to go out with an ambulance, but daren't ask; the doctors are far too busy, including Dr. Yik, who swings himself up on a monster rushing by.

Only the medical superintendent is free, and drives me home, looking very pale and sad. He was in England during the war, he says; he loves the English. Jerkily we start talking about that, and about things in Europe that have happened since then. It all seems so simple, and so sad.

"We've thrown away all our chances."

"No . . . I can understand it. It was hard to deal with. And the Germans in their own place are terrible. They will knock you off the pavements." His lips are quite white.

Ring on stick. . . . At the station, where Paul and I went to reserve my sleeper, the stationmaster said: "This is a great pity. You should have gone up last night, when twenty-five American bluejackets travel on the train, or it is better still to have gone up when the British Ambassador went up. Then, you are quite sure, no bombs."

There were several stories about the new British Ambassador, Sir Archibald Clark Kerr, who arrived in Shanghai in February. The frantic interest in his politics now seems rather naïve. When he entrained for Hankow, Canton got the legend that the Japanese had been given ten days' notice, together with a plan of the train showing where the Ambassador sat.

We thought they should have carried it further, giving a plan of the Ambassador, marked: 'Don't Poke Here.'

But the funniest-if-true story was provided by the Japanese, who, allegedly, did not bomb the train, but stunted. They flew over and around it, alongside, in front, and when they were tired they went off and bombed the horizon. Everybody got off that particular train in a nervous condition.

Paul and I got outside the main building, a handsome station with leather chairs, steam heating, and superabundant pot plants. We came out into a population which flung down the sugarcane it was sucking, and ran.

We tried to catch up. The few laggards looked upwards, yelped, and joined in too. Somehow it all felt very unpleasant, though it was only a matter of three circling 'planes. A Chinese soldier passed.

"Where shall we run?" I yelled. But he only smiled in a pale way, and tore off round a corner.

Paul began: "Better roll under a damn carriage," and then pulled up, nobly.

"No! Why should we?"

Unfortunately his heroism had no time to seem effective, as the rest stopped running, almost at the same moment. Some pointed out that the 'planes had flown off. We took a jitney-car, whose driver, spitting scornfully, blew his horn at full toot all the way to the ferry, till I could have cried with the pain of him. We had both been well scared, Paul and I.

Slowly I was being squeezed to death in the corridor of a train whose carriages were all locked up, because ticketless people came and hid in them. I stood against the wall, expanded and flattened. Ordinary luggage, huge string kits, livestock, and people dug into me. The guard took a look at my ticket, said it was out of order, refused to open a carriage door. Aysgarde and Paul went out to see if they could bribe an official. I remained crucified, but surprised at nothing.

Mr. Edward Bing-shuey Lee then arrived, and matter, in some peculiar way, dissolved before him, though he still looked westernized and rather sleepy.

A door opened, a porter gave me a lower berth and said: "Chow soon, Missie." An inspector of railways and a nice-looking young Chinese couple were also allotted to the cabin, and squeezed in, smiling. I told Mr. Lee that Aysgarde and Paul were lost, so he went out and produced them from the bosoms of hundreds of coolies, old women, soldiers, ducks, and pigs making rude noises from string kits.

"Budget for a week," advised Paul, who had heard that hotel rates in Hankow were 40 dollars a week.

Canton had done much to my 40 dollars Mex., and I didn't want to trade in my one other asset, the trans-Siberial ticket.

So I kissed them and said: "Yes, a week." When I saw them again, Aysgarde would feel all right, and we'd laugh and tell stories.

We had had a run of fine sunsets over Canton, if you like the kind where the sun plunges down, a naked red ball. There's much the same kind on a white flag, but the Japanese call it the Rising Sun. I don't think I liked it, our last sunset over Canton.

But I liked them, the one Chinese and two foreign faces, little and gone so quickly in the narrowing cylinder of lights and darkness.

CHAPTER TEN

Interlude with Azaleas

MR. P. KOO HAD some business along the corridor, and Mrs. Koo and I could only bow and smile, she speaking no word of English, nor I of Mandarin. So the Inspector made the running, and, discovering that I was a New Zealander, asked if on our trains men and women were allowed to sleep together.

I said: "No," adding hastily, "But we all think it's very old-fashioned."

"Well," contemplated the Inspector, "not in China, either . . . not until this war came."

There was a quiet, golden-smiling optimism about him which removed him a little from this world, as he sat dangling long trousered legs from his top berth. Even when apologizing, he was bright. He apologized for the train.

"It is very little and very dirty," he said. "We had some good trains, especially for this line . . . very up-to-date. But now we have taken them off and hidden them away, in case of damage. It is because of the bombs. The journey, however, is no longer very dangerous, because most of the dangerous section we run through quickly, by night. In the morning, we are too far away for the Japanese to get in. Oh, yes, I can guarantee that."

He beamed, and Mr. P. Koo, a young man with a face so exceptionally thin and pointed that, for a Chinese, he looked delicate, came back and struggled to raise the window. We pulled up in blowing darkness, a few yards from a small station.

"That has *all* been done to-day," said the Inspector, thrusting his head out like a tortoise. "When I came down this afternoon everything was level. They have been using some good big bombs. I must go and see."

He vanished. In the swelling darkness loomed a hole about the size of a nice swimming-bath, heaps of bricks, some bars over a window showing a glim, and a scared-looking little kid in uniform, trotting up and down, waving a lantern.

Surely the Inspector had gone a trifle Coué? He came back, golden-smiling as before, nodding, "It has *all* been blown to pieces!" and took from Mr. Koo's outstretched packet a Chienmen cigarette. In far northern places, so isolated that the most avaricious black trousers sold nothing else, two things were still sold . . . peanuts, Chienmen cigarettes. The Chinese soldiers of the Central Government troops seemingly never smoked anything else (just as the Japanese stuck to Spear Brand, put up in Tokyo). Sometimes on a road there was nothing remotely human, except soaked, grubby and empty packages, Chienmen and Spear Brands. The British, by the way, sold a brand cheaper than either Chinese or Japanese: but this was notorious.

Mr. Koo, who said he was reporting to Hankow after visiting England and Geneva, apologized about his wife.

"I can speak a little English," he said, in accents much nearer the clear stream than my own, "but she, none at all."

She, whose round-faced curly head lay back lazily, knew she was under discussion, and smiled at him, like a cat which would like to bite its master's thumb. Grey gown, ankle-slit . . . they always come through the wear and tear of travelling so immaculate, these women. You can't wear a waistless Chinese gown, which shows everything you've got, unless curve-control means sweet meditation for you, not anxiety. Her husband smiled back with his eyes.

'Well, he's just home after six months,' I thought, feeling lonesome.

He began to teach me Mandarin equivalents of Cantonese words . . . face, eye, hair, nose, beautiful, jade, green. . . . The characters, you see, are easy to make. To prove this, he makes some with a pencil. And high up in grey-flaky darkness, far beyond us, appeared a small ruby ring of fires.

"What are those fires?" I demanded.

The Inspector answered, with his inevitable golden smile: "Oh, the people of such a very little place like that light fires at night, because they are afraid of tigers."

Lovely tigers!

Suddenly we were all going to bed. Mrs. Koo and I kept on our top layer, and took off underneath things under cover of the scraggy blankets. The men swung to the top berths, there to arch and murmur. They dropped their trousers: long vistas of shank, suspender, and sock.

"I must tell you story," said the Inspector, popping his head down in an acrobatic way, so that like the business end of a boa constrictor it swayed before my berth. "Story about American missionary husband, travelling with the lady, his wife, first time in China. The boy put these two in sleeping-car with Chinese men. The missionary husband shouted very angrily: 'Take us somewhere else! American lady does not sleep with Chinese men!'

"So the boy goes away. Some time afterwards, he comes back, and tells missionary husband please to bring his wife along, carriage all very nice now. So he puts them in a carriage with two more men. One is a Finn man, one is a Japanese.

" 'What is this?' says the missionary husband, very angrily.

"Then the boy is quite cross. He says: 'You only say to me: "American

130

lady does not sleep with Chinese man; you don't say she will not sleep with other man." ' "

Giggle. . . . The rounded face of Mrs. P. Koo is quite asleep, its mouth wide open; she snores the ghost of a snore.

After this night, there was not much to be seen of the Inspector, except when he came back to sleep. I suppose he had duties: the food, for instance, gave out in the first twelve hours, excepting eggs, and I fear and shrink from the way Chinese boys cook eggs foreign-style.

Old red-yolked pickled Chinese eggs, such as we had coming from Australia, are not bad; their middles taste like salty cheese. But the foreign-styles! Something between fry and poach, the bare yolks gleaming and slippery, fringed with whites as tough as shark skin. There is no salt. As one draws north, hospitable traditions become unshakeable, especially that of the saltless, foreign-style egg.

"Special for you!" beams the host, his cook-boy producing never fewer than four iniquities (which he may have wanted and needed quite badly for his own supplies).

All the while you pant for cooling streams . . . pickled bamboo, sliced beans, savoury green onion-tips, peas diced with chicken broiled pink . . . the commonplaces of Chinese repast, which everyone else is absorbing without discretion. But when you have forced your digestive organs to curl round four Specials For You, all that looked so tempting is gone.

How can you explain? The Chinese is more courteous, as a rule, than any foreigner: but only the lowest foreigner can insult Special For You. So there is never any explanation.

Half-way between Canton and Hankow, the traveller leaves the rice-bowl and strikes into noodle country. Experienced writers like Edgar and Peg Snow, Agnes Smedley, James Bertram, coming back from the north-west, lived mainly on noodles. The Eighth Route Army soldier is supposed to feed himself on under four cents a day; peasants of the north-west, too poor to go beyond the noodle as staple, make up their vitamins with chopped vegetables, and are a tough race, with first-class teeth.

North-easterly, far up beyond Hankow, one runs into light-soiled wheat country, which also produces millet, soya bean, and peanuts, cropped in rotation, the bean-shoots spindling up before the last wheat is stooked together in low stooks. Here will grow grapes, melons (the first of which herald the dysentery season), little pink drippy apricots, a few fine peach trees, flowering ash and roses, from whose petals the peasants make good confections.

There's no romance: when an American missionary, one of the half-dozen or so scattered in the immense yellow plains, imports and, with great labour, brings to birth a new rose, the peasants look, smell, and say: "It is good to eat," or "It is no good to eat." Every successful grower is a grain-hoarder, stacking millet and other grain on huge wicker trays.

It might almost laugh, almost be fruitful, this land. But every few years it meets the Yellow River in flood and when it has shaken that frothing dog from its back, the landmarks and stores have vanished. Then comes famine, the long cry seldom clearly heard, because in this country the people are illiterate and poor, and have not so many politics; the cry sinks without recognition, except that missionaries of different Christian sects have little wars, snapping about which should take the most grain-sacks sent for relief from various centres.

There are other natural troubles; torture (*legally* abolished more than thirty years ago) lasted long enough to reduce and frighten the once immense armies of bandits. There are, of course, still plenty of bandits. All but the young women of thirty or so still have bound feet, another popular thing put down by the Chinese Republican Government. Some provinces, such as Kiangsu, were waving, curling masses of opium poppies, pink, white, and red, until some years ago they were included in the limited but still increasing areas where poppy-cultivation and opium-smoking were prohibited . . . though all poppy-profiteering was not . . . by Generalissimo Chiang Kai-shek.

Every three hundred years (say the wiseacres) Huang Ho, River of China's Sorrow, must change its course. Then the north-eastern villagers, who happen to be caught between the dead and living arms of the waters, see a rage let loose that might carry them back to fabled scenes, if they were given that way.

But they are much more practical people. At Hsuchowfu, once surrounded on three sides by the Huang Ho, and still part-girdled by a thin stream showing the old trace, they have a bronze cow, which perches up among houses and small shops, with mouth wide open, drinking the waters.

While the cow keeps her mouth open, the flood will fall back before the city.

When I last saw Hsuchowfu, the bronze cow was still there, but either the bombardments or subsequent events had caused her to close her mouth. I am told that at Peiping there is another such monstrous drinking-cow, but I never saw the cow of Peiping.

In spite of these floods, the soil of north-easterly plains remains always sandy and shifting, its surface fertility blown or torn out in a night's wreck. The white dust begins in Hankow, where everybody who does not wear dark glasses (very capably manufactured by the Chinese themselves, and just as popular among them as with the foreigners) wears pink-rimmed eyelids, and probably suffers from a dust disease, of which you can take your choice, beginning at blepharitis and pinky-eye, ending at complaints which really do give you a God-forsaken air. Foreign employers deal competently with pinky-eye (which is catching and prevalent among boys who don't literally mind their eye). They fire them, and don't re-engage until cured. This causes so much fuss among the dependants that the boys take care not to catch pinky-eye.

Hsuchowfu is dream, conveniently far off in futurity, hundreds of miles north-east beyond Hankow. Here is a little dirty train forging its way into morning towards Hankow, and all the foreign-style eggs have given out. Also some soldiers, boarding us while we slept, commandeered and drank the beer. They travelled sitting up, thin young chaps in bilious cotton, looking too happy. The beer, perhaps.

Passengers could buy food only from station vendors, and Mr. Koo took over the responsibility of seeing that I bought nothing "from eating which" (as he said) "you will die."

He liked the English. "But you are all too much afraid of the Japanese.

Temporarily his concentration seemed less political than (a) on Mrs. Koo, (b) on diet. I bought some millet patties, pretty things, marked with large black characters on both sides.

"The meaning of this character is Ground. The meaning of this character is Sky. Much better not to eat them, they are made in the dirt."

From a waif he procured hard-boiled eggs, their yolks greenish-black, also Chinese meat pies, which turned out a success. They are baked with a milky outer skin, which you peel off, leaving hygienic, or at least hopeful, what lies beneath. Good little new-baked loaves may be procured deep in the hinterlands, special for you!

Ground and Sky; Chienmen cigarettes; eggs green at heart, roasted chickens and ducks, cooked with their heads on, and looking so frankly miserable. Don't eat wayside poultry, or you will die. Seaweed dries black on a shaky sacking roof, where seeds, sprinkled over big trays, are drying brown. The huddle of poor dwellings, too small to be named a village, clings plastered like martens' nests against rocks, high above a green river.

Fighting the rapids, with high torn oblongs of matting sail, long poles, or both, are a few small rivercraft plied by boatmen in peaked hats. Naked to the hips, they throw their weight against the bending poles, while the water's weight, in solid and in spray, leaps high against them like a jade fish.

The world rolls out of my hands, like tousled knitting-wool. Foreign artists often say Chinese landscape has no perspective. I wonder if Einstein, taking a look up and down these gorges, would feel that they have *another* perspective, his fourth dimension, and that the best of the country's art is simply-co-related to this?

Then I remember, too, a funny little thing about some Cantonese paintings . . . how one artist makes the yellow reed, another paints the bird with wry neck, a third the hovering dragonfly. A couple more have lovingly brushed in characters, black or scarlet. Good writing is to them more beautiful than any other form of painting. When I asked the Cantonese boy to show me the best painting, he led me straight up to a character-scroll, where the black characters spoke up from the white.

The differences between us, east and west, make me laugh, but it's not an unhappy laughter. Could *we* do that . . . five famous artists all work together, making the one painting? What an idea! If anyone in the west does anything nearly as well, or nearly better, how it hurts and prickles, how the school -masters sling in their healthy spirit of competition ' muck, how the pale critics goggle 'imitation,' how everybody pants until exhausted by spite, and the work, the real thing, is never looked at at all!

I try to teach Mrs. Koo (whose grey slit-gown unfairly turns out to have another blue one, quite unruffled, concealed beneath it) English words for parts of the body and face. We can easily say 'Tea.' We have small train-cups provided for this purpose, also longish pots perpetually refilled by Boy with warm greenish water. The Koos know a trick with tea-cups. Seize, take border of clean white cloth, dip in methylated spirits, rub cup inside and out: pour in a few drops of green tea, rinse, hurl from window: refill, smile, and bow.

There is no milk, no sugar, but the faintest fragrance.

And we are out of rice-pond country. Stone and clay villages remain rather similar to those of Kwangtung, but the clay walls flung round them make them more compact. Over the large conical grave-mounds, in rows which cut away a fourth of a man's field, glistens some substance white as limestone.

Never was a land so be-sunned. Yellow is taken up, deepened and shaded in the outcrops of millions of wild azaleas, which streak hills and valleys. Colours apparently keep their tribes, for after the yellow come long strands of salmon pink, after these an apricot colour, and, at last, turning the green hills into wine-sopped napkins, the wild red azaleas. It is a colour like blood from a wound, yet it strikes back. Memory, thought, and enchantment are pierced, and flow out to meet it, and what can bring them back from the Chinese soil again?

Closer, on the cutting's edges, runs a straggling wild rose; a daisy-species waves back. And I always loved wistaria, but here I saw what I never quite expected, whole drifts of fallen wistaria petals knee-deep, filling the grooves and gutters of dark red soil. Above the fluttering of petals rose the vines, so thick and sturdy from growing without support that they were like trees rather than vines. Now and again, flashing past in silver mail, shone an archangel tree I took for wild almond, because of its whiteness.

More common were the small thorned acacias, white-flowered too, and sweet-smelling, that march on through Hankow, five hundred miles easterly to Hsuchowfu, and beyond, for all I know, to the Gobi desert; hardly another tree follows them in any great company except small basket willows and pomegranates. But a village or station may be celebrated for its two or three fine fruit trees, or even for one fine fruit tree. A station near Hsuchowfu was renowned because it had a remarkable peach tree, which bore such very good peaches; but nobody ever quite explained why the peach-stones were not planted somewhere else, as charmingly recounted in Pearl Buck's book, *The Good Earth*.

About azaleas, the Chinese are almost irrational. When the National University of Hunan was bombed, in Changsha, the Japanese said it was because Chiang Kai-shek was visiting the university, and had been gravely wounded.

The Chinese, in a rather pathetic appeal sent out to the whole civilized world, said they had only come to visit the azaleas.

Chiang Kai-shek said nothing, but appeared next Sunday evening in Hankow and gave a public address, at which he showed not even an inch of sticking-plaster. The azaleas survived. A fair total of civilians, including some students, did not.

Mrs. Koo addressed a remark, which her husband translated simply: "She says, 'Now I must go away, and you go away.'"

I did, wandering off to the dining-car, where Chinese who had no sleepers were lying on or between the marble-topped tables; women's tired heads had fallen, resting against string kits, and the little naked, scarred behind of the baby dangled from its mother's shoulders, the head wabbling, always a piece of sugar-cane plugging the mouth. There was still no beer.

Life going on, springing from rusty spores of pine, from the big crooked thumb-joint of the wooden plough, squeezed into mud. A silvery ring, where picks of a hundred coolies chip at red and blue cliffs . . . one of the many gangs keeping this death-watched road under repair. An old woman has two pigs, and one is sick, and she keeps it tenderly covered in a blue cotton quilt, which heaves up and down with its pink waves of fever or emotion. Such huge pigs, she such a small Black-Trouser, and gone for ever!

I try to sleep sloping backwards, but that hurts, so I go to sleep on a little boy and a string bag.

The little boy seemed not to mind, until we both woke up, and I tried to be matey with him. Then he just howled. His mother, with a kindly smile, rammed his sugar-cane into his mouth. The soldiers also endeavoured to get some head-and-shoulders sleep, waking up to slop a little more tea down their throats. The flies crawled on us; we all caught one another's diseases. Fair enough.

Mr. and Mrs. Koo looked charming, she in a fresh gown, with paint on her cheeks. They were chipping eggshell from our greenhearts, dropping the bits into the spittoon. I put it down to Mr. Koo's great credit that he never spat all that time on the train. She spat . . . not profusely, but still, a spit. Kindly they offered me some greenhearts.

We were now definitely a military objective, having taken on a large company of soldiers, and some carriages said to contain munitions. Not a sight of a bomber. For the first time, instead, I saw sparrows in China. We still had no beer, and the Inspector said we would arrive in Wuchang rather late that night.

"*Very* late, perhaps," he hinted, with his golden smile, "if you like, since it will be hard for you finding good hotel, you can sleep in the train all night. Only you must be locked up."

Somehow I disliked this idea, and said I'd rather chance the hotels.

Afterwards, it still seemed the wiser choice. Next to aerodromes (with which Wuchang was well supplied), standing trains and train-sheds continued to be the military objectives most frequently tried for by eager young Japanese fliers, who had more success than was printed in Hankow papers, Chinese or foreign.

At this period there were fair numbers of eager young Japanese fliers visiting the Wuhan cities, Wuchang, Hanyang, and Hankow; mostly they kept to Wuchang, both because of the aerodromes there, and because, when they did come to Hankow, Chinese 'planes, supplemented by Russian ones flown by tough Russian pilots, invariably drove them off again.

Hankow was the only place where I saw the Chinese 'planes have any luck against the Japanese, though I saw a Chinese gun bring a bomber spinning down over a little place called Naishan Mountain. This was because, in most cities wide open to aerial attack, such as Canton, Chiang Kai-shek's definite policy was to concentrate on defending and attacking military objectives, while leaving the defence of civilian targets to anti-aircraft guns . . . when there were any anti-aircraft guns. A hard policy, but beyond criticism.

Wuchang, on the edge of the Yangtse-Kiang, was journey's end for the little train from Canton, and one of the three Wuhan cities, the Chinese heart and Fatherland. Hankow held the greatest importance. It had been the capital, was westernized and rich in trade, and even now, when the transference of the capital to Chungking had already seen the exit of several Government departments, it was the most vital artery of political and wartime activities, the place where military and civil policies were shaped, re-shaped, established, broken.

It was also the rendezvous of generals and politicians; in Hankow, perhaps, could best be seen the window-dressing of the Chinese United Front, reputedly a little more united at the Communist end than at Generalissimo Chiang Kai-shek's end.

The Generalissimo had a house of private address on the Bund where he could sometimes be interviewed, Soong Mei-ling, his beautiful westernized wife, acting as his interpreter. W. H. Donald, an Australian, was among intimate friends.

Frequently the Generalissimo and Madame appeared in public, and he made addresses, sometimes connected with Christian church activities. His baptism in Shanghai by the negro Methodist evangelist, Mr. Carter, is an old story.

Debatable, none too accessible (after the attempted assassination of one of his trusted advisers, he would seldom allow any but his own camera-men to photograph him), he had established, from Hankow over China, a reputation for personal courage and for sudden appearances in dangerous territories where even the spies did not expect him.

On these lightning visits, Madame was usually at his side. . . . Madame with the Chinese elegance and grace, the nervous vitality, who sometimes let herself be photographed in western slacks and slouch hats by Hankow's omnipresent camera-men; Madame, whose portraits could sometimes be reduced down to a taut, sensitive mouth, a pair of beautiful eyes.

The New Life Movement was Chiang Kai-shek's plan for creating a Chinese mentality to which the new industrialization would be acceptable. It rested, very simply, on the premise that in the west abstractions have for many centuries been successful in diverting the main current of human thought from more material considerations: its revival is chiefly that of the old Confucian virtues. There is, of course, far more than this to be said of and for the movement. The Youth Movement, chief subsidiary of the New Life Movement, with women and war-work its especial fields, was Madame Chiang Kai-shek's hobby.

Soong Mei-ling, Soong Ching-ling, Soong Ai-ling . . . the names of the three Chinese sisters, names meaning Beauty, Purity, and Love.

Soong Ching-ling, who had been the wife of Dr. Sun Yat-sen, and who now lived in a Hong Kong apartment, was half an exile from the war, though her whole interest, the whole deep feeling of a nature capable of much passion, lay in this war. Throughout China she had an indestructible prestige, though some said that Chinese people were a little afraid of her.

Others said that Chiang Kai-shek was keeping her back from the dynamic part in the war she could so easily have played. Her name was vaguely associated with the Third Party, which had no direct relations at all with Communism, but lay between the extremes of both sides. It was more than ten years since she visited Hankow. She was a little over forty years old, and very beautiful. Her Hong Kong apartment looked steeply down past the gardens to the junk-fleets, which sailed out and were sunk or burned; and although she did not visit Hankow, before the fall of Canton Mrs. Sun Yat-sen had paid a public visit to Canton.

Wuchang looks older than Hankow, a city of open shops, great red pots, factories, much less westernized than the sparkle of lights facing it across the Yangtse.

It is one leg, say the legends, of a mighty tripod, supporting the ancient and sacred Fatherland. It has Snake Hill, on which old Mr. Lay gave me good advice; and the Temple of Hell, depicting a thousand hideous tortures, which I tried to see, but was barred out because it was occupied by the military and a large, intractable man with a bayonet. And stately Wuhan University is there (or was there) where the black-gowned Professor of Literature (dusty acacia petals clinging like moths to his dusty gown) told me of the translation of Katherine Mansfield's works by a young Chinese airman, who died in a crash even sooner than dark Katherine crashed and died. Icarus for Icarus! Pagodas, pines, an old broad lake glistening, full of bullfrogs and germs.. . .

But when our train arrived, an hour off midnight, we saw only darkness. Chinese people crowded down steps leading to the river.

The Inspector came up to say good-bye.

"One time," he said, "you must visit far north, in the Mohammedan country. It is so hot, we have trains whose sides are only matting and leaves. I will now say good night."

Good night, Inspector! But Mr. and Mrs. P. Koo took me under wing.

"In any case," he assured me, politely, "to-night, coming so late, I cannot arrive at my home."

Somebody kicked an empty oil-drum. A pile of them slithered from the top step to the bottom, leaping, booming, clanging, and quite mad.

Automatically, though unreasonably, all the tired, chilly people decided: 'Now we are being bombed. If we run hard, maybe we can escape the bombs.' We tore down the steps like Hindoo widows escaping half-cooked from burning-ghats. Half-way, we realized that nobody was bombing us, and stopped running. Some laughed, but everybody was a ghost.

We crossed the Yangtse River by moonlight . . . a moonlight of midnight, half rubies, half pearl.

Oh, sleepy enough! The breaths and vague presences of soldiers halt behind the saloon windows, their faint curiosity, though most of them remain out on the deck. One soldier has a wolfskin collar. I can hear our primary-school voices chirping up, like idiotic birds behind the wire-netting cage of the tall windows. Among the great waterways of the world is the Yangtse-Kiang. It seems queer, but any vinegar is taken out of the pickle by the nearness of Mr. and Mrs. Koo.

On the Bund we procured rickshas, tired coolies. Acacias in full white blossom, staggering lamp-flames, and no hotel; Chinese or foreign, no room at any inn. I didn't mind; my green coat was heavy and had a big fur collar, and I felt willing to sleep out, but Mr. Koo was quite upset by the thought. Something had to be done, and yet we were like three yawning cats, two amber tortoiseshells, one grey-white. Our ricksha boys, quite done in, complained, bargained, and then struck. Mr. Koo looked worried. Perhaps Hankow brought back to him the importance and dignity of his mission.

At last we found the all-night teashop which was gaudily lit up, and had at one end a fruit stall, still open. We were sitting up on chairs, and Mr. Koo seemed to hope that later on the tea-shop might let us have a bed. Mrs. Koo's round chin lifted and dropped in her restless doze.

Some people came unevenly out, and the proprietor beckoned us in. It was a big, bare room, with a marble-topped washstand, and only one double bed; but the bed had an awning, supported by pillars of lattice-work interlacing blue things like hearts. The sole bedding was a mattress and a quilt patterned with more hearts. There was a spittoon, but no water to wash your hands.

I thought: 'It looks rather like a brothel, doesn't it?' but was certainly not going to criticize my benefactor's great teamwork.

"I've got an overcoat," I murmured, "blanket."

Mr. Koo murmured something in exchange, and we covered Mrs. Koo, who lay asleep like a doll. With clear affection, I thought: 'This couldn't possibly have happened without him,' and went to sleep.

I suppose he had time to think, just for one bitter moment, 'This couldn't possibly have happened without a foreigner.'

In early morning he sat up and looked at himself, or, rather, separately and somewhat coldly, at bits of himself. His hands, socks, trouser-buttons. He certainly looked slept in; and now like a sick man, surveying yesterday's cold scraps on a plate, he got up very quietly, walked to the spittoon, and spat.

I knew how he felt, because I wanted to spit. That dark-brown taste. But I thought for the time being, I'd better not be awake.

After about ten o'clock that morning, I never saw Mr. or Mrs. Koo again.

Without noticing, I had worked over into the zone where not to see nice people again was the norm, especially if they were Chinese people. Normally, if you like people and they are good to you and you don't hate them for that, you date them up, however casually. Here you didn't, so the zone into which I had worked was the war zone. That finality is a part of war (particularly since war has got in among the civilians) which helps give it the gently smiling, gently staring gaze of a mental defective.

After all we couldn't sit rubbing our eyes on the blue-hearted counterpane for ever. I suggested the British Consulate, though the day was Sunday. Mr. Koo looked wearily relieved. While I called for rickshas he translated my good-byes to his wife. Then it was hardly five minutes of acacia'd dust before my coolie stopped outside the consulate, which had shoddy old crumple-petal roses behind its gates. For all our sakes it seemed better I should ask the British Consul where to look for a bed, though to date, I had kept away from consulates.

The P. Koos drove away, waving, smiling. I wish I knew that he got an Order out of his English mission. Whatever it was, Mr. Koo deserved an Order.

CHAPTER ELEVEN

The Fires for Taierhchwang

HANKOW, AND THE FIRST WEEK of April. I had missed by a night the giant torchlight procession with which the Wuhan cities celebrated the second battle of Taierhchwang, that famous victory written down by military experts as the sharpest knock the heavily mechanized armies of Japan had ever received in open field.

Everybody in Hankow demonstrated . . . honest citizens, soldiers, intellectuals, progressives, die-hards, die-not-at-alls, Communists, students, some of them prisoners for years before the outbreak of war and declaration of the Chinese United Front.

Like the New Lifers and Youth Movement, the old radical societies, of which the most important was probably the National Salvation Movement (open to all shades of political thought, but somehow attracting no Blueshirts), hung together, affiliating into something called 'The Fourteen Federated Political and Cultural Societies of Hankow.' If you wanted to go creeping around bushes looking for Reds in this organization, you would find yourself at one moment in a society for promoting better relationship with the French; at the next, bumping your head against the piano-legs of a musical society.

It was all extremely Chinese: and the aggregation of youth, whatever their politics, as they waved their torches on Taierhchwang's night, had behind them the consciousness of a well-developed, vivid, and efficacious war propaganda, caricature, war-songs, patriotic oratory, fund-collecting, recruit-catching, the very important literacy classes, the comforting of wounded and lonely soldiers, the assistance of refugees and care of wounded men.

Madame Chiang Kai-shek's Youth Movement, a subsidiary of Chiang Kai-shek's New Life. Movement, had set out to establish an orphanage for war orphans in the south. The opposition group (or perhaps I should call them the opposite group, since within the United Front a definite opposition did not exist) were doing the same thing in the north-west.

There was a backdrop of bitterness, the years between '27 and now; but although among many of the older people that must have been ineradicable, in Hankow's United Front it was all far pleasanter, with less bickering and jealousy, than one might have expected.

They were all so young (the oldest, usually, in their twenties), and all, once provided with a war job, so gloriously busy. Ceaselessly, so far as I could see, rival societies stole and toned down one another's thunder; and either the Kwangtung students' village organizing groups had borrowed heavily from Hankow, or the northerners had been cribbing from the Cantonese.

This slight confusion and overlapping was of all things the most desirable. The mass mobilization, after all, was China's.

But there was, or seemed to me, no immediate desire of the young to break apart, to personalize or politically to segregate the force of their efforts from the mass effort, resistance against invasion. The point had arrived where when they spoke of an enemy they meant Japanese militarism, though scores of them, having studied and lived in Japan, had a liking for Japanese people.

Hankow even had its Japanese apostle, Wataru Kaji, the celebrated young author and friend of the great Chinese leader and writer, Lu Hsun. Lu Hstin was dead: his friend worked high up in the Chinese National Political Council, under whose auspices receptions for foreigners were held, and the most fiery oratory usually proclaimed. At the beginning of the war, Wataru Kaji, then in Shanghai, had hairbreadth escapes from Chinese who misunderstood, and Japanese who understood only too well. A White Russian gave him a hide-out; but the Chinese chased him into Japan, where, collecting his wife and disguising himself, he promptly set off again for Hankow.

I pointed out to the Chinese orator who was telling me this that such a thing might be possible if New Zealand, for instance, went to war with Australia. But before the Australian had a chance to open his mouth and explain, he might be shot as a spy.

"Well," said the Chinese, expanding, "a lot of people here felt like that. But, anyhow, what is there to spy on?"

I thought, if this war ends in the right way, China should do a lot in revolutionizing the psychology of Japan. Meanwhile the famous Japanese author, who was small by reason of his slender build, like a Chinese cut vertically in half, surveyed his audience with quiet, critical eyes; then got to his feet, and made one of the best speeches of the afternoon. Disciple or not, a very brave man.

Obviously this still hall wasn't in any hurry for Sunday visitors. On the back of a second visiting-card I scrawled: 'Call has no financial implications,' and handed it to the floating yellow leaf who appeared on request.

Slept-in slacks, navy; large red fish leaping aggressively on crumpled silk shirt; hairpins, and not enough of them; an ugly determination to get a bed, whoever suffered. Whenever I looked down, back stared the soles of my English shoes. 'Think yourself funny?' sneered the soles, which by this time were arched and frayed, like trick convex mirrors with nasty faces.

I began to think that the complete passivity of the British Consulate, even though this day was sacred and Sunday, was a little queer. Of course, Britons notoriously loathe getting up on a Sunday morning. I'm with the majority, I loathe it myself But . . . but . . .

But just then, walking by way of her garden, came the British Consul's wife, a slim lady in worn blue jumper and skirt, escorted through the slipshod old roses by two large, spotty, starchy dogs.

"Down!" she kept telling them, and they barked happily, and upped. Lord! For ever, even now unmistakably, England.

I told the Consul's wife (who was a nice woman) about having bed trouble, and she told me that when the Consul-General got my second card, he thought if it wasn't a money matter it must certainly be politics, and turned over and pulled up the sheets again. The lesser, or younger, Consuls also did this. She couldn't find anyone who would get up; but it seemed to her that somebody should, and so she had dressed herself. Now she seemed genuinely worried over last night, which was all so long ago.

"In such an emergency, you should have rung up the consulate," she breathed. "Really, you should have rung up the consulate."

Suddenly she asked, Had I breakfasted yet? Well, no. For a moment she thought, then her small, wrinkled face lit up.

"I will get you some eggs!" she cried.

I thought: 'No, don't tell me. They will be some fried eggs, and your Chinese cook will do them, so they will slip about the plate.'

Anyhow she told me the way to a bathroom and lavatory. Oh, China!

So I washed upstairs, in a great porcelain lavatory adjoining a colossal bathroom, and saw (enviously) the empty bed, almost sacred because Peter Fleming had slept in it, before going up to Hsuchowfu. John Gunther was still in Hankow, and in hospital, very sick, people said, of the lobster. Auden, the poet, with Isherwood, the playwright, was somewhere in, or near, Sian. Agnes Smedley, after cave-dwelling in the north-west, now shared the roof of the American bishop. Anna Louise Strong had come and gone in the early part of the war, and Edgar Snow was still in Shanghai. It sounded interesting, and as if some French genius, Cocteau for preference, should now arrive and write a play called *Troy Without Tears*.

Nobody seemed to know if there were any Chinese writers about, and if so, where they were or what they had written. But they were all in Hankow, from poets and short-story writers to straight-out propagandists; and the only woman journalist permanently at the front was Miss Ting Ling, who was up with the Eighth Route Army.

Her stories of peasant life in the district where she was born had once got her into hot water with the Central Government officials, who felt these books were revolutionary. For a long while nobody would betray Ting Ling's whereabouts; but eventually, some pressure was brought to bear on the right person . . . her husband . . . and she went to prison. But with the beginning of the war she was released, like all the survivors, and was now moving about with great courage and freedom.

"Also she is married to somebody else now, I think," happily concluded Mr. Yeh, who told me this. He was a writer of short stories, but interested in verse as well, and I think it was he who, with another Chinese poet, meant to translate some of Auden's verse into the Chinese. He was young, happy and a Leftist, and when he talked a long black lock of hair fell over one eye.

Stepping down the Consul's stairs, between walls hung with exquisite old paintings, grey and white, hard green; landscape and flower within, and the British roses without. The Consul's wife took me by car to be seen by some Americans, who might know of a bed.

"The Americans!" she murmured, "so wonderful about anything like that."

Between us a dog, immaculate though spotty, reared his collar. He looked like Baldwin, Chamberlain, and Eden.

This was the American Bishop's house; they were all busy, but tired after last night's concert, given by the Bishop's daughter, who was going away. Even her bouquet, when they auctioned it off, brought in over fifty dollars Mex.

Agnes Smedley, who had a room upstairs to write in, walked in and out: square-cut, with cropped chestnut hair, good shoulders, and grey-blue eyes. I made a date for an interview between tea-cups. This busy place, concerts and delegations, looked like where you got completely lost and rattled, or else came alive. The fund-raising was mostly for the north-west Civilian Partisans.

Meanwhile the Americans snapped off their attention from the Bishop's daughter and rang up Edith, saying reassuringly: "You'll like Edith; oh, yes, she's a grand little person Edith. If only Eppy isn't coming back this *minute!*"

I dug out the fact that Eppy was Edith's husband. If he hadn't yet come back from Taierhchwang, I might be allowed by Edith to frequent Eppy's bed.

It was like that in Hankow. Unmitigated bed trouble. You couldn't leave your bed alone for five minutes, without somebody snaking into it.

Missionaries were doing it.

"Well, tell her I'll be glad to pay anything I've got," I said; hotel-beds were up to forty dollars a day.

But back over the telephone crackled Edith's voice: "Tell her, if she pays for her meals, she can have Eppy's bed till he gets back."

"Oh, that's grand!" said the Americans, breaking off their conversation about a picnic they were getting up for the Bishop's daughter.

The Bishop's daughter had made one of the first foreign goodwill delegations to go up from Hankow to the Eighth Route Army Headquarters, where Communist soldier and peasant were welded together.

"You should go up," they said. "Up there you'll find the real spirit."

I thought they were wonderful, all right. The queer, the rather dear, the startling American generosity!

Things were going round in funny-coloured circles when the chauffeur dropped me outside Edith's; (big chilly building, lift, a sudden cosiness of small flats). She was a dark spot on a red silken coverlet, and she said: "I expect you'd like to lie down."

So I said "Yes," and then was falling into sleep, like a little tram from a cut steel cable. Outside, in a balcony room, she had a lot of pot-plants and canaries, and I didn't understand that. Afterwards it devolved, quite naturally, that the missionary who really owned the flat, as Lessee Number One, had gone away to Hong Kong, leaving the way open for Edith and Eppy, who at once grabbed the beds, while failing to ditch the begonias and canaries.

Usually Edith was out by day, teaching English to bulky Soviet airmen who took it like lambs. Their class was round in the new U.S.S.R. embassy on the Bund. The old one had been burnt, and often I passed it, matting flapping over its blackened sockets.

This was after the international air corps, other than Russian pilots and mechanics, had been disbanded, and Madame Chiang Kai-shek had handed over her position at the head of China's Aviation Commission to her brother, Mr. T. V. Soong, who had come up from Hong Kong.

T. V. Soong, head of the Bank of China, had on his own account a tremendous political and financial prestige, abroad as much as in China, and many people were impressed when his address temporarily changed from Hong Kong to Hankow, and pleased that his participation in the war was a more direct one.

Of Madame Chiang Kai-shek, it remained true that she was doing the work of ten normal people, and doing it with a very brave heart.

Regarding toughness, I never saw anything in Hankow tougher than some of the foreign women who hadn't been evacuated. Early in the year there was a scare around Hankow. The Japanese said: 'Watch us, we're coming over!' And the Chinese said: 'Little brothers, if you do come we shall only break the dykes, so where will that get you?'

But on many special trains foreign women were evacuated, few taking the trouble to return, perhaps to go through the whole thing over again. The few English and American women who remained were diplomatic corps, Red Cross, relief, religious or kindred workers, and a small company of business wives and daughters, who played tennis, and once a week rolled bandages.

And of the Germans who stayed, many were so large, with such guillotine scarlet lips! And of the Russians, many so life-flattened and sad. (Though at Mother Pheraie's a sort of brightness stayed on with the beer.)

I hadn't been in Hankow for three days without seeing that I'd have a lot of hard work in making this part of the journey the slightest use to anyone. The only foreign women in Hankow, except notables who had their purpose and their place, and those in the categories given above, were the whores; and the foreign supply, together with a limited number of Chinese girls, seemed to be doing well enough in that respect to fill any requirements.

So far, in China, I'd had things easy. I'd been in Hong Kong, which was offside from the fighting, though it showed certain aspects of war; in Shanghai, where the fighting was superficially over, though Shanghai showed more aspects of war; in Kwangtung, which was in its preparatory stage, quick and kindling, willing enough, within limits of discretion, to show the foreigner *its* special aspects of war.

Now, in Hankow, there was a very fait chance that if I didn't have extra-special good luck, 1 would go away having seen nothing at all. My capital was ridiculously small, and though a number of highly important political and military movements were here, working at full swing, their staffs were busy people, much too busy to advertise.

The big pink cardboard arches, marked with gilt characters and picturesque designs, run up in the street to commemorate the Victory of Taierhchwang, still stood erect, but rain was sapping the colour and stiffness out of them. They stood in the least westernized street of Hankow, the one with most beggars and the greatest number of photographers' shops, all showing immense photographs of Madame Chiang Kai-shek, costumed now east, now west.

The Japanese were very much annoyed about Taierhchwang. In revenge for the Chinese victory, they declared that they would bomb Hankow every night of full moon week; they came as promised, but though they got over

Hankow, they did no damage in the city. The searchlights and pursuit 'planes had them chalked out every time. It was rather beautiful to watch . . . first the slender, feeling searchlights, a nebulous mass of clouds, high up, changing to a golden fleece, then at last the 'plane . . . a moth, silver and gold, pinned against the fleece by fingers that looked so gentle and sensitive, once having found and fingered this bimetallic creature they sought. The moth shot high, looking for dead midnight blue; but always now two searchlights had it, and quiver as they might, pretending to be nothing but harmless antenna, they nipped round its body like death. The pursuit 'planes drummed up. Somebody cried: "There!" Edith and I, hanging out of a window which gave us a good view, sang:

> 'There'll be pie, in the sky,
> There'll be pie in the sky when you die. . . .

waiting to see the frightened moth, now shooting up and down, suddenly sizzle burning gold. The cheek! To inconvenience our city every night of full moon week, to bomb Wuchang's hangars, to blot out the road-gangs whose collective lives kept open the way from Hsuchowfu to Hankow, Hankow to Canton!

Anyhow, we could laugh, while right opposite, in the sudden complete air-raid blackness, ricksha-pullers slithered down like dead golden leaves between the shafts. Queer to hear them, slithering and whispering, their lights pressed out by the one big word of alarm.

And the second battle of Taierhchwang became officially 'The Victory of South Shantung'—because Taierhchwang was such a little place, although such a bad name to Dai Nippon. Next the Chinese Central Government troops were billed to capture Yihsien, an important town to the north-east.

Down south, Canton, deliriously excited at the news of the Chinese victory, proclaimed a night of rejoicing for Talerbchwang, a great torchlight procession around the Pearl River.

So on that day, some Japanese 'planes had an ' accident' over Canton, dropping their heaviest 1000-pound stuff on a big sewing factory in the heart of the city, a place staffed almost exclusively by sewing-women and little girls. And that place, with a roar, burst into flames, setting alight other premises.

Much of the walling caved at once: but all the several hundred aggregations of woman-flesh and child-flesh did not succeed in being buried, knocked out, or cooked in that first bursting glare. So a mindless, hopeless screaming, that still kept a few human words, escaped like a poor lunatic from the factory. And burning arms and legs crawled out, clutching rubble, but before they had any hold, the bodies seared to them crackled up. And men outside went mad, and clawed with their naked fingers, as the women and little girls were doing inside. But rescue work was almost entirely useless, as the, bombs dropped were not those kinds that can be cherished in scoops and put out with squirts of cold water and sand.

But with night's coming, and the digging out of three hundred bodies, whole or fragmentary, the rush on coffin-shops equalled the earlier, triumphant rush on wicker lanterns and torches. Besides the ornate coffins of normal trade, many plain coffins were knocked up, receiving bodies that could not be identified. And lifting their coffins to shoulder-height, while other men spaced between them slowly lifted the great lanterns and torches of victory, the men of the City of Rams walked slowly along the river-banks of their city, celebrating as a festival without laughter, without applause or feasting, the chief major success of an army desperately ill-equipped, against an army very well-equipped, well-rationed, and well-clad.

As the sparks from their torches, trailing back, rained gold into the blackness of the Pearl River, so were the bodies of these women and girl children brushed into blackness from the history of their race . . . sacrifices innocent, untimely, and unknown. It was done, neither can any act of vengeance or pity in the future alter it, nor anything intended as reparation ever overset the marking of that work. So let it be said, and so left.

CHAPTER TWELVE

Pa Ta Chia

BEFORE I LEFT CANTON, Mr. Edward Bing-shuey Lee had given me an introductory card to Dr. T. T. Li, Director of the Publicity and Intelligence Departments. This, shown to Dr. Li, who arranged all the daily press conferences and weekly 'specials' on Wuchang side, gave me admission to as many Press gatherings as I liked.

What happened at the daily meetings was that Chinese and foreign reporters . . . some interesting figures among both . . . ate chocolates and a very nice kind of Chinese jujube, and drank tea. If it was a Wuchang side conference, usually addressed by at least one General, there were also foreign-style cakes, which the foreigners abandoned, and the Chinese journalists slowly, thoughtfully munched. General Chen Cheng, in charge of the Fifth War Area, frequently gave out the Wuchang news . . . a smiling man with a little bristling moustache, talking rapidly in Chinese (interpreted by Reuter's Chinese pressman), his hands moving coloured stud-pins about a map; nearly always, now, a map of north-eastern war areas, where Hsuchowfu, key city and junction of the Tsinpu and Lunghai railway lines, was the focal point for many radial lines of battle, including the line marked out to Yihsien. We didn't hear so much about the imminent capture of Yihsien. There was a restlessness, a waiting, foreign and Chinese: slight boredom for us, death for them.

After ordinary meetings, those present were issued with a leaflet containing the news of the day, put out by the Chinese official news agency, Central News.

Central News was more accurate than Domei. It would be as silly to claim perfect accuracy for either as to say that the British reports of German corpse-factories during the 1914-1918 war had the slightest measure of accuracy, or, for that matter, the German reports of Canadian and Australian atrocities against wounded prisoners.

After the issue of report, 'T. T.' (otherwise Dr. Li) sometimes gave a brief discourse, explaining troop movements on a map with the inevitable pin-studs. We then dispersed, and about three hours later, at their private addresses, the foreign correspondents all received fat budgets of Chinese 'human interest' stories, which had gone quite well in the first few months of the war, before China was off the front page. Now the poor kids who worked ten or twelve hours a day at Pa Ta Chia, their black hair flopping into their eyes, their fingers madly racing along the keyboards, their brains

149

racked for *another* angle of some non-existent or unimportant story, might perhaps give some foreign correspondent two lines which once in a month he would bother to work up into an inch paragraph and shoot over to his paper.

"Even if there's another Nanking," one American reporter told me, during Pa Ta Chia's chocolates, tea, bulletins, and *bonhomie*, "what of it? There's already been one Nanking."

The first time I went to a Press meeting (the afternoon after arrival in Hankow) I came away exhilarated.

Meeting Dr. Li in the morning, I had mentioned that I would like very much to go to an active sector of the Chinese front.

"To be able to see a little of actual living conditions among soldiers, villagers, and refugees," I added. "That is all more important than anything else I've been able to approach here in China. Of course, the writing of articles for magazines, Chinese or in a distant country like mine, is of no importance beside the work of the daily correspondent. But my country, though small, is very friendly to China, and interested in the war."

At this first interview I had hopes of convincing Dr. T. T. Li, who didn't raise any serious objections.

After that we had the Press conference, at the soft yellow time of a summer dusk, and a couple of reporters saw me home, past a Russian Cathedral with an onion-shaped, gilt-starred dome, a Sikh temple with rich yellow tiles. Both reporters were Australians . . . one working at straight-out Chinese publicity, fair-haired and nervy, an enthusiast about Generalissimo Chiang Kai-shek, and the glamour of the Orient. The other was going to the front soon; he was actually a New Zealander by birth, but Australia seemed to have adopted him with some force. He wore khaki shorts, sweater, and slung camera (as all the men did when they were going to the front), was dark, quite young, and definitely a war correspondent. He was taciturn, but liked being a war correspondent.

The Hankow street along which we swung was bitter with a piecemeal air of dust, and though at first you'd never have suspected there was a war on, the listless shops soon showed it . . . Chinese and Indian shops for foreigners, with almost nothing to sell, and ridiculous prices for everything, especially clothes or edibles.

The kids with the red trousers open behind and before weren't so strenuous about begging as might have been expected, but still there were beggars enough; a slim Indian woman, lissom and brown as a cat, with half a dozen Chinese kids runny-nosed about her slim ankles, and jewelled studs in her ears. She wore a *sari*, transparently thin, and her eyes and slender lounging body had a special self-assurance.

On the other side of the road, which was banked up over the wharves and junks of the Yangtse-kiang, coolies jogged along under huge loads, wool, rope, wool-matting, the breath jerked out of their bodies in an unending rhythmical refrain, 'Ha-*Hao*-Ha! Ha-*Hao*-Ha!' It sounded exactly like the same phrase repeated in the 'Song of the Volga Boatmen' . . . probably the only authentic phrase the boatmen ever did sing, no musical conception, no aristocrat, but a proletarian jerk of hard grunting breath from squeezed lungs, body trying to save itself by keeping in rhythm.

Besides these, whose feet scuffed up the dead white acacia blossoms, there were always soldiers, in lorries or on foot, their cotton uniforms coloured from bright tan or mustard to the colour of coffee-grounds. Double-seated Mongolian pony-carriages, with the red paint worn dull or scratched to nothing, the shabby little ponies raw-patched but quick between the shafts, rattled along. Chinese laughter floating back high and sweet: officer on leave taking his girl for a drive round the Bund. The French Concession is further along. Its sentries have always those swarthy faces, young, but never boyish like the light-coloured English boys.

He only wants some money, ten cents at most; probably a couple of cents would buy him off. As for looking threatening, you'd look threatening, having to pull that soggy wreck, his hat, over the black, threatened, lost-to-pity caverns of his eyes, the huge black hole where his nose used to be.

The hand he holds out is covered with sores, and all he wants is a little money to go and get some food. Barefoot, wretched. A leper, maybe, like the lepers in the Bible. Being perpetually glared at, having that gap where he once had a nose, has given his sunken eyes their look of rage.

We're all cowards at heart. Threatened, not threatening. To him it really happened. You can see, in spite of his ruined face and having nothing but blue cotton rags to cover the starving slave-body nobody will pick out of the gutter, he is just a young man, and mayn't have observed the reality of what has happened to his nose any more than according to many religious sects a dead man knows straightaway what has happened to his dead body.

I'd like to give to this beggar, but the two Australians, becoming protective, stand in front of me; and shout, and threaten the place where his nose used to be, ordering it out of sight, back slinking to the gutter. They don't speak in Chinese, they shout nothing but English, but the noseless beggar gets it, and turning his blue cotton so that his face can't be seen any more, he slinks away.

"Dirty, obscene beast! He ought to be locked away."

"I suppose it's leprosy."

"You can take it from me, that man deserves all he's got. He oughtn't to be allowed out in the streets."

"Well, if it's *that*, it's completely a matter of luck, isn't it?"

This wasn't the right thing to say, and I was tired of the two Australians, and thought 'Damn you!' instead of 'Good night.'

But Edith was inside, just up four flights of stairs. She was lying on the scarlet silk, because her Russian aviators also made her a bit tired, though in another way. They were so thorough about everything. Teaching them meant that she had to concentrate the whole time; they asked so many questions that she was usually an hour late for every meal. We ate our meals together, sitting on the balcony, with the festoon of canaries and begonias about us; I had got to like it.

I told her I had hopes of getting up to one of the front-line sectors, and she showed me a letter from Eppy, who was having a very good time at Taierlichwang.

Eppy had scooped the Second Battle, getting up farther than any other foreign correspondent, and arriving in the little battered city itself just a couple of hours after the last of the Japanese had departed, smoking. He was the sole reporter, accompanied by Captain Evans Carlson, of the American Legation, and Jack Young, a Chinese explorer. The Chinese authorities, though nearly in a fit at the idea that a foreign correspondent should be risked so near a large, unrestrained battle (which might *not* have been a victory), were nevertheless delighted, as Eppy could cable immediate confirmation of their fullest claims. So now the Chinese, having furnished Eppy and his companions with an escort of hopeful soldiers, were doing a tour of the battlefields while everything was still hot; and Eppy was having the time of his life, and not coming home immediately.

'My bed, my bed!' I thought. 'Well, thank God for that.'

Wandering about in Hankow, from minnie golf courses to tea-gardens. Scrawny Chinese poultry seemed to have a good deal of licence and no self-consciousness here. And a wharf notice-board read, black down a pointing white finger: 'To Shanghai.'

It used to be quite easy, before the war days, to get by river from Hankow to Shanghai, but now the only way was back to Canton, by rail, then to Hong Kong on the little Canton-Kowloon express, whose guards were all armed with huge Mauser pistols, and after that a boat journey of three days, up the dulled cold shimmering of the never-unclouded China Sea.

After the first few days, things weren't going so well. I was feeling gloomy, and faintly scared of bad joss. Dr. Li's oncoming attitude towards the idea of giving me a pass for the front had faded, from an initial polite regretful puce to a grim pallor. Somebody among the reporters or on the publicity staff, I never knew which, had strongly advised him against it.

I still argued, because by then I felt; 'Yes, certainly, that's the thing I really have to do.'

The matter slid into a minor topic of discussion with the foreign men reporters. Already I was the only woman at the Press meetings, the larger Wuchang conferences . . . the only girl in the Pa Ta Chia world, and representing, when all was boiled down to cold fact, such a small bunch of periodicals, not even dailies, in such a distant corner of the world.

The one thought of the foreign men reporters (fighting, themselves, for their chance to get into khaki shorts and shirts, sling cameras over their shoulders, and happily label themselves 'For the front,') was, it became plain, 'Will we really have to handicap ourselves by taking *this* along?' They had been so cheerful, so breezy, on that first afternoon! Now the breeze blew cold.

It was not serious, but it was prickly. In an English April there are allegedly bluebells, primroses, swallows. I hadn't ever seen any swallows. I should, by due date, have been in England long before April. In a Hankow April, there is life and death, the westernized concrete buildings are ugly, everybody's in too much of a hurry to tell a stranger—unless an important delegate, or, better still, a whole conference—the pattern of things, the way they go on. There is always the white, infected dust, and though I had taken to wearing dark blue glasses, that little precaution was several days too late. I couldn't see, my eyelids were hot pink rims ornamented with excrescences nobody could like, there was the slight fermentation of something going wrong.

I think I might have given up and gone home then, except for Edith, who was still reading me bits from Eppy's letters, which were the best descriptive material I'd heard for years, and made that elusive zone, the Chinese front, sound more tantalizing than ever.

Yet I very nearly quarrelled with Edith about something in one of these letters: it would have been such a fool quarrel. It was about a Japanese soldier, whom I insisted into making a martyr. So he was, but only because either his obstinacy or his suicide-code obstructed him from being anything else. A month later, I had seen too many Chinese martyrs, of the kind who really love and honour the small facts of daily existence—and those martyrs, surely, are the kind to respect first—to make much fuss about Japanese martyrs who die because they refuse to do anything else but die. But at the moment I couldn't see it: everything except the man's sheer bravery and the odds against him went out of my mind. Incidentally, it is perhaps worth recording that if he had added common sense to courage, he could have joined the seven hundred Japanese prisoners who, after the second battle of Taierhchwang, were sent down by the Chinese to Hankow, together with a great deal of captured military equipment, including tanks.

What were-the facts? Commonplace enough. An escort of Chinese soldiers patiently showing their three foreigners around the battle-fields, some days after the victory at Taierhchwang; a rotten old blanket lying over a hole in the ground; and chance, which made one Chinese soldier poke his bayonet through the blanket, just as a boy with a stick is impelled to poke the end into the sand.

The blanket then sat up, and the Japanese soldier who had been concealed beneath it (he was wounded in one leg) didn't make the motions of surrender. He fired off his pistol, shaving the cheek of a foreign correspondent the surprised Chinese were beginning to like and value; one of the escort put a bullet through his wrist, but immediately he switched his gun to the left hand, fired again. Somebody threw a potato-masher bomb, which failed to explode. The wild duel continued for several minutes, until a second Chinese bullet put the Japanese pistol out of commission altogether. Even then, there was no offer of surrender: and the bursting of a hand-grenade meant the end of things for this son of Nippon.

.   .   .   .

.

Edith said: "I used to feel awful when they came down in burning 'planes. Only look what happens underneath."

"Anyhow, it's men who make the wars. In the long run, men will have to pay."

"Suppose so."

We went out to one of the French cafés and had a sort of cabbage dish mixed up in a floury roll, and something to drink. That was the first night of Full Moon, so the Japanese had to come and bomb us, else there wouldn't be any honour left in Japan: too bad! And the German girls still wore their big dough faces, Bloody Mary fingernails, peroxide hair; and the White Russians still had that look of being done out of tuppence in early youth, this setting up a complex where the tuppence should have been; and the good-hearted gorillas of the U.S.A. and French marines and English sailors still looked as if they didn't notice they weren't getting served with the very best. As for the respectable, you couldn't generalize. That which they had to do they did privately, indoors. The lights went out.

"Come along," said Edith. "If we're lucky we'll get back home without a fuss; if not we'll get stuck in the stomach with a bayonet. Put out your cigarette."

The Chinese sentries who lined the streets, standing with fixed bayonets the moment an air alarm (*ching pao*) whizzed into the skies, had sometimes very extraordinary ideas of audibility and visibility. Sometimes they didn't seem to care a hoot, and let you along, gruffly indicating that you should keep to the shadow. Sometimes they made you take off anything light-coloured. North in Hsuchowfu the Japanese, probably by accident, had let a bomb drop near a flock of sheep, and after that light-coloured animals got their throats cut regardless of expense. I hate to think what would have happened to a company of platinum blondes, and I know what was happening to roosters and cockerels, who added the crime of audibility to that of visibility. Notices requested women to wear dark colours, such as red, green, indigo, in place of light ones: white was definitely unpatriotic. Much of this was founded on the facts of experience, but I think the Chinese (who were getting all the bad luck, down below) were inclined to attribute vision and hearing near the supernatural to the Japanese zooming down the skyways.

CHAPTER THIRTEEN

Chinese Movements

TO PROVE TO MYSELF that Hankow wasn't labour in vain, I ran about interviewing people.

One day it was Agnes Smedley. That was a queer interview, as I arrived with a huge bouquet of wistaria, acquired from one of the pleasant-faced coolies who squat chattering in front of the Lutheran Mission, and couldn't think of anything to do with it except present it to Agnes.

She kept looking at the flowers as if she expected them to turn into string sandals, munitions, or a small donation for the Orphans' University in the north-west. But in spite of her preoccupation, she convinced me . . . as she would have convinced anyone . . . that no foreigner in Hankow, male or female, could exercise a more vitalizing influence over the fence-sitters who couldn't make up their minds whether or not to cash in with ten dollars. She was as effective with Chinese factory-hands or engine-workers as with bishops. She had even got the British Consul down. The British Consul had a keen, cool-headed dislike of Communists, but he never got round to disliking Agnes Smedley.

"Ah," he once remarked to me, "that's a *nice* girl. Communism . . . all a mistake!"

I told Agnes that, and she was a little upset. But the finest truth one can say about the girl from old Kentucky and new China is this: she had the courage, not only of advance . . . which is any fool's courage . . . but of retreat. She didn't want to come back to Hankow, when the combination of her injured back, and quicker military moving on the part of Chu Teh's army, made it necessary for her to do so. Forgetting the civic charms of Hankow, she cried: "Don't send me back to the cesspool!"

Arrived in the cesspool, she worked, talked, wrote for the Civilian Partisans, with more concentrated activity than anyone else I heard tell of Chinese or foreign.

Interviewing Miss Yuan, of the Youth Movement, was different. Miss Yuan spoke no English, only French: my French was tattered and dog-eared, though sufficiently intelligible: we could have roped in an interpreter, but wanted to keep the dinner small. It was a dinner entirely composed of Mandarin dishes, in honour of Peiping . . . I think that was Miss Yuan's city . . . and although the diced chicken and green peas were good, also the wine, what haunts me is the Mandarin duck, roasted whole.

For weeks I hadn't touched a pair of chopsticks, and to the foreigner this art, unlike swimming or dancing, doesn't 'just come back to you.' You learn and forget, learn and forget all over again.

This duck! How in the world could I, while concentrating on a conversation in my worm-eaten old French, also concentrate on making my chopsticks tear its skin from its rather difficult flesh? It had a tough, shining skin, not at all a non-skid skin.

Miss Yuan and little George Wong did their best to keep me happy, and we all drank more and more small cups of wine.

But still, that duck! . . . I couldn't get on with it, over it. If only they had given me the burnished beauty alive, waddling in curved plumes of amber and bottle-green! I should have been so proud of it.

Youth Movement is New Life Movement's favourite daughter. It has attracted the women leaders to organize their country and its village life in every way (say the apostles), both for war and peace. It is the animating spirit of all such movements, whether or not it takes part in them direct. Madame Chiang Kai-shek is Youth Movement's highest leader, and her organization is co-operating with New Life.

Youth is organized according to district and profession: in Hankow, the Youth Movement groups were arranged north and south. Silk factory hands, mill workers, students, and railway workers were organized, their training concerning patriotic and wartime assistance. Students were graduated as section teachers as soon as possible.

Youth Movement in the publicity sphere was one big card: there were sections in charge of posters, singing, playing, organized again into corps, which split up into groups of five or six people, all attaching much importance to the affairs of wounded soldiers and refugees. Small, mobile groups visited the soldiers, 'comforting' them with patriotic oratory, letter-writing, and, other attentions. At this time the Hankow Movement was centralized in city and suburbs, and under control of the army.

"New Life is a thought, not an organization." (Pretty Miss Yuan.) "The Japanese are hostile to the Party directing the movement, therefore to the New Life and Youth Movements."

"Of course we can still send messages by mail or special courier to any occupied area. We find our movement functions much better where the Japanese are there, to rouse the people. The New Life Movement is directing guerilla warfare to a great extent, and always functions better where the villagers have come directly in contact with the Japanese.

"The biggest hope for China lies in the fact that every peasant and worker is a guerilla fighter. We get our munitions from the Japanese. We will get our food from the Japanese. Peasants, appearing as innocent villagers, cut the lines and seize the trucks. The. Japanese can attack only the communication lines, therefore at any time they can be cut across the wrist. The countryside belongs to the guerilla fighters.

"One unit of one hundred woman soldiers from Yunnan is already in uniform under organization here. Chiefly, they will support the armies, but they are ready to execute every order of their commander's. We refer to these activities as the Women's War Service province. Mostly the women are students, not yet trained to use the machine-gun. An interesting subsidiary exists in Honan province, where all the women have trained the prostitutes to watch for spies and traitors. Seven spies were trapped recently in one day. This is not yet in Hankow, only on the front.

"Difficulties? Finding money for refugees willing to work. Finding the work itself is our worst problem. The Mayor of London contributed to this, but all is swallowed up in the huge demand. The Youth Movement has this resolution: 'Give the refugees a chance to do practical work, opening mines or building railway lines.' This has been brought before the Central Executive of the Kuomintang, but a huge capital is wanted. Perhaps we will begin first on light industries, and reclaiming lands.

"Our hand and rural industries are looking up. I am a member of the Organization for Productive Work. That specializes in the hank rope industry, besides cigarettes. About one hundred and eighty factories, formerly in Shanghai, are now in the interior, so we didn't lose too much. Before the war can reach our big factories, the Productive Committee removes the machinery. I'm one of the Youth Movement's promoters and organizers, a sort of idea agent between the lines. Boycott? That could not function successfully before the war, it's getting on better now."

Little George Wong is funny: he made a cable story about the organized prostitutes of Honan. (I thought that strategy was hard, myself. A bed is one place where one ought to be able to count on rest.) George came in, eyes lit up, his wire stating that two prostitutes, Fragrant Guitar and Pretty Lotus, had just succeeded in trapping twelve important spies. Nearly midnight, he arrived again, with a wire which said: 'Keep posted any more developments similar Pretty Fragrant affair.'

The Fourteen Federated Societies of Hankow, headed by the National Salvation Movement (whose leaders were all in gaol for political reasons, until the war and Chiang Kai-shek released them) have their own propaganda department. It does not differ very much in the *type* of propaganda put out. . . . That is clear-cut stuff, on the anti-Japanese issue and no other, and bodies of a semi-communistic nature have adhered to this resolution rather more resolutely than some on the Central Government's side.

But they have fallen into their own groups, prefer to work by themselves, and aren't so easy to find. Seven propaganda artists are devoting themselves to painting striking cartoons. I'm afraid that with wartime plays, it may be a little different, if a foreign audience is required. And with Slogans. The Chinese has been hard hit by the word Slogan, hurtling simultaneously from U.S.S.R. and U.S.A. But what the Chinese thinks of as a slogan is not what U.S.S.R. or U.S.A. thinks of as a slogan.

The thick stirring-up of Chinese movements, ideas, and slogans, during this present century, is easiest localized between two periods. First lies the stormy time of 1924-27, when the Kuomintang-Communist united front was followed by the Nanking *coup d'état* of 1927, which put the Kuomintang very definitely on top, and left the Communists hard pressed by the military power of Chiang Kai-shek and his Whampoa-trained officers. The second period lasted from 1934 (which saw the revival of many student movements and re-establishment of confidence in the Soviet districts) to that day of August 1937 which saw the Japanese strike down over the 'incident' of the Marco Polo Bridge.

As with all states of being in China, states of opposition, definitions of hostile movements, are loosely knit. The National Salvation Movement, being open to membership of all political colours, could not be called a Communist body. But when the Communist nob was hit in China, unfailingly the National Salvationists got hurt as well. With them were associated progressives of the Students' Unions.

The Nanking Government sponsored some of the rivals . . . the Boy Scout Movement, Officers' Moral Endeavour Society, New Life Movement, Right Wing Students' Movement, Blue-shirts.

The Blueshirts, right-wing extremists, came from landowning and capitalist families, and their methods were not always gentle.

There is something fatal, these days, in a Shirt. Any Republic or Monarchy with its head screwed on would settle the issue altogether by putting a ban on shirts.

In Shanghai, the Blueshirts played rough, and were not guiltless of association with gangs who played much rougher. These gangs, descendants in a sidelong way of the ancient tongs, specialized in kidnapping and armed robbery, usually concentrating on the sons of wealthy Chinese, beside whom the foreigner was small beer. And they had gone Hollywood, sailing about in armoured cars, using machine-guns, forming intimate contacts with certain highly-placed officials of the police (the association of one Shanghai police chief with the city's best-known gangster was notorious); and, as a final touch, specializing in banquets, at which many well-known foreigners were regular guests. Little parting gifts of ivory chopsticks were a friendly touch.

Obviously Shanghai's gangs and their over-lords (now so useful in making the pace for the Japanese, and, yet more, for the Chinese Ta-taos) could be useful acquaintances, or the reverse. During the 1927 troubles, their function, partly inspired by the Blueshirts, was intolerable to the students and many others.

But allegedly the Number One gangster of Shanghai (who is a friend of the highest in China) used his influence in securing the release of the Seven National Salvation Leaders, when in Shanghai, November 1936, they were arrested, accused of Communism.

Sze Liang, one of the Seven Leaders, was a lady, and a celebrated barrister. The others were writers, bankers, lawyers. So many thousands marched on the gaol that the Seven, for fear of demonstrations, were sent to Soochow, where the gangster leader demanded their release, and judges apologized for their arrest.

The National Salvation Movement was an all-China affair, a group elected from every province, and with head offices in Shanghai, until the war swept them to Hankow. Chinese of all classes, political opinions, status, could at least theoretically be active, and on the outbreak of war the Movement declared for a whole-time campaign against Japan. Curiously enough, though the Government made no bones about picking off its celebrated leaders, the Movement itself was never suppressed.

Lu Hsün, whose stories were held by some of his admirers to resemble Tchekov's, by others to be the work of a Chinese Gorki, died nearly a year before the war, on 19 October 1936. Whichever one takes as closest resemblance (and certainly the Russian group, including Tchekov, Tolstoy, and Gorki were close to him), his individual work gave him the name of a leader of modern Chinese culture; and modern Chinese culture, in just that simple form he chose to extract it, is so intimately mixed with the rise and fermentation of recent Chinese politics that no man can dissociate the two.

Like the Russians, Lu Hsün took up the dust of his own land; and following a legendary precedent, the Chinese mingled it with spittle and tears, and blew on it, and it had being. He was a fighter against feudalism, with great influence among the heady young rebels of his day. To some extent he crossed the Government's path by becoming a strong supporter of *Pai Hua*, the spoken or colloquial language, which is used by modern writers and journalists in place of *Wen-li*, the old-style classical Chinese, to understand which a knowledge of many thousands of characters is requisite.

The new Thousand Character Movement can be learned in a few months by an illiterate Chinese; and, as illiteracy in China, varies from 75 per cent to 90 per cent in some of the more isolated provinces, illiteracy is a cruel problem of the nation's future. But the various simplifications have not yet received much official encouragement from the Government, though those movements and student groups influenced by Generalissimo and Madame Chiang Kai-shek are also conducting valuable literacy classes in many fields.

The Latin *hua* (romanization of the Chinese script) was formerly identified with the Communist Party, which has not been abolished by the United Front in China.

The Wade system of romanization, generally adopted in China, is enough to make an English or American convert cry. If you mean to say 'P' you say 'B'; 'D' naturally works out as 'T'; and to think of 'Hs' except as 'Sh' shows some mental trouble in your family.

Not are you safe by simply mixing the consonants; every now and again, a romanized consonant takes a nostalgic liking for its usual western pronunciation, and reverts to type.

Chinese are hurt when westerners suggest that their language cannot be romanized. They themselves are not only good linguists, but beautiful linguists. Their clear voices take a language so well, and they seem always to know the word they want.

Kuo Mo-ju was there in Hankow, a famous poet and writer and a medical graduate, a Szechuanese by birth. A romantic story is the poet Kuo's. The Japanese beat him over the head before he escaped from them, but it's still a handsome head, with sparkling brown eyes, and he speaks in the Wuhan University like an orator. He studied in Japan, and escaped imprisonment in 1927 (when he was among proscribed Leftists) by heading for Japan. There he was interned . . . pleasantly enough, as he acquired a wife and five children.

Early one morning, after the war began, Kuo dressed himself as a Japanese peasant, and set out, very secretly, without telling even his wife. His diary tells of his escape. He was in Shanghai first, then back in his native Szechuan, before he came here to be a propagandist in Hankow.

'Tchekov and Tolstoy come first; a few are for Gorki, Whitman, and Verlaine; German or Russian translations are better liked than American or English ones'; I feel so pleased with the flop-haired boy (a writer himself) who is telling me about what he calls the Realistic Movement in literature, because although the Chinese choice may seem a little dated, at feast it *is* a spontaneous choice, it hasn't been pumped into them. Katherine Mansfield's books are all here, in the beautiful library of Wuhan University.

But the black-gowned Professor, talking among the acacias, is depressed. "I'm afraid the Japanese will soon be here and bomb all this."

He doesn't think there is any such thing as a really perfect translation of Chinese verses. Arthur Waley? He gets the *sense*, but what about the rhythm? Nobody ever gets the rhythm!

A small disconsolate figure, he watches from the green heights where we were all photographed, everybody laughing.

Rogoff, the big Russian, one of the Tass News Agency men in Hankow, is the only man among us who speaks and writes Mandarin. He has translated some Chinese stories. When he went down to see the bombed University of Hunan, and outside the smashed library saw all the books lying, soaked and charred, Rogoff coined a good phrase: "Wounded books crying out for help in the different languages of the world."

In its literature and general culture more than in space, China is a Far Eastern country. A month or less takes you to China; but the scholars say it takes four years for you to learn a bit of written Mandarin. One can imagine what the moderns have already done, and are doing: first raising up the immortal pagoda of old-style culture, then, in this present time, making articulate their country, giving its yellow dust, human dust, a voice and a cry. It is annoying to hear them quarrying and chipping away in there, and not be able to read. But one can tell a little, even from titles or chance phrases in translation, of what materials they draw upon . . . peasantry, the life of the conqueror, the life of the conquered, the life of revolt, the iron of militarism, the silk of politics: and people, men and women, still recognized finalities, I suppose.

On a bend of the road from the wharf-steps into Wuchang city stood a huge wooden billboard, propped up on high legs, covered by a poster from one of the propagandist art departments. It showed, in vivid colours, the immense figure of a Chinese. Out from the folds of his gown came flying as many gifts as if he were a rather crazy Santa Claus.

There were gold dollars, representing the wealth of the rich; books, for learning; guns; small adroitly-drawn aeroplanes; jewellery, for the trifles accumulated by women must not be left out; finally, the gown disgorged little soldiers. It had a splashed slogan, but didn't need one.

'Give!' shouted the poster, 'give whatever you have to give!'

This was now being dinned into Chinese ears throughout every one of the provinces. The old proverb, quoted in Pearl Buck's *The Good Earth*

('You don't take good iron and make it into nails; you don't take a good young man and make him into a soldier'), was smashed and discredited in China.

Eppy was expected back from Taierhchwang any day, and Hollington Tong, the Vice-Minister of Publicity, whom I had clung to as a drowning man's straw, hoping for a pass to the front, would say nothing except: "What would be said about us if we sent a lady like you up there?"

I told him I had never been so insulted before in my life, but he only smiled and repeated that I was a lady, and could not get a pass for the front.

It was a hot day, high and blue and sunny. I wanted to get away from anyone who might possibly speak my language, and walk about among strange people, or sit on a patch of grass I had never seen before, nor would again, and think: 'What a lot of fuss and trouble! Then, why make it?' So I took the boat for Wuchang, hoping to get away from my own kind.

There were soldiers and sweethearts on the boat, soldiers and sweethearts; among them sat several black-gowned girls who had trachoma. One was blind, her pink lids had sealed up. That was another little thing . . . my eyes.

But we had seemed to be drifting rather wide of the steps at Wuchang where we usually landed, deeper down the river. Without thinking, I asked a soldier: "Will this boat touch at Wuchang?" and though the soldier, of course, made no reply except to goggle his eyes at me, immediately an old, white-bearded man replied: "Yes, we are going to Wuchang."

We passed one or two complimentary remarks, then the boat touched the steps, and everybody, soldiers, sweethearts, old man, blind girls, and myself marched off. I got as far as the poster, and stopped there, thinking Then the old man came up, and gave me his card. He was a Mr. C. Y. Lay, and he told me he was interested in engineering, and knew a number of people in England.

"But most of my neighbours don't know that I speak English," he added, "they think, 'Oh, he's just an innocent old native.' "

I don't know what it was about Mr. Lay, or why; he did look, as he said, just an innocent old native; but he was also a wise, simple old man.

Mr. Lay and I were presently walking up Snake Hill, and he told me that Tortoise Hill lies with its head out on the other side of the Yangtse ("You see? It looks something like a tortoise from here"), and that both hills were considered very sacred.

We passed by a pagoda which had been burned down and restored in an ugly way, though there were hopeful picture post cards on sale. Then the road ran to a track through grass, green and tender, as there had been a lot of rain lately, making the clay soil very slippery. The track ran through a forest of small trees, edged by huts whose uneven roofs all ran together, over cracked dwellings with little black-clad people staring from the door.

Soldiers and sweethearts . . . soldiers and sweethearts. There were hundreds of them, strolling about through the living, flowing green and coolness, in couples or small groups. As we walked along, I told Mr. Lay everything . . . about coming from New Zealand to this place, about trying to get a pass, and failing.

"Well," he said, stroking his beard, "maybe they think you are somebody the Japanese have bought up."

I admit that several times, especially in Canton, I had wondered why people did not decide that, but had then turned back to the restful conviction that I needn't worry about it, because if Chinese people thought you were a spy, they would shoot you and say no more about it. But when it came to the point, I was somehow surprised that an old Chinese man like Mr. Lay should even consider the idea.

"Do I look as if the Japanese had bought me up?" I asked, "For one thing, I would want a lot of money. Besides . . ."

I told him the various ways in which New Zealand was friendly towards China, and he sat on a bench, nodding his head.

"Well, you had better write to them," he said. "You can't expect them to guess."

He was friendly; I can't describe the difference it made, his look of friendly, unruffled wisdom, as he sat there, and the light slanted between leaves on the small wet trees. We walked down a great number of steps, by a road which passed General Chen Cheng's military headquarters, and back to the big poster, where he left me. An elderly beggar passed, and I turned back to give him a few cents. Mr. Lay said: "Ah, you have given the old man ten cents?" but I couldn't answer him, only to smile and say good-bye. I could see I had been doing several stupid things in Hankow; getting off with the wrong foot foremost.

A few days later there was Eppy. It no longer mattered about bed trouble. In fact, I could feel genuinely happy to meet Eppy, because I had found a room for myself in the same building as Edith's flat, a quiet little cave, high up, and haunted by a kind of White Russian prophet, who roamed about the corridors, wearing a long beard, a long white nightgown, a staff, and spitting constantly. I found out that he was White Russian from some younger female relatives who were always in his room. They chirped incessantly and wore good clothes, not at all prophetic. Besides this establishment, there were shy Chinese in all the bathrooms, for ever.

Eppy was wise, too; short, thin, fair-haired, blue-eyed and only twenty-three. It was a long time before I knew his age, and I would have taken him for at least ten years older, not because he had had the sense and intuition to hang about and scoop the battle of Taierhchwang, but because, without being in any way over-serious or dull, he was grown up.

He was neither light-weight nor heavy-weight, but capable of either. Besides that, there was something behind him, some truth. He had a sense of humour and could talk his descriptive articles, impromptu but without show or parade. All that seemed a good deal for twenty-three.

"My wife," he said, "isn't a human being. She is an elf or a fairy." Edith, trying to slant her eyes like an elf, laughed at him. She wore some sort of red thing, which suited her, and looked very happy. They were going off to the café where you ate floury stuff mixed up with cabbage.

During the next few days things for me moved on a fair wind. I went to see an oculist about my eyes, and he, a very bleak, expensive old Scotchman, first hurt me abominably, then told me my eyes were a filthy mess, but lastly said the trouble was pinky-eye instead of trachoma.

That afternoon Eppy had asked me to come around to a reception given by the Fourteen Federated Societies of Hankow to three foreign film-makers, Joris Ivens, Capa, and John Furno, who had been at Taierhchwang making the first part of an eight-reel Chinese war film, and were now going back to Chengchow.

That was all very well, and these young men, who were locally known as 'The Three Musketeers,' were very popular in Hankow. But when I got into the hall, where beneath the most lifelike war cartoons sat row after row of young Chinese, men and women (as well as some little girls selling patriotic lollipops), Mr. Chou broke the news that I was a guest too, and the first speaker.

I began, Mr. Chou interpreting, by telling them I would have run a mile if I had known I had to speak; that made them laugh, and then I felt not so bad inside. So I could talk.

Afterwards Mr. Chou said cordially: "It was a very good speech, though a little too long." *Ta Kung Pao* and another Chinese newspaper gave the speech in full, calling me (vertically, of course), 'Robin Hy-ed,' and some of the girl delegates in patriotic blue asked me to speak at their societies.

But the sequel was hard on the last speakers on the programme; as a matter of courtesy many important Chinese now got up and made speeches in reply. There were two Generals, one in khaki, one in blue, and the khaki one spoke for over an hour, with such wild rage and force that, catching the name 'New Zealand,' I was terrified.

'My God!' I thought, he has seen a copy of our immigration laws . . . and no wonder he feels as he does. . .'

But when I could get back breath enough to ask Mr. Chou: "What is happening?" he said: "It is only the Japanese. This speech is a good deal too long." The General, it appeared, started fighting the Japanese a long while before anyone else. It became more of a passion than a hobby with him, but the only difficulty was that he *never* stopped fighting the Japanese.

At the end of the orations Joris Ivens, the director and producer of the film outfit, who had a good speech prepared, had wilted like a branch cut down. Beret, dark hair, dark vivid face flashing up . . . he looked his role of a musketeer, that young man; but the speeches had him beat.

The reception nearly ruined my pinky-eyes. The hall was full of nippy little camera-men, who crawled about squinting up at queer angles, taking flashlight photographs. The white flash was murder. I took off the deep blue goggles, leaving the parboiled casualties beneath to weep and protest as they liked. Incidentally, this horrid custom of flashlighting in Hankow's public places was introduced, or, at least, officially permitted first, by an Anglican bishop. It would be. He was having a New Year Service, fully choral, and let himself be swept off his cathedral's feet. Since then the flashlight photographers were as bad as the spies.

Eppy and Rogoff were going away again, first to Changsha then on a trip west. A fairly big party of reporters, foreign and Chinese, had left for Hsuchowfu. Hardly anyone remained except, in a top room of Pa Ta Chia, the half-dozen poor Chinese lads, whose typewriters clicked away so madly ten hours a clay, turning us out stuff we wouldn't even send away to foreign newspapers . . . because there had already been one Nanking, 'so even if there was another Nanking, *what of it?*

"We would all like to go to the front," said one of the Chinese ruefully, "but we are wanted here."

But for myself I could walk out of it quietly, the big house with bicycles and a green vine outside, with Little Girl in the gutter, screaming catlike, her small happy mouth wide open, and the coppery dust of sunset powdered over Wuhan.

This was all over, because now I had my pass. It was issued by Generalissimo Chiang Kai-shek, and bore his big red seal, which would be valued, in the original, at thousands of dollars Mex., not being susceptible to forgery, as are writings, whether brushed or penned.

If a Chinese somehow feels he has to sign a paper, but doesn't want to sign it, he may get out of it by brushing his name, or writing it, without the red square at the end of the message. Then every other Chinese knows, 'This man didn't really mean a word of this message.'

Some of the pass was in English as well as in Mandarin, and gave me permission to go to Hsuchowfu and other places. As it happens, I was the only foreign woman who had had this pass; but that was because other foreign women, not dust on the wind, and able to spend long periods in study and intelligent co-operation, had turned north-west.

The reasons I turned north-east were partly because of these women . . . the little time I could possibly spend at any place would be like a penny plagiarism of their work . . . and partly because of something a Central News man, a young Cantonese named Yao, had said at one meeting.

He said: "At the time we won Taierhchwang, General Tang En-po's and General Kwan. Lin-cheng's[1] men were doing quite as well farther over to the east. General Tang En-po was Number One General over there, and General Kwan Lin-cheng, whose name was associated with a victory at Lanfenchang, only just his junior in military rank. These troops fought very well, with no trenches at all at first; but they never got any sort of publicity, because the place where they were fighting was so badly cut off that no reporter could make it.

"I tried" (he concluded) "to make it myself on a mule. By and by, my two guards stopped and said they wouldn't go on any farther. So I went on alone for a while, but after I'd been stopped by about thirty sentries I got sick of it, so I came back."

I leaned over and said: "Will you take me next time, Mr. Yao?"

He said: "Would you go?" And I said: "I'd like very much to go."

Mr. Yao then shook hands and said he'd take me.

But as it happens it didn't work out like that, although both Mr. Yao and I eventually got to the place we were looking for. Mr. Yao was now in charge of the party of Chinese and foreign reporters who were up at Hsuchowfu; he was head of the Central News Agency, and therefore an authoritative man on the Chinese side. He was rather good-looking, with a high-spirited face and deep-set eyes.

It was brave, the way he got out of Hsuchowfu after the fall. He walked quite alone into the Japanese frying-pan, and was challenged, but he told them that he was a Filipino named Fortunato, and they, for some peculiar reason, believed him. Of course, he had mother-wit. Anyhow, he got across country, and then down by river-boat, right to Shanghai. I liked him for

---

[1] Also spelt Kwan Lin-tseng: I have used the spelling preferred by General Kwan's secretary.

being Mr. Fortunato.

I had my pass, and all I felt about it now was that I wanted to be quiet. So I got home, and though the prophet was filling the corridors, as usual, and the shy Chinese all the bathrooms, I managed to lie on my bed, thinking about nothing much, seeing nothing except the coppery sunlight still pouring in.

Eppy, or the bit in *Ta Kung Pao*, or the letter I wrote to General Chen Cheng, or persistence, or somehow, invisibly, old Mr. Lay? . . . I hadn't the faintest idea which of them got me the pass.

In a glass of water I still had my rush prawn, and its pop eyes looked red as ever, but its tail had come off. Before that it was a good prawn. A Chinese sells them for ten cents each in the big Hankow park at the other end of the city, the park where there's a stream under willows, and all the lovers go boating, or sit about in little teashops; and you never see much in the way of flowers, but the Chinese have been so loving, faithful, and kind with their arrangement of rocks.

You feel: 'Those rocks are going to do well here,' or 'Isn't that old pine just the very place for those beautiful rocks?' There are a few low pine trees, twisted and kind.

You wouldn't think one could see New Zealand in such a place, but I did. There was a huge blue globe, cut in halves, each half standing upright in grassy ground, protected by barbed wire. I looked down the Pacific, and there it was . . . Te Ika-a-Maui, the Fish; Te Wahe Pounarnu, the Greenstone Place; and the little tail-end island, the Land of Ruddy Skies.

After this, George Wong had come up with his camera and a girl-friend, and started taking photographs of us, against New Zealand, against the big stone models of the Arc de Triomphe, the Houses of Parliament, London, the Eiffel Tower, George Washington's birthplace. The Chinese had all these celebrated structures in their park in the Wuhan city. Not that nations so honoured seemed to care.

CHAPTER FOURTEEN

Interlude

FOR ME THE HSUCHOWFU EPISODE lasted a little over six weeks. I went up by train on the Lunghai line, 1 May 1938, leaving the key city again the night after I arrived there for Yun Ho, the railway terminus, which is about thirty-five miles from Hsuchowfu.

Next day, Chinese soldiers from General Tang En-po's headquarters, which were at Yun Ho, took me about another thirty-five miles by camouflaged motor lorry to the large walled town of Pihsien. We walked the last couple of miles to the village headquarters of General Chung Yao-ruing, of the 25th Division, who kindly received me as a guest for the few days I was at this part of the eastern front.

The rest of my travelling was on donkey-back (really very comfortable with string stirrups, and much preferable to Chinese wheelbarrow, which I tried later). My donkey and I saw a little artillery fighting from the top of Naishan mountain, which had been visited the day before by a Tass News Agency party, including Miss Chang Yi-lien, with whom I shared the same grave-mound during a bombing on the way back.

The little actual fighting that we saw did not, unfortunately, indicate that this sector was now a healthy or peaceful one. Its soil had been soaked with the blood of ten thousand Chinese soldiers about a fortnight before this visit.

Less than a fortnight later, in Hsuchowfu, I saw very large numbers of Chinese troops from the Pihsien area swinging along the Hsiaohsien road to the south-west. So remarkable was their discipline that none of us . . . a small body of five foreigners in a city which for days had been racked by aerial bombardments from fleets of up to sixty heavy bombers . . . guessed that these troops were no reinforcements, but soldiers in retreat.

Young front-line Generals had said: "We can guarantee Hsuchowfu,"; but General Kwan Lin-cheng, who was Tang En-po's second-in-command, told me: "If the Japanese come back here they will come back with very heavy reinforcements." This, apparently, had happened. At about the same time, on 14 May, Japanese troops cut the Lunghai railway line to the south-west, severing Hsuchowfu's connections with Hankow.

Most of the fighting at Hsuchowfu, with the exception of some crosswise shelling during the last two days, was done outside the city, on the surrounding hills, and of this I can give no details. But the worst of this final phase of aerial bombardment started on 10 May and continued until 19

Part Two

Game

CHAPTER ONE

Defeat of the Very Likely

AT CHENGCHOW, THE HALF-WAY HOUSE to Hsuchowfu, Joris Ivens and John Furno, two of the filmmaking outfit who were going to turn out a Chinese war-film on the lines of their 'Spanish Earth,' got off and tumbled away into darkness.

An Americanized Chinese, Jack Young, who has done a great deal of exploring in Tibet, stopped to explain where I should cross to the far side of the station, and how buy a ticket onwards. You couldn't buy a full-trip ticket in Hankow . . . only as far as Chengchow, which had been very badly bombed, but was still habitable. Jack Young looked more alive than the others, as we sat and drank authentic lemonade at one of the slopped-over tables. I wanted Ivens to tell me the story of his life, which he wouldn't, as he had been to a farewell party the night before, and now felt bad.

"It is a pity, though," he said, with deep seriousness, real or otherwise. "It's a great pity, for it would have been very interesting."

We passed some refugee trains on the downward tracks, crowded like ants on the tops and cindery black sides. Refugees from south of Hsuchowfu. Running away from that department, which the foreign correspondents took so lightly, seemed strange.

I asked Jack Young: "Is it really so bad?" and he replied: "So bad that most of those people are leaving everything they've got."

The carriage, which was hot and dusty, I shared with a narrow-eyed, narrow-faced, curly-haired young girl of northern looks. She had a sienna gown, but was stripped down to clean white singlet and blue cotton drawers, and sat up smiling on the dusty berth. We couldn't speak a word of one another's languages, so smiled, bowed, and drank little cups of tea. For a while I lounged about, but it was so stifling hot, so dust-on-the-desert's-path: I got sick of that and went back to drink more cordial waters with the pallid Ivens and Furno.

A moment after we struck Chengchow, even the thought of anything foreign seemed to melt away in the large Chinese darkness. Jack Young, eyes and a smile, was off too. I found the ticket-booth, which was lantern-lit, surrounded by vague Chinese, who all roared with laughter when I had almost to undress myself, getting out the fare. I had no luggage except a very small handcase with a change of clothes, also a blanket, Edith's blanket.

Eppy had used it for Taierhchwang. Then, when I hadn't a blanket, and apparently had to get one or die, she said: "Goodbye, blanket!" kissed it, and handed over. I had the same old slacks and blouse, my heavy coat, my good English shoes, and a tussore hat which a Chinese boy in Hankow very reluctantly let me have for seven dollars.

It was his last hat, foreign-style, and he didn't think he should hand it over for less than ten dollars. I wanted one of the peaked coolie hats, about forty cents: but he was firm over that. "No, no, Missie! No good for here. Maybe do for the hills."

Nothing could be seen of Chengchow's battle-scars; somewhere behind this storm wall of darkness sloped off the big western detour to Kaifeng, where there were a good number of foreigners, mostly missionaries and doctors. A very faithful Chinese Travel Service man came with me to the place where I should catch the train; there was no regular service, the idea being to stay with your station (unless bombed) until a train arrived. The boy settled in to wait beside me. Station pitch-black, crowded with ghostly soldiers sleeping on their packs. The great saucer-shaped mouth of a dug-out. Sudden mad running, urged on by China Travel Service man, under the wheels of a stationary train, to grab the Hsuchowfu express, which had inexplicably come in on the wrong side.

Right under the train, I bumped heads with somebody, and even in the dark recognized the slimness and narrow eyes of Sienna Gown, who laughed. We ran for it together. Doorways all jammed. . . . Chinese, bundles, string kits.

I yelled: "Lift me up! Lift me up!" to an enormous soldier who wore a wolf-skin collar on his coat. Of course he didn't understand a word, but grasped the meaning of my passionate gesticulations, towards hips, towards the train's open window. Seizing me triumphantly by both legs, he waved me aloft like a banner for a moment, then tipped me head foremost through the window, where, unable to steady myself, I landed on an awful shriek. Shriek belonged to a pig, done up very firmly in string. Crosby Garstin says the passage from life is made pleasant for Chinese pigs, by giving them opium. This pig was no drug addict.

Well, it might have been worse, and really nice was the sight of Sienna Gown, following me, more neatly, through the window. From that instant, we were long-lost sisters. Soldiers gradually erected me, and squeezed us into a compartment, where we slept with one Chinese soldier apiece curled up on the bottom berths; but there were more on each of the top berths, more on the floor.

One civilian top-berther was a very fat Chinese boy who spoke good English.

"I was hastening to assist you," he sighed, "but then I saw you lying on

174

the floor."

To me, that seemed no explanation at all. However, he was cheerful enough at this stage, for the Hsuchowfu express was (comparatively) a fast train, and he thought we would be there sometime before morning. Also he translated enough for Sienna Gown and me to say "Good night."

We slept, and should have woken up at our goal; instead, we were roused to the horrible dust of the little station, Liu Ho, and sat there for two days, while a couple of stations farther along railway gangs chipped picks, repairing the damage caused by one of the worst bombings yet. Two hundred people, wiped out in as many seconds!

Liu Ho and the dust. . . . Liu Ho and the beggars. . . .

" Have a kind heart!"

"You eat alone!"

"Take pity on the baby, she is dying!"

"I haven't eaten all day, give money!"

"I want only big money!" (This last from a white-haired, serene old lady who knew her scenic effect, a sort of beggar-queen, supported, tottering, by two lusty young women.)

I got the fat boy to translate what some of the beggars said; but he was more interested in the bandits, who, he said, were thick and very fierce all about here. Sienna Gown had found friends on the train, two young and small Chinese soldier-boys, and as we choked more and more, miserably trying to cool our throats with little wild cherries, she had the idea of going on by ricksha. But the rest said this would be madness, because of the bandits. Only a few days ago, a man had gone ten yards from a darkened station, and had been robbed and beaten.

Sellers of peanuts, inedible poultry, no eggs. In spite of the beggars' ceaseless insistence, we ate very little, alone or otherwise. The cook-boy's first deed was to stick his head round the door, leer, exclaim "No chow!" and retire to his cabin. From sounds issuing thence towards evening, he simply became drunker and drunker, joined by a chorus of soprano village belles.

There were villages, yellow clay, walled and high-gated, one squatting on each side of the railway tracks. The Japanese 'planes were still making themselves a pest, farther along, and what part of the first day we didn't spend hating the flies and the dust, we spent in being chased through wheat-fields towards willow trees, driven out by air alarms. Queer to see, squatting among the very sparse, dusty-bedded ears of green wheat, the poor old black-gowned peasant women. Some of the old ladies and half-naked youngsters were very chatty and likeable. One, white-haired, indescribably wrinkled, was so cross with the Japanese, because they had interrupted her when she was doing her washing. But the common need interrupted her. Out came small brown claw. Have a kind heart! Have a kind heart!

"In the south," pronounced the fat boy, "the people like to eat and live well. But among these people there is more avarice. They don't mind what they eat."

Anyhow, they had a very good dug-out, concrete, deep, and camouflaged with dying willow boughs. Willow boughs, often dead or decrepit, were expected to work wonders in camouflaging not only citizens, but very large lorries, which had, however, the initial advantage of being painted a muddy green. The village on the other side, which I went to see alone, had dark shops, frizzling pots and pans, blood-bladders, and only one beggar, the whole of its other population having gone up to concentrate on our train. It was here I met the station-master of Liu Ho and two more Chinese railway officials, and discovered that French is spoken on the Lunghai line, which was built by the French, and for some time operated as a French possession. They gave me fried eggs, vastly improved by toast.

During the night, one set of rails was repaired; but that didn't help us, as ours was not a military train, though plenty of soldiers were on board.

It seemed to me a matter of certainty, so clear that it was almost admirable certainty, that we should stick there at Liu Ho for ever, and the light turn that peculiar tortoise-shell cat yellow at dusk, and dust sweep up round the legs and faces of the beggars, who tried vainly to beat it back with branches of willow. The fat boy bore out what I said: looking like one who is going into a decline, he announced that the rails might not be fully repaired for days, and meanwhile only soldiers could pass, not 'the common people.'

But the beggars didn't treat the soldiers as uncommon people. Some train-loads of wounded men were brought down, held up, then bodily shunted to trucks further along the track. They had no beds, no attendants, no rations at all. Those who could stand propped themselves up in the doors of the cattle-trucks that carried them, staring out. With one accord, the beggars of Liu Ho fell on them, like lice.

"Have a kind heart! Have a kind heart!"

Have a kind boot! . . .

In mid-afternoon I was saved, all because of Sienna Gown and her two little soldier-boys, who, seeing some troop-trains pull in, suddenly gathered their bundles and indicated that they were off. I implored them to take me, and they quite understood. Dashes beneath stationary trains, awful leaps up the sides of the troop-trains. This, as it turned out, was largely an officers' train, and because we refused to forsake our little soldiers, we all had to sleep sitting up on wicker seats; but it was a very good train, with real lemonade, beautiful dust-proof lemonade.

There was food to eat; I ate a steak, swimming in a red aureole on a plate, and then wondered, 'A steak of *what?*' It didn't matter, it couldn't matter, because we were so happy.

I forgot to say that just before we pulled out from Liu Ho, our cook-boy came running up, thrust out a grimy paw, and remarked in perfect English: "I want tips!" But by then our blood was roused.

Singing. . . . My singing is a little like old-style Chinese music, and Sienna Gown wasn't so good either. Of course we could only try to follow one another's tunes, which climbed ridiculously from our 'Old Kentucky Home' to 'Chi-lai, Chi-lai, Chi-Ial.' Just on the ragged and fantastic edge of darkness, an old beggar, propped up on crutches, who plays a wild flute . . . a wild young flute from the bamboos, not a tame one. He has to coax it.

Between the weary lids of morning, a station slides by, its one side still completely covered by a wistaria vine. But nearly all the blossoms have fallen, it is green again.

A young officer, tough and in command, comes along and wants to make us get off. We might be spies, and, anyhow, have no business here. Persuasion no good. I show him my pass with the big red seal, and though he still makes himself frowning and important, in a few moments one of our little soldiers gesticulates very cheerfully. We can stay on, but go and sit with a truck-load of wounded men, who agree that they want to have us. Nearly all are stretched full-length on the floor, nicely bandaged up, well fed, and not half so forlorn as those we saw at Liu Ho. We buy them greenhearts, wild cherries, and pastry (You will die!), which they accept with a pleasant courtesy. After that, we are flying on again, it seems only a few minutes before the train slows almost to stopping, as it goes round a sandy bend, and to my great horror I find that we have to jump while the thing is still moving.

Our party is not the only one. Some peasant hitch-hikers have been bumming their way in a back carriage, and drop off like locusts; there is even another man who has been lying between the wheels.

Certainly I can't jump; so I throw my handbag and coat into the sand, dangle for a moment, then drop. The white sand is quite easy and pleasant; Sienna Gown, two unknown soldiers, and I, with our very small belongings, have come within walking distance of the east gate of Hsuchowfu. Of the city there is nothing to be seen, but besides the sand-drifts and continuing railway tracks, there are hard, meagre, shaly hills, all sloping their shoulders the one way. In the far distance is a little stone watch-tower, and steadily forging along the railway tracks (to reach which we plunge down the sand and scramble up a gully's other side), is the long line of black-coated, black-trousered bound-footed women, the richer of whom have hired a coolie to carry their bundles. Everything feels heavy, because this day (the sand underneath dying to drink) is pale blue, but most sweltering hot.

Very politely, one of the soldier-boys carries my coat, which I would never allow, but that very politely, the other soldier-boy is carrying Sienna Gown's luggage. Along the railway tracks, naturally we make good going against the other women, who one by one fall behind. Sienna Gown would take, perhaps, a Size Two. There was never any need for Chinese girls to bind their small and pretty feet; even the men take a small size in shoes. My dark green coat, streaming over the shoulder of the soldier-boy, looks like a wild Tartar banner. The white soil opens its mouth and says certain things: it has a kind of coarse primulinus, dark velvety blue; a leaf-flower splashed the colour of sorrel, and trembling and nodding from golden-coloured wires above the sand, the same catkin-grasses and convolvuli we knew around the Wellington bays.

The misty and dusty mountains, mud ramparts, and the pagoda. The first person we meet on the road is an old woman, selling peanuts. Then come a few mules with bells and bright saddles of cloth or scarlet, and immediately behind these, stalls where radishes gleam with a wet freshness, as if they had just been dug up. You can see, the moment you get into Hsuchowfu, how it has been smashed up. A large number of sun-coloured clay walls have their corners knocked off, or holes through their middles. Brick walls are boarded up, where the bricks have been, and everywhere the enterprising and economical Chinese stack the bricks in neat piles, as soon as the bombs have finished knocking them down. One brick wall has been re-erected, quite perfectly, except that no mortar has been used. There is only one ricksha in sight, and another enterprising Chinese grabs that before we can shout to it. . . .

Here is an illustration of the way in which Chinese people take pains to look after foreign ones. Sienna Gown and her soldier-boys, not far up the street, came to a hotel with blue decorations, and waved to me to come within. This was the Garden Hotel. But I had been advised to go to the China Travel Service Hotel (whose name I had with me, written in Mandarin), because its owners and managers had all run away, and the boys were running it on their own, very cheap indeed. Cheapness had to be my one consideration in Hsuchowfu, though when I got to the front, I wouldn't be able to spend any money even if I wanted to. Naturally I expected that Sienna Gown and the soldier-boys would smile, and say goodbye. That always happens. Instead, they conferred for a moment, then picked up their bundles and came with me to the China Travel Service Hotel.

The front entrance was boarded up, but round at one side we found an open place, and I did my best to wrestle with a boy who knew no English. Then down some stairs and into the open came running a tall bronzed youth, shirt, shorts, zipp fastener, camera, who looked as if he had been sun-tanned beneath glass for months.

"Welcome to Hsuchowfu!"

That was one of Mr. Fortunato's big foreign and Chinese party. There were three foreigners upstairs, including the one who was born in New Zealand, adopted by Australia. I could have embraced him. We went in, the three Chinese, now a little shy, following upstairs to one room, I to another.

Boy looked grey and wearied, and when he brought tea it was not tea, exactly. I met the other reporters, who were amiable, and we drank the health of everything in thick, sticky port wine, poured out in thick, sticky glasses. I had some soup, which tasted very coldly of burnt flour mixed up with burnt fungus, but when probed revealed nothing but a little rice.

To go to the front the correct procedure was to call on General Li Chung-jen and meet his secretary, a nice man named Mao, who spoke very bad English: then you went back to your hotel and waited. General Li Chung-jen had kept the party kicking their heels all this time: but they thought their journey was set for to-morrow.

"That's good," I said, more or less happy about the port, though troubled about the soup, "I'll be able to come with you."

They went out, leaving me prone on a spare bed; Sienna Gown came in, to smile and make things clear by her language of gesture. She was going out now, downstairs. Presently, in the evening, she would come back again with the others, and we should see one another. All right?

I lay still, but couldn't rest. In a little while I went downstairs myself, summoned a ricksha (noticing that every Hsuchowfu ricksha had on its back the insignia of a huge nail-studded copper and brass butterfly, which made it look gay), and showed the boy a second Mandarin writing, the address of Central News Agency.

These streets of Hsuchowfu were quite different from any others I had seen in China. They were crazy-cobbled, for one thing, and almost everywhere the system of open shops prevailed, shops so tiny, so queer. . . . One stored grain, whose colours ran all the way from orange-red to black; in another the potter was screwing up the necks of his high jars, his hands

179

gloved in soft clay; there was a bird shop, with larks, canaries, finches, and enormous sparrows in cages, and money also blew about caged, all the greasy notes fluttering in their compartments behind iron bars. One or two clothing shops looked unusually good, with flowered cottons for summer unrolled for show, just as in western shops, and many silk umbrellas.

Besides all that, the warm clay walls (Hsuchowfu was a poor man's city, one could almost call it a city of clay huts with black-tiled roofs), and the occasional gates over which dragons were coloured like the most beautiful marzipan. I know of no other Chinese city where the little girls wore roses in their black hair, but this was very common with the Hsuchowfu young; the boys, of course, had their heads shaved for summer, with one lock or a bit of fringe left on to deceive the demons into thinking that here was a useless girl, not worth stealing away. Many of the tall Chinese men shaved their heads all over, and old scars and patches showed where the razor had gone too far. Made for the women and little girls were those fine wooden toothcombs, painted at the tops and sold in the street.

The way to find a Chinese place you are looking for, but can't quite find, is to go through yet another courtyard. Then you find it. Pomegranate bushes were in harsh red flower down at the bottom of this mud slope, and such big roses swayed about their heads, pink and red, roses almost the size of peonies. A woman with a baby came out from the room, where I could see stools before the little altar, and when I showed her my paper she went to a matting-covered door and banged loudly. Her children, of mixed sexes, came to hang about her black trousers and make remarks, but she smiled kindly. The door opened, emitting a large, plump Chinese man who had stripped to his shirt, and was yawning, still half asleep. This was Mr. Hsiao of Central News.

"Oh, come in," he said, friendly, "oh, come in, do, co-o-ome in!"

He stretched and yawned so loudly that a full pink rose toppled over backwards. But when I did come in (the place was cool and low, with earthen floor) nobody could have been more affable. And the first thing he said was: "I think we will keep you here."

"Oh, no, Mr. Hsiao! Oh, not at all, Mr. Hsiao!" (Though privately, I like Hsuchowfu's looks, and can't see why not.)

"But I want you to meet Miss Shih . . . one of your Youth Movement leaders, very famous. You see, she is visiting Hsuchowfu just now."

"I should love to meet Miss Shih when I come back. I could only go to the front for a few days, you see."

Miss Shih settled this by walking in immediately, with her husband and a small company of happy warriors. We met without hesitation, agreed to

180

meet again, to drink tea. Then Miss Shih had to leave, to be very busy in another place. Obstacle No. 1 politely dealt with. I explained how fortunate it would be if I could go with the party, quite a big party, who were going to-morrow.

And Mr. Hsiao, yawning like a dozen cats, said: "I don't see why you can't go."

Indeed, indeed. . . .

"As a matter of fact," said Mr. Hsiao, "I think I can say where they are at the present moment. Let us go. Then we may arrange."

About twenty minutes later there were tense feelings between myself and the Press. Especially the former New Zealander, who made the explanations.

"They are too polite to say so. But can't you see that you'd be a encumbrance to them?"

I don't like any reference to women as encumbrances, chance or otherwise.

"Go to Hell. We'll see whether I'm an encumbrance."

"Later on," pronounced Mr. Fortunato, regretfully. "A Chinese lady will go up at a slower speed, travelling with her party. You could go with her. I think this is a good idea."

I said I wasn't going with any Y.W.C.A. delegation, and got down the steps at a remarkably nimble speed, in a more remarkably pepper-and-salt temper.

As a matter of fact, the crack about Y.W.C.A. delegations turned out totally unjustified on the results, as the Chinese lady was Miss Chang Yi-lien, who was acting as interpreter for one of the Tass News Agency men, Mikhail Koublinsky. The third in the party was a Mr. Lee Kai-sheng. And Chang Yi-lien was a nice girl, besides being an interesting one. Moreover, they got to the place we were all looking for a day sooner than I did, going direct from Hsuchowfu by lorry. But going alone, though not a purely objective method, had its points.

I remember I saw a beggar-woman in the Hsuchowfu streets, and she was kissing a rose, or, at all events, rubbing it softly and with such appreciation over her drawn old mouth. I didn't know what to do now, except that I didn't want to see any more reporters. But I had one or two cards; a couple of them directed me to the American Presbyterian Mission's Hospitals; one hospital for men one for women.

Writing, I have the clearest, queerest feeling of actually passing through the gates again. Men's hospital first. Dr. Mac. It was early twilight, summer twilight, the breasts of the Hsuchowfu roses were broken to grass. Like a flock of small ragged goats stood up the white irises between the grass and broken flagstones. There was a terrier dog, running and barking, standing up to be friends. Dr. Mac's figure looks dark, probably because it was evening. A round-faced, bald-headed old man, who should have been rubicund, if something hadn't made his face and hands a little tremulous. I don't remember what he said, only that he had an American voice. We walked over the now dampened grass to Dr. Nettie's house, and he left me there.

"Well, now! . . . Come right in! . . ."

She was seventy the day after I left Hsuchowfu. It was a bad place to be seventy, just at that moment. Dr. Mac was sixty, at the least, and the other Americans, the Franks, very little younger, though Mrs. Frank was plump and good-natured, and any other where would have been comfortable. She was the most human of them all.

Behind the ivory-coloured face and blue eyes of this old American woman (she came from Greenville, U.S.A.) there were small candles pricking up their wheat-sheaves, showing in soft gold a cabinet of good china, a rocking-chair, a piano, Dr. Nettie's clean high-collared dress of blue linen, made in severe Chinese style, and over the piano a picture of an amphitheatre where some lions were having the time of their lives with some Christians.

We had coffee served up by a nice-smiling middle-aged Chinese (a Christian, like all the mission servants and hospital staff), as well as small cherries in a bowl. Dr. Nettie had a huge solemn female dog, a brown retriever, whose name was Brownie, and who never had any pups. Brownie kept looking at us solemnly, eyes of syrup, and paddling the carpet with her flail of a tail.

Dr. Nettie, and not only Dr. Nettie but the old Chinese matron of the hospital, who came in for a while, thought I was the image of Miss Cora, a girl who used to live with them, and of whom she was very fond.

"Miss Cora! Miss Cora!" exclaimed the old matron, clasping together her small, fat hands and looking up at the sky, as an indication that Heaven had sent me. I had a look at Miss Cora's portrait later on; there was no real likeness.

Suddenly I remembered Sienna Gown, after Dr. Nettie had insisted that I should come over from the Chinese hotel to stay for the night, and was saying, alongside the invitation: "Perhaps, my dear, if you're not too tired, you will come to see some Chinese pictures with me . . . war films, of course. It's a long time since I've done anything so worldly."

But we never did get to those films. Not to meet Sienna Gown and the boy-friends, and thank them for bringing me to Hsuchowfu, seemed unbearable.

Sienna Gown's slim northern face and body came flying out of the dark near the hotel. Dr. Nettie told me she was a young bride, whose husband was a Szechuanese soldier, and was meeting her next day.

I said good-bye to her, my sister, my two young soldier-brothers, and that was that.

Come home. On the wash-stand are china toilet articles, flowered with violets. I try to have a bath, but the Hsuchowfu well-water is full of grit, and makes little impression on my griminess. There is another rocking-chair, I never before saw so many rocking-chairs, and a row of books, none of them worldly.

Poor Dr. Nettie! She is now training young Chinese girls as nurses, but all her trained ones ran away, besides another doctor, two obstetricians, a technician, and . . . saddest of all! . . . a cook. Also a younger woman, who was apparently the life and soul of the little station, is on furlough, and Miss Cora quite ungettable, and the only daughter remaining in China is in Soochow.

She is lonely and troubled; there are too many bomb cases, besides which she has endless confinements and ordinary female complaints, eye-cutting daily for the trachomas, and once a week a kala azar clinic. The kala azar babies are interesting, from the medical point of view. They have a spleen trouble, which causes their tummies and eyes to pop in an astonishing way: but they are quite curable by hypodermic injection. Hsuchowfu, a bad place for sicknesses, a place surrounded still by shadows of ancient sufferings, superstitions, cruelties. Once she nursed the wounded of the famous bandit warlord, Chu, whose army was so great that his wounded men alone numbered 25,000. Chu was buried alive, and Chiang, his rival, was shot by his own men.

About four years ago, bandits carried off some thirty Hsuchowfu schoolchildren, keeping them in the icy caves all winter, for a ransom the parents could not afford to pay. When at last a deal was made, most of the children had died. The little survivors were carried down: they did not walk, they did not smile, for the frosts had rotted off their hands and feet.

But thirty-eight years ago, when Dr. Nettie and her young husband came here, the punishments meted out to bandits were the punishment of farmers for weasels and stoats. One day she came on a quivering pulped heap, and it was man; it was bandit, just flayed alive. Bandits have been greatly reduced.

In 1900 the Boxer year forced the missionaries to flee to Japan; the Chinese begged them to go, saying the presence of white people would bring trouble on them all. That was a strange year, with the Japanese calling almost every evening, to sit for hours, polite to the death, unfortunately unable to speak a single word.

In 1911 young Republicans were snicking off queues at the western gate, till the whole street was thick and soft with the plaits of outraged old Chinese, who screamed like cats. There was the poppy waving and streaming over the hills, beautiful in colour, dark and terrifying in the after-glaze which beset dreamers not quite awakened from their dreams. Even now, some of the young countrywomen were addicts. They brought 'in just a little,' to the hospital, tied to the roots of their hair.

Quiet behind us, willow sifting light to the yellow grave-mounds, there lay the old execution grounds, where the people, even the young children, used to swarm like shrieking flies.

"Ai! Ten feet high, ten feet high!"

Splash of the ruby blood, shadow of the huge naked executioner. But almost as near were the old Examination Halls, where honour was born in China before the beginning of the new Money Dynasty. The old teacher, his Button achieved, dreaming in sunlight! the little boys screaming, yelling their lesson, now and again waking him to wild life: the closed cells where candidates sat for their examinations, and there were many suicides among those who failed.

General Chang Hsun, of the pre-Republic days, is a man whose prestige is great, and so is his army. Everyone knows how he won his power. He was the carter who drove the old Empress-Dowager, the Big Buddha, out of the lashing city behind her, hidden away in his cart: and for part of his reward, she gave him his bride, a Manchu Princess. This yellow butterfly kept him faithful to the old regime, for when Yuan Shih-kai (afterwards President of the Chinese Republic) was casting about for a way of displacing the now doubly tragic little puppet Emperor, Chang Hsun was one of the men he decided to win over. And a cartload of silver dollars came with Yuan Shih-kai's envoys to Hsuchowfu, where Chang Hsun received them with a great banquet.

In spite of this, for the first two nights of the banquet, nobody dared to approach the subject of the visit, but it was decided that on the third night, bribe should be offered and overtures made. Now Chang Hsun's spies were as good as the next man's: and when the guests came, that third night, there was a great banquet, yet none of them mentioned the bribe. For in a place of honour upon the tables, there was the portrait of the little Emperor.

And this General Chang Hsun, as he was one of the most famous sons of Hsuchowfu (which is mentioned in Marco Polo's account of his travels) was also thoughtful and progressive. On one occasion, coming with his army through Nanking, which had installed its electric light plant, he stole the electric light plant for Hsuchowfu, and Nanking never succeeded in getting it back. Moreover, he allowed the plant to be connected immediately with both the mission hospitals, and the houses, making his theft as near Christian as anyone could ask for. His great house and grounds were in use as a barracks to-day.

Now it was twilight on an evening of 1925, and a Chinese policeman told the ageing American missionary that she must not go by the railway station; and she knew why, she knew that the body of Dr. Sun Yat-sen was slowly being brought through in its special railway carriage to the place of burial. Only one hundred appointed representatives of Hsuchowfu would be there, to make gifts to the dead man's son, when, for a few moments, the train stopped moving. But she begged with the policeman, "I have a patient on the other side of the railway station," and in the end, he told her to keep very much out of sight, and let her pass.

Slowly the train came in, all painted blue with steps gold-leafed: but that carriage which carried him, the lost leader, the author of *San-Min-Chu-I* (*the People's Principles*), was massy and shining with blue and gold, and over it hung velvet curtains of a deeper blue. These were drawn back, showing the coffin where he lay: and over this casket, great silver palm-fronds joined. their stiff fronds, bowing, though no wind swayed them.

Then Sun Fo, the son of the man who was dead here, came out and stood on the platform. One by one, citizens of Hsuchowfu came to him, and bowing deeply and speaking the customary words gave him their funeral gifts, which were very rich, as it was fitting. One hundred and one stood on the platform, yet only one hundred brought their gifts to Sun Fo, and the odd one gasped, twisting her hands, afraid to be noticed, for she had no gift at all. So she shrank back, glad it was not a bright time of the day, and very slowly the train began to move again.

And she saw the many temples go down, and the poppies go down; and a young child died, gasping, while they sat and waited for a little diphtheric anti-toxin. They were driven out twice from the city, saved once by a bandit's retreating army.

But her husband died, and American members of the family put up a stone memorial church with a rose window, where she had a Chinese preacher she liked and trusted a good deal, Pastor An. All the preachers were Chinese, most of them still young men, trained up by the missions. At one time there was a lot of trouble between the Presbyterian and Catholic missions, each one swearing the other was doing the grain-thieving in time of famine: but that, thank goodness, seemed to be all over, and on the committee of relief all got along well with the Roman Catholic Bishop and priest, and the monks of the Red Swastika Society. . . .

All the bad times had been bad: but there was something alien about this, and she had never seen anything like the bomb-wounds and great sweating burns, and already the hospital was so full. The Christians wanted to open the refugee camps (which were in the deserted schools) at once, but the Buddhist monks, who would have to provide food for all refugees, were against that, and said the camps must be kept closed until the last minute.

Anyhow, it's a lovely house, I thought; and, also in a clean bed, went quietly to sleep.

CHAPTER TWO

The Rain Prayer

A DOG BARKED, and I wished it wouldn't: a cock crew, and I wished it wouldn't crow.

Well: the one thing I mustn't do (though Eppy said it was the one thing I must immediately do) was to pay a courtesy call on Li Chung-jen, Commander-in-Chief of the Tsinpu front. Because though General Li Chung-jen was the biggest General I had approached to date, and might even give me an interview with something about those German military advisers in it (I heard they had all gone back to Hankow), he might also be just another voice saying Woman, and Encumbrance.

I went downstairs, and found Dr. Nettie up already, smiling from the pages of the enormous Bible. Her boy brought in eggs and coffee, cookies and cherry jam, and Dr. Nettie said a long impromptu grace before we ate, smiling and talking across the roses.

The Americans brought the short-stemmed roses to Hsuchowfu and had a time making them grow. Also the best peanuts; that happened God's way. A missionary brought back two handfuls of peanuts to Hsuchowfu (where peanuts already grew, measly, but biscuit-coloured pretty on their low green bushes) and gave one handful each to two Chinese.

One of them ate his handful, as I would do, one planted them—and lo, the finest dandy peanut crop since creation, in a yellow soil which was very unreliable, but also produced the hollyhock buds which knocked against the windows, like hard red door-knockers, all the time we were talking.

Old Mrs. Ma, the hospital matron, waddled in smiling and pointing to the skies. Hymns now at the hospital, Dr. Nettie explained.

The Chinese women sitting in the hospital porch were all black-clad, and many wore their hair in absolutely wispless beehives, made from finest coiled plaits, coned under a little veil with a stick-pin. They had good-humoured, round, healthy faces: the shaven-headed little boys ran about, their horse-hair charm locks tied with red wool. The little girls, bobbed or plaited, flirting with their soft amused eyes, were honies. In a room inside, they sang and prayed in Mandarin, to the more straggling and discontented hymn tunes.

Old Mrs. Ma, so fat, smiley and suffering, appeared to have charge. After her early days, a child in an opium-smoking old devil's house, she was sold to a husband who gave her V.D. And then she got converted. But the queer thing was, *he* got converted, and I have seldom seen a man with a better, cleaner face than this shaven old Chinese. They were both patched up in health, she remaining a faithful-hearted, authoritative old figure around the place, whilst he, with a serene, bony face, good eyes and silvery skin, sat on his chair for hours at that green hospital gate, smiling at folk with lips which held the short stem of a pipe, but not an opium pipe.

Dr. Nettie and I went across then to see the last batch of bombing cases, in the women's wards. There were children also, of course, as this was a small-sized hospital.

Perhaps the ghastly red solution used to paint those burned with sulphur and phosphorus made them look worse; but they all looked very bad, and seeing a stranger, moved or cried out, for they wanted their cases to be seen. The youngest was a baby who had lived three weeks with a bullet in one lung, a boy, too little to know a thing. Dr. Nettie threw back the cover, and I wondered if he could somehow know, if nothing else, that whenever he breathed he made a shrill little terrible whistle. But he lay back still, not asleep, his pale mouth wide open, not whimpering. There were two fracture cases who were pregnancies, one very near: and it was her hip that was splintered, so close to the great swollen mass of her belly, she didn't have much chance; but she was in little pain, just now, and seemed shyly pleased at the importance and interest of her case to strangers. She had a white hospital shirt, and could help to twist this up. Her dark hair was spread against the supporting pillows, her lips smiled.

The other pregnancy-fracture had only a break below the knee, and besides that was only seven months gone, so with any luck she might sail through. Another big white-shirted woman upstairs was shot through the lungs, and hadn't a show; she was now semi-conscious, beating the bed a little with one clenched fist.

Then I saw, uncovered at the end of two padded boards, two little feet like goats' feet, with all but the great toe and the next one crushed against it and turned down under the semi-translucent skin of the sole, and the great toe disproportionately large, with a sharp dirty horn on it. The heels were too large, a wrong shape, red and bulging from bandages. Some of the toe-nails had atrophied, and all were dirty. The poor little feet were unbound at the end of legs fractured by the Japanese.

Yes, said Dr. Nettie, that's dreadful, but you've seen nothing yet, my dear. So we went and saw some livid red-mercuried burns, and a woman from whose side the nurses were slowly twitching, between forceps, yards and yards of stained yellow packing, pus and a little blood coming out of the wound.

This woman was crying, and she believed in foreigners. She wanted me, because I hadn't ever seen or touched her agony before. Oh, all right, I said, I'll help; and taking the forceps, continued to make the packing come out like a flattened yellow worm, taking the weight of it as it unfolded. But when a Chinese nurse told me in Mandarin to do something at the finish, I was embarrassed and helpless, and putting the stuff in a basin, slithered off the bed.

But nobody seemed upset, and the woman with the running eyes squeezed my hand; so I smiled and went away to the old lady from Taierhchwang, who was a sort of trick patient, because she ought to be dead.

She was sitting up, old and grey, wispy as a witch from the hills, having a raw soup-plate on one shoulder dressed. She was bare to the waist. She had a head-bandage too, and a simple fracture of one ankle, and her right breast had been torn off. The ragged red place where her breast should have been caved in, bare.

She wasn't crying: she was so aimless, so harmless, so fond in her skinny limbs of the sun that she wanted to live. It wasn't for any reason. She had a little house in Taierhchwang, said Dr. Nettie, and a small bomb almost blew it to pieces. Her son, her daughter-in-law, a daughter and three grandchildren, were all killed. I looked sideways, but Dr. Nettle's serene old face as obviously couldn't tell a good lie like that, as George Washington's could and did.

There were only two other cases I saw and remembered after that, and two more I didn't see. The first was the girl soldier, Mrs. Wong. I think she was from some other place, not Hsuchowfu, because instead of the round, smiling, wrinkled faces here, this girl, who sat up thin and clean in her shirt, had straight hair cropped to the shoulders, a long oval face no darker than olive, schoolgirl's big white teeth in a schoolgirl mouth, soft and loveable, but not knowledgeable. Her eyes were exactly like those of an eighteen-year-old who used to come up to me and talk in a New Zealand book-shop, always about the more starry poetry: light brown eyes, so big and startled, looking for what she wouldn't get. It was a faint shock to meet this girl again as Mrs. Wong.

"We're all very proud of Mrs. Wong," commented Dr. Nettie. The missionaries were all very proud of the girl soldier, because she had worked so hard at the un-ornamental jobs that both her knees were up like balloons with sinovitis, and she couldn't walk.

The girl soldier smiled and talked, her toes poking up bonily under the counterpane. Dr. Nettie translated back from the Mandarin, but what was said I can't remember now, except that there was a Mr. Wong, here in Hsuchowfu, and a little girl, Lo Ti, eight by Chinese reckoning.

"A jewel of a child," said Dr. Nettie. Mr. Wong could speak some English.

The other case was only a woman lapsing from unconsciousness to death, her head splintered in by bombing, and I can't think why she comes back. The two unseens were Japanese rapes, one over seventy, one a young married woman, daughter-in-law of the first. The son-husband was with them a month before, when they came close to a band of soldiers: both women had bound feet.

The raping of the old one seemed queer: the scrawling, perhaps, of a very plain signature on a letter to an elusive man who keeps refusing to accept one's letter. Or else the Japanese soldiers were drunk, and wanted to bait an old, black scarecrow, skewered terribly between green wheat, blue sky. Sometimes, Bushido notwithstanding, just that happens, the savage baiting of old helpless women.

The old woman was still in hospital, because drunk or sober, the Japanese had knocked her about very badly. The younger one because, after a month, they still weren't sure if she was pregnant, and her husband, quite untouched, was hanging about declaring that he didn't want any Japanese babies.

The mission were grieved; but the thought of procuring abortion shook them to the core, because all human life is sacred.

But we were walking the curt, springy grass, untamed though chopped by boys, and against the windows on one side the hollyhocks pressed their bobbins of dark and pink silk, and we walked on sunlight white as almond blossom, while a big blue and grey bird with a black tail rustled out of greenery, and yawped at us.

"Bluejays," said Dr. Nettie, "a fearful nuisance."

She bent her head among the luncheon-table roses again. Everything clean and white, silver and glass, shining.

Brownie thumped a tail like a kangaroo's on the carpet. There was chilled asparagus, and Aunt Nettie had put a tin of tomato juice and some eggs and cookies into the handcase I was taking up to the front. Hollyhocks nuzzled white and red, opening mouths on the windows. In a fortnight, wide out. Oh, I said silently to the smiling pictured eyes of Cora, I am a swine to criticize at all.

Cora looked over to where, above the piano, hung the print with the Christians and lions. Certainly there was that.

Dr. Nettie wasn't in the least opposed to my going on alone to the Chinese front, for two reasons. She was a feminist (she had had to go alone, against men's opposition, to a good many queer places herself), and besides, I had told her the exact truth: I was going, I felt I had to go. I knew, too, that the fuss was over nothing. I would be all right.

That was exactly as positive for Dr. Nettie as it was for me, and nothing further need be said about it.

She thought for a moment. There was Mr. A. Liu, formerly stationmaster at the East Station, Hsuchowfu, which was the one I wanted, as it carded the last piece of the Lunghai line to the terminus, Yun Ho. Mr. Liu was grateful to the mission hospital, which had recently, nursed his wife back to health. Mr. Liu spoke very good English.

I went out into the sunshine, and in a ricksha with a butterfly on its back along a cobbled street; cloth on the loom, a whole row of brass shops where men tapped shining dented bowls and spoons, every size, then a man making lovely little pots, like a great artist's elves, and boards embossed with golden or red characters telling the nature of each shop. I saw a donkey going sadly in circles, grinding stones in a dark inner room. But what he thought he was making, God knows!

Finally my card was handed from one clicking soldier to another, at an old stone *yamen* where veranda'd buildings led from courtyard to courtyard. There was nothing sprouting in the courtyards, except pomegranates in flower and youthful soldiers, and at last I found the office of Mr. Mao, General Li Chung-jen's private secretary. We talked a little, and I told him (though he knew such scanty English, it is almost true to say Mr. Mao knew no English) that I was very anxious, owing to circumstances, to visit a Chinese front as quickly as possible: but nevertheless, I was very anxious to visit General Li Chung-jen as quickly as possible.

He said: "General Li Chung-jen has gone home to-day," as I thought he would, for the hour was past five.

So we drank tea and smiled; after which, somehow I persuaded Mr. Mao to write me a paper describing me as a safe person to have wandering about, and I knew enough by this time to ask him if he would mind using his red seal. He used this and I left by the same ricksha. In Hsuchowfu it costs nothing to keep a ricksha back waiting for half an hour, there is no shouting, no roughness, no sense of people in any tearing hurry.

By the way, the original name of the place was Tungshan, or Brass Mountain, and the Chinese Government was for no reason whatever trying to change Hsuchowfu to this old name. It wasn't even as if Hsuchowfu had any special repute as a brass-making place. Brass was made there, certainly, but the Hsuchowfu speciality was a long, slender kind of pipe.

In dusk Dr. Nettie got me away, aided by Mr. Liu's portly blue gown and little bowing boy. Dr. Nettie had brought a lot of tracts for the soldiers, who, to my amazement, simply ate them up: they had no saintly reputation otherwise, they liked girls and wine, and were very nice, agreeable lads, very good, underpaid, underfed soldiers, dressed up in cotton 'khaki.'

The fact remains, they left Dr. Nettie not a tract, and I could see her starched blue linen gown wandering about duskily among them, while the station-master waited.

Everybody at the East Station was feeling pleased, because two days before the building had been bombed, with several direct hits; but as it happened, the staff were at that time in the front of the building, waiting for an incoming train, which was delayed. The back of the building was a shell. They took us in and showed us the shell, feeling very proud of it.

The station-master told me, through Mr. Liu, that the Japanese were puzzled and distressed, because although they broke the rails so often, still the trains kept running.

"The fact is," he said, beaming, "we've a loop here, which can't possibly be seen from above. Oh, it is such a clever loop!"

He told me, too, that I was the first woman who had ever travelled in such a way, alone on his troop train, and I must travel in the cook's cabin, and not go into the other carriages at all.

And it seems that now, this minute, I am waving back at them. We had to cross a high bridge, and then I mounted and got into the cook's cabin, which was dark except for a candle-lantern. Every time the door opened the flame rushed out. Dr. Nettie's wave and blue gown, Mr. A. Liu, and the little boy.
. . .

As on the other Lunghai trains, I could make myself understood with the senior officials here. I had a thermos of coffee (Dr. Nettie's) and at once tried to be amiable by offering drinks all round, which were accepted by everybody, including the cook-boy. Then I was moved from an uncomfortable stool, to the cook-boy's bed. The rapid, non-stop train simply tore through the dark, showing nothing but country of shadows on both sides. From time to time, French-speaking officials popped in, the lantern-flame popped out, and when the cook had struggled to re-light it we drank more coffee.

We arrived at Yun Ho so suddenly, with such a jerk, that I was startled. Quite black it was, almost midnight, and all happening so quickly; the train didn't wait, I was dropped off on the station with a sentence shouted over my head, and then, I think, the train ran on into a shed, where the men disembarked.

Anyhow, I saw no more of them, but two or three Chinese soldiers held up their lanterns near my face, and then two of them took me by the arms, and led me by some steps down into a dug-out. It was a very good, big dug-out, quite the size of a room, and not mud, but walled with concrete. It had two telephones, both in use by Chinese who rattled off what they had to say at top speed. Besides that, there were Chinese officers, most of whom looked big and boyish, and stared hard under the electric light. Some of them were grinning.

Then the man who had been using one telephone put down the receiver, came up and stared, and started talking to all the others. He didn't look amused. They all looked inquiring, under the electric light, and I, fumbling for Chiang Kai-shek's pass and the little red seal kindly contributed by Mr. Mao, wondered whether it would have been wiser, as well as much more polite, to pay that courtesy call on General Li Chung-jen. Eppy, after all, had told me. . . .

I tried speaking in English, but that was no use: then I tried my bad, my almost viciously accented French, and it was all the good in the world. They broke up the suspicion party and started talking in a friendly way. Being Chinese, of course they brought fresh tea.

There was a big General living less than three li from here, they said; but for to-night I must stay with them.

'Right!' I thought, ready to sling my legs up in any part of that comfortable-looking dug-out. But the station-master, after more argument, said I had to sleep in his bed. So I went along some earth passages to his bed (dead sleepy now), and he spoke very bad French indeed, a sad, dark, heavy kind of French, but seemed to want so much to talk. He got a neat room ready, while the cook-boy brought some fried eggs, with toast.

Suddenly I was dying to be asleep, but I couldn't take any clothes off, or wash, because people kept coming in and looking at me, as if I might explode with a bang. I was happy and loved them, and wanted them to go home now and go to bed; presently I kept saying this, in English and French; there is no Mandarin for 'Good night.'

All rippling white: and a zinc bath-tub, whose water I can see. The water keeps giving funny little bubbles. After a bit, this worries me enough to make me sit up, take a look, scream. The cook-boy comes bobbing cheerfully in.

Cook-boy (following my accusatory finger): "Fish! Fish!" Me: "Snake! Snake!"

Cook-boy grabs one of the slimy horrors by its middle, holds it aloft. I suppose it is really an eel, but won't give up the point that it must be a snake. In late afternoon, little boys of Yun Ho kill a snake, frankly admitting that it is poisonous.

Early on, the station-master takes me round the little village. It is two months since any rain has fallen at Yun Ho, the meagre roots of the green crop seem to be shrivelling yellow. Small galled donkeys march round and round, round and round, in the blinded shops. Over the fields comes a noise

I have never heard in wartime before, and know immediately . . . the noise of big guns.

They are shelling thirty miles north of Yun Ho, says the sad man at my side. I like talking to him, but somehow it's a responsibility, his inarticulateness and effort to be understood. As if he wants to say more, and can't.

After breakfast more soldiers arrive in a lorry to take me to the headquarters of General Tang En-po, only a couple of li away.

This looks like incredible luck, as General Tang En-po was my chief official quarry; but when we tumble out at the gates of a very big Chinese house, with several stone moon-gates and courtyards before we reach the long balcony where, under a flare of wooden character-banners, a group of officers are sitting at table, the luck breaks off snap.

Neither French nor English is any use. In a few stumbling words, we make one understand.

She is looking for General Tang En-po.

Well, Tang En-po is away, it is no good, he is superintending troop movements.

She wants to go somewhere or other. But she can't speak any Chinese. She has a pass.

Well, better keep her sitting here, otherwise she might walk off and walk into some bad trouble. If she walks far enough, she may walk into some Japanese.

This is a bother. Well, better send for that fellow Yuan, from Number Five Building, he speaks very good English.

Yes, but it is a bother. Foreign men will let foreign women go anywhere, because . . .

Has she eaten yet? Well, we might as well have something now to eat.

Sumptuous repast, really sumptuous, mostly Chinese, with the beatuiful little new-cooked loaves. Tang En-po has Sheffield cutlery, Sunkist oranges; and all the time, in the great deep balcony, swallows ply their blue shuttles to and fro over our heads. At least, they are like our pictures of swallows, though we were always taught, 'You will see the swallow in England,' nothing being said about China. Paul Yuan arrives, puffing a little, mopping his rubicund good-natured face. It is all right; Paul Yuan can speak very good English.

I can't interview General Tang En-po, for the moment, as not even his own men know where he is, except that he is personally directing very big flanking movements from east to west. So I interview his secretary and some of his officers instead, and they are riding an up wave.

194

Only yesterday, in sorties out in these peaceful-looking fields, they brought in a pile of Japanese trophies, which I am shown. Rising Sun banners, silk and cotton, swords, a gun, the tiniest playing-cards in the world, with a flower, bird or fish marked on every card; Japanese 'thousand-stitch' charms and joss-papers, humorously ugly; letters, diaries, cards; little switches of dark woman-hair, tied with red ('Japanese people very sentimental') well-cut overcoats, with shining buttons of plain brass. A lorry-load of larger stuff has recently gone down to Hsuchowfu, and ten after Taierhchwang.

Then, just for strolling in and eating a magnificent meal, I get the pick of the trophies . . . the white silken Rising Sun banner of a leader, Ei Tang, they call him, whose name is marked in Japanese characters down the side; some of the little cards, joss-papers, pictures, a snapshot of a young father with plump, happy Tokyo kiddies, a tiny tragedy.

I kept the notes of this interview, but they, unfortunately, are among the missing: chief burden of Tang En-po's officers (who seemed to like the General very much) was that he was always coming up against some special Number One Japanese General, and wherever they fought, the Japanese 'never had any luck.' And they were in high spirits about sorties, and this conspicuous house (which I called 'The House of the Blazing Characters') had not been bombed; but about tanks and heavy mechanized equipment the soldiers who smiled and waved as we drove away said nothing. Paul Yuan was under instructions from General Tang En-pa's vice-regent to drop everything, and take me to the front, himself acting as interpreter. We had a bunch of Chinese soldiers as escort.

First, of course, we had to have a banquet. The station-master's heavy sad face lit up, and he said in his difficult French: "Are you coming in here?" but the crowd swept by, and I had only time to sing out: "On the way back."

The banquet was given by Transport-Marshal Chang, and was notable for me in that I now had my first taste of *pai ka'rh*, a white grain-spirit which the Chinese peasants, in their hardy way, drink from huge earthenware bowls.

They served it to me in a glass goblet, the kind that might be used for brandy, very large; one mouthful, and my legs felt peculiar; two mouthfuls, and they felt certain; three, and we lost contact. This stuff had terrible effects on the morale of the Japanese . . . twelve hanged themselves in Hsuchowfu, and I don't blame them; it later on became a good place to get hanged in . . . and even the Chinese soldiers seemed to know they had tasted better in the good old days, for they had a proverb: 'Foreign *pai ka'rh*, Chinese wife.' This seemed to mean: 'Your foreign whisky will do.'

White blown rose-petals drifting across the doorway, and on one wall a picture of a Frenchwoman in a hat, period about the nineties. Bored, she was, incurably lonely and bored. I could believe she had lived in this tiny mudpie of a place, and never had any hope of getting out again. Outside, kids were shouting over their trapped snake. Inside, a railway official was explaining to me about one photograph of the railway staff, and another showing the great, wide lily-pads of Peiping.

"Peiping," he said, "it was all right there on a boat at Peiping."

All Chinese people talk as if they loved Peiping.

We hung about so, because there had been an air alarm or two, and on one occasion we went down into the dug-out. Makes you feel bored, languid, hanging about: doesn't make you feel: 'Now, to-morrow-moment, I'm going to be blown all to red strips and pieces, an eye here and a stomach all over the place.' It might, only for the baked yellow clay with rose-petals drifting across its oblong mouth, Paul Yuan saying: "Go in there and lie down," and my taking his word for everything.

I wish I could convey, somehow, the good-humoured reliability of my new guide.

Not a bit handsome, in the first place. A little over middle height, thick-set but not fat, with a round, red-cheeked, jolly face.

Hair quite straight. Wore uniform and a big sword at hip, as usually worn by commissioned officers: but I'm not quite sure if Paul Yuan was a soldier, or if, as on many parts of the road from Kowloon up, he held a commission because he was a senior railway official.

I think, however, that he was a soldier, and he told me he had been trained at the Jefferson Mission College.

"Mission college," he added, "very good indeed . . . to teach English."

With us now, besides Paul Yuan, were two boys from Siam, reporters and members of an overseas Chinese delegation. They were coming to the front.

One I don't remember well, except that he was fat, small, and friendly; but the other one, Mr. Lung, could speak some English, though it had been buried so deep it had to be hauled out of him.

He wasn't a real Siamese, but a Chinese born in Malaya (he called it 'Mēelia,' name softer than honey), and working now on a big newspaper in Siam. Somewhere he had picked up smallpox, and was badly pitted: so it sounds wrong if I add: 'Mr. Lung had a beautiful face.' Yet it was true. It was a small face, with small dark eyes, which glowed red at night, like a forest animal's.

Our dirtily green lorry at last oofed itself out of hiding; I was somehow jammed inside, not on a seat at all, but lying on a shelf or ledge above the driver's neck, propped up on one elbow. I don't think anything could have felt more uncomfortable, but I could see the forthcoming strips of road, bordered by willow.

Mr. Lung and Paul Yuan sat in front, and the other reporter and our military escort piled in behind.

We had travelled less than five hundred yards like this when I saw another dirtily green lorry coming.

"Hold on," I said, "it is all right. I know these men."

For the lorry contained the Press, none others (except *their* driver and military escort), and as we rolled towards one another did they look suddenly startled!

Passing, I thrust out my head, and blinking painfully said: "How are you? I am doing very nicely."

The young linguist of the party, the Belgian, said limply: "All right, thanks," and we were gone in two clouds of dust, never to see each other again.

But I had brought bad luck on us, behaving like the worst apparition in *A Bad Child's Book of Being Beasts;* very soon after, though we heard no sound, the lorry stopped with force, and immediately the military escort hopped off like crickets, literally melting into the background.

There was no background but green wheatfields, and they were hiding in the wheat as fast as they could hop down. Paul Yuan ran farther than anybody . . . I know, for I found him later. But Mr. Lung and two or three of the soldiers stood by a ditch under some trees, looking up with smiling indifference, refusing to run away at all.

I did not refuse to run away. The only reason I did not run much more quickly was because I couldn't.

A voice spoke out of the wheatfields, saying: "Well, why don't you anyhow sit down?" and I sat down, catching a glimpse of Paul Yuan's sunburnt face.

Over my own face and the too-vivid top part of my clothes I began to weave, in and out, a nice little nest of cool green wheat-ears, and presently felt relaxed under this.

"Hullo," I called, "it's quite nice under the wheat-ears."

"If you make any noise at all, the Japanese will hear you and come back," replied Paul, in a voice positively oily with comfort, "they always do that. The audibility, from the ground, is very great indeed. The Japanese have heavy bombers, which can stay in the air thirteen hours without refuelling. They do not come from Nanking, as people say . . . that is all a mistake, Nanking is much too far. They come from a great mother-ship."

We had three 'planes, spinning bright silver in the air, creatures of light. It was extraordinary, but under the green hood dwelt no fear, not the slightest fear. Yet I'd been scared white that morning on Canton station, with the other Paul, that morning when the 'planes were only circling. Again, I'd felt quietly sick about getting into the train for Hankow, not so much at the idea of being bombed as at that of being trapped in a burning carriage. Anyhow, in the green peaked hood, neat as an insect's, I. wasn't afraid.

The 'planes unloaded with a crash, not far away, and Paul's voice said: "Come along to the lorry." Our military escort, plus the boys from Siam, piled in.

They had bombed a poor old yellow village, from which dense clouds were rising.

"Maybe they think some soldiers are in the village," said Paul, "or maybe they think it is us."

Either way, there was that dense dream-cloud, and also the fact that they had held us back three hours. We went hurriedly, jerkily over the rutted road, passing the serrated walls of Pihsien. I always wish I had stopped and wandered about Pihsien. But the last civilized thing after that was a stall where an ancient woman sold peanuts, and then a little village.

I think I remember it right: a stream curled between the upper and lower bank, and on the lower bank there were fringed palms, like banana palm leaves when they are sallow. Small naked golden-brown boys played about in the mud, and one screamed, afraid of me; but the old man told him not to be such a fool.

From here the lorry went back. If we went on at all, we went alone, on foot.

"Well," Paul said to me, "what do you think!" Here is Pihsien, just down the road. Do we go on, or go back?"

"Oh, let's go on," I said; and without a murmur, whatever they felt, the reporter-boys and Paul Yuan set their faces towards some pine trees and fields, not very good fields, because they, like everything else, had suffered from the drought and the dust.

A village of this sort, in the interior, is built on a system of courtyard opening by clay arch and step into courtyard; small low-roofed houses facing into each with open doors, like oblong mouths.

Every courtyard has its own convenience, which may be a natural, time-saving passage between two places, or else an L-shaped erection of high bound straw. Both are cleaned out at least once a day, and the fertilizer used.

There is no special playground, but the children too young to work may play almost anywhere, under their mothers' clotheslines, among the fields where the little donkey labours, and the oxen among the steady pine trees, among the agricultural instruments of grooved wood and stone. Stone troughs, great stone rollers cut in grooves, stones erected like chopping-blocks, wooden ploughs, long wooden instruments like elongated spades, and wooden forks made by the cutting of two young branches so they will grow the right shape, just there, below the crotch.

The women labour in the fields with the men from first youth. And yet I saw a book in the village, and it was handled by a child of about eight, who wished to know words like 'flower' and 'wing,' and was trying to study, his little back crooked into a curve.

There seemed practically no money in the village; despite this, when I gave a few dollars to a basket-maker's children (because he and his wife were kind and let me stay in their hut) he really had a hand-out with the children, and told them to keep it. In the hut were masses of clean wicker-work in various stages of advancement, a bed with legs, and a matting stretcher, and nothing else. A candle-stub stood on a wooden box. On the walls were stuck coloured pictures that looked like demons, but were probably Buddhistic good spirits, friendly to have about.

In the middle of the night, somebody felt so excited and curious about my being in this village that I heard a cry; and with a lamp blazing before him in came a huge peasant. He didn't come a step nearer, do anything but blink like an owl, but some other villagers immediately came and hauled him out.

A larger village would almost certainly have had some kind of shrine, probably a school: but here there was nothing, no building of importance except the bandit-tower and General Chung Yao-ming's headquarters, of which the first was the one of permanent importance.

The bandit-tower, as well as being the only double-storied building in such a village, is the only one where guns may be stored, and the only one so built that its clay walls aren't easy to batter down. Outside it is thatched all over with small, thick overlapping squares of brush, much as a watch-house in parts of Polynesia and New Zealand will be thatched. The top story of the bandit-tower is where the guns are stored . . . most likely they date back to Rider Haggard . . . and when the bandits are coming the villagers go up by a ladder to this top part, and shoot down through narrow glassless windows, not much wider than arrow-slits. This is not a good way of fighting the bandits if their band has come in large numbers, shouting and screaming so that they can be heard miles away (and can send all the small beasts, terrified, running into their jaws, like that other sensible tactician, the African lion); but it is a better way than not fighting at all.

General Chung Yao-ming's headquarters were two of the village huts, one for himself, one for guests and for his staff to use as a rest-chamber. We ate our evening meal in the nearest courtyard, with pomegranates at one end, harsh scarlet trumpets, the bats a soft fluttering darkness in the clear air, which ran like a blue water between the fingers of those pine trees, against whom the darkened shape of an ox or donkey showed heavily now and then. To fight this darkness, the crescent new moon, silver against all dross, rose cutting with her sickle the huts where the children had stopped shouting and shrieking and begun to taste dreams. There was a low table, piled with food, but not nearly such opulent food as we had in the morning . . . just a little soup, a few dishes of vegetables, and for me some Chinese bread.

Paul Yuan: "Special for you!"

Everybody laughed at me because I had forgotten how to use chopsticks properly. But I did not feel hurt, and have seldom seen a handsomer soldier than this young General, who had grown his hair to a thick black bush, in spite of summer heat, and whose eyes danced and sparkled like champagne.

"The sufferings of one who does not understand a dialect must be very cruel!"

Then he told Paul it was just as well for me that he was here to translate, and Paul started to translate.

All the Chinese Generals talked so much of the three phases of the war . . . Retreat and Disorder, Men and Blood (then supposed to be well advanced), and, lastly, the third phase, the hour of which they would know on Chiang Kai-shek's word. In the third phase, Chiang Kai-shek intended to use aeroplanes, and more than aeroplanes.

But this General, like some others, wanted to know why foreign nations should show sympathy with China, instead of Japan. I had the idea he thought there was a joke in it somewhere: if so, yes, yes, I'm afraid there was a joke. But the greatest part of the joke was, so few foreigners ever remotely suspected the joke.

Sleep. The soldiers and reporters are making a great deal of noise, playing a gambling-game. Every few moments they all shout together. There is a small lavatory built in a stable.

'Special for you!' Paul is very proud of that. The saucer of the candle looks up, swimming gold, at the paper gods or demons, who have such ugly pink and butter-coloured faces.

In the morning, they all come stepping warily through the puddles. (It has rained during the night, the whole courtyard is splashed with long, spattered water-stars, two or three inches deep.) The children come first, hand in hand, the girls much bolder than their brothers, and the eldest of the lot not above eight years old. I sit up, like a revived corpse in a fairytale; immediately they yell, and start to retreat, but one *fat* little girl's courage is of the stolid, rather dignified kind, and she stands there pulling against them, a thumb stuck like a lollipop in her mouth.

Oh, blast it, I never thought about lollipops!

The children begin their approach again, until they are all just inside the maw of the clay house.

Suddenly a woman runs in, calling out some name, and seeing Paul Yuan in his shirt and trousers across the way, just having washed himself, I call over, to find out what the woman wants.

Paul comes over, and says: "That is the name of her girl. She is called Little Horse."

I ask the names of the other children, and they are all said out loud, with several women now inside the house, laughing and joking together.

The children (boys) are Field and Chinese-equivalent-to-Spade, the girls are Plough, Miss Flower-That-We-Eat, Small Moon and Little Horse. These are their milk-names. ,

"You see," says Paul, "the people up here call their children very plain things, the same sort of thing they see about them."

I tried to get a shorter definition of Miss Flower-That-We-Eat, because she was the fat, stolid little girl who wouldn't run away; but Paul only laughed, and seemed to become a little embarrassed. I think he had the right flower-name at the back of his mind, but there it had stuck, as happens so often. Anyhow, Miss Flower-That-We-Eat was quite temptingly named, and unique in herself. The other children, once they felt sure that I wasn't going to bite them, started gently to feel my clothes and everything I had all over, and so did the women, who seemed particularly impressed by my big fur collar. But the children wouldn't let me touch them, the one exception being Miss Flower-That-We-Eat, who suffered herself to be picked up and joggled.

The mother of Little Horse was a nice woman, still quite young and slim, with a silver ear-ring in one ear, a soft voice and laugh. She adored her little girl. But she worked too hard: there on her finger was a Chinese thimble, much the same as ours, but topless.

"Aiyah!" she sighed, with the pretence-look of the good-looking woman not too old to bear a bit of flattery. "How can I be pretty, when I have to work so hard in the field?"

"That only shows you are good, as well as pretty," I said, restraining an old peasant lady, who was smoking a cigarette from the volcano of a small pipe, from getting off altogether with my fur collar.

The mother of Little Horse had bound feet; and though Little Horse had not, Miss Flower-That-We-Eat had dirty white bandages welling up to her ankles, so perhaps that was why she seemed such a slow, determined little girl. All the other children, both boys and girls, wore trampled coloured slippers, and looked clean and bright.

I asked Paul Yuan about the forbidden custom, and this was his story. A long time ago, he said, an Emperor of China had had an exceptionally beautiful concubine, who at most times had the power of making her lord feel very cheerful. Naturally she had to watch out, lest some other concubine (of whom the Emperor had plenty) should make his heart light to a greater degree.

"And so one night, when they were dining together in the pavilion on the lake," Paul explained, "she bound up her feet very lightly with her gauze scarf . . . pretends to bind them, you know . . . and danced for the Emperor on a great golden lily. Made lily." (That one was easy: artificial lily.) "So then, the Emperor was very happy, he gave her many beautiful things, and all the other young ladies started to bind up their feet. It became the fashion. Then the mothers started telling their babies: 'If you let me bind up your feet very young, the Emperor will marry you.'"

I don't know whether this is an accepted version of the story, How Bound Feet Began, or whether it was a Chinese Apocrypha.

After a courtyard breakfast, we all rode over (followed a little later by General Chung Yao-ming) to where, three li farther on, General Chien Yi-chih was established in his blue-painted front line camp, right underneath a small, shale-sided, very steep and hot mountain, which was, by title, the front. The fighting at the moment had resolved itself into night sorties, mostly on the other side of the mountain, and to an artillery-duel, limping along in a one-sided way, as the Chinese had captured most of the big guns, including Japanese cannon pieces from the rocky breaches built at the top of this mountain, in a battle finished less than a month ago.

That was bad fighting, and until General Kwan Lin-cheng turned up from Taierhchwang, with heavy troop reinforcements whose first job was digging themselves trenches, times were hard for the Chinese soldiers, who had not more cover than a lump of stone gives a hare, and nothing much to eat. Now the mark of the mountain-base Chinese trench on the far side showed in a red line (the soil was clay).

The Japanese remnant, being bottled up in three villages, which for all their sun-coloured earth and willow trees looked like death, the windows and doors of them being cut-out holes of shadow, were busy entrenching too. It looked and sounded as if the Chinese had got them this time, all right; and maybe the Japanese in those three villages they did finish off, before the bigger, waiting trap snapped just too late, giving the Pihsien soldiers time to skip out of the road. But what didn't skip, what could hardly skip, remains a ghost . . . the little village, the basket-maker's hut and the other huts: Little Horse, Field, Plough, Spade, Miss Flower-That-We-Eat, and Small Moon.

I was riding past green wheat, happy as somebody quite drunk, and riding, at that, on an ass with string stirrups, not on one of the Chinese horses. There were some pretty tall horses in Chung Yao-ming's camp, though the Chinese cavalry unit everywhere moved best on its stunted-looking weeds of Mongolian ponies, which were quickest in every place, but in the slippery north-west cold, I am told, indispensable.

I couldn't use a stirrup, and everybody agreed one of the tall horses would spill me, so General Chung Yao-ming said: "Give her this man's little donkey," in a handsome way, and there were my ass and I, edging our way through green which was like a lake, rustling and whispering.

But no water flowed there, on account of more than two months' drought, from Yun Ho to Pihsien and Pihsien to this mountain.

I thought, deep back, of that old song, 'The Rain Prayer,' which they played on Chinese classical instruments one night in Shanghai. You couldn't remember it and whistle it, as you could any sort of tune, because, though it had repetitions and cadences, it hadn't got our idea of a tune. Only it seemed to be there and close, while the air bubbled and grilled with heat and near-by was the smell of some dead thing, perhaps an ox; and then the piled-up weed stank as we were riding, several of us drawn close together, over a small bridge spanning a tidal creek. The foundations of the bridge seemed to be rotting bamboo and branches, and the top of it a rotting mess of weed, but nobody cared, least of all the serene white-haired peasant woman crossing the bridge, while we held back.

Detour round a high wall, and we pulled up inside a courtyard of General Chien Yi-chih's camp. The General had almost a family likeness to General Chung Yao-ming. The night before, General Chung had presented us with uniforms for general utility in scrambling about. The uniform cotton was cooler than slacks, and I wore it whilst astride the ass. I thought General Chien Yi-chih might find this brazen, especially as about a yard of puttee had come undone, and slithered off in the serpentine way of puttees tied by the uninitiated. But instead he took me within his wooden house, and gave me an immediate lesson in the tying of puttees.

In here (it was a cool little house, very neat, the whole encampment built for its purpose, instead of being a village, like Chung Yao-rning's), we met the Tass party, Miss Chang Yi-lien, Mr. Mikhail Koublinsky, and Mr. Lee Kai-sheng.

They had arrived yesterday, by lorry direct from Hsuchowfu, climbing the mountain without stopping to pick any daisies. Now their one word of advice was: 'Don't go up the mountain!' which did indeed look a hot, steep griddle. But we had come so far; our one wish, our only and trivial wish, was to climb the mountain, because it had some Japanese on the other side, and with luck we might see a Japanese (though not from the wrong angle).

General Chien looked a little worried about my climbing potentialities.

"All right," I said, with the calm ferocity of another Peter the Great, "I'll ride my donkey up the mountain."

Mr. Lee Kai-sheng declared plaintively that he wished *he* could have had a donkey to ride up the mountain, he was still aching from yesterday's climb

Chang Yi-lien, straight-gowned, is in blue cotton, her black hair unusual in that it hasn't been cut off, her face remarkably like one on a fan. She has bought a pistol for the occasion, a big one, very stiff and hard to grip, and has a proper pride in it. And though she looks quite delicate and must have ached last night in every slender bone, she is the first girl to climb the mountain with her party.

She is from the Yenching University in Peiping, an American university which kept to its original schedule most courageously, after the bloodless fall of the city. She has since been working in Hankow, mostly at newspaper work and interpreting for Mikhail Koublinsky, who, like myself, doesn't speak Chinese.

Anyone, in any country, would find Miss Chang attractive. She speaks not only her own language and Russian, but good English, rather delicate and graceful like her own make-up. And Mr. Lee is a young man who speaks English exceptionally well, far better than Paul Yuan, who yet contrives to understand and express so much.

We keep on drinking warmish water, which isn't particularly refreshing. But this is in country where tea is so precious that it must affect millions of peasants like Pearl Buck's thrifty old character: 'Aiyah!' Drinking tea! You might as well be drinking gold!'

Neither General Chung Yao-wing nor his Sub-General have any tea at all, for themselves or anybody else. That stamps them out as not being luxury Generals, who wallow in comfort while their soldiers make the best of rice-gruel, memories, hopes.

Theoretically, there is a wine-ration for soldiers on this front; both Generals impressed on us the fact that the soldiers were contented, well-treated, and had a wine ration. None of the soldiers looks really wilted, but on the other hand, none shows signs of a wine-ration, even at the top of the mountain, where Ground and Sky are two enormous energy-sucking leeches.

Our escort turns up, very smart, one youth wearing a great plume of pink wool stranded from his Mauser.

"Why does he wear that?"

"For pretty," promptly replies Paul Yuan. It shows that male vanity, like the female brand, can function well enough, any time, any place.

Mr. Lung's compatriot, the young reporter from Siam, is going on alone to-day to Taierhchwang, a good long run by lorry, but in spite of this he decides to climb with the rest . . .

Nothing but shale, a once burnished rooster dying hard and reproachfully outside the gates. No bacteriological examination will be made: one more for the pot. The mountain started with an enormous black goat, her kid pulling at her teats. We began to look human again, alive, idiotic enough to enjoy ourselves.

The ass sweated very much. She was such a clever little thing for keeping her humble feet on the shale, finding a foothold where there wasn't one. There were some erect old charactered slabs of stone, Chinese memorials, looking away to the west, and round the mountain-head, which was crossed by a track, a bastion-like griddle of stones piled up. This was where Japanese artillery had been mounted, and Chinese now had big guns (not cannon, the really big stuff was under cover at the base of the heights), and a giant telescope looked over the deathly villages.

Soldiers in tin hats and cotton suits slightly thicker than the usual slept up here in dug-outs scratched like small caves under the rocks. They had mats, and those who weren't on duty lay with helmets off, arms wide back in the shadows, sleeping, or imagining, perhaps. One or two were reading books.

"Look," said an officer up in this desolate place, "over there you .can see the Japanese. There, in white."

The Japanese wear white cotton suits under their uniform, and on occasions when they can relax, such as in a troop-train or a bottled-up village, they peel off to this sensible white suit. The brass eye of the telescope sweated; I couldn't see any Japanese at first, but watched the hill-slope, where Chinese soldiers, flattened against rocks like enough to the colour of their uniforms, scrambled about without bringing down a stone. Below, the yellowish-red ribbon of the Chinese trench; the clear rhythmic singing of Japanese picks, driving into another trench, but out of sight.

"Our artillery doesn't like that," said the officer. "We want to find what they're doing down there, so now we are going to give them a bang. You are very lucky."

I expected to hear Paul Yuan say "Special for you!" but he was prone in the shelter of a rock, talking with one of the tin hat soldiers, and trying to get cool again.

The whole way over the mountain-top and on its shaly sides was growing a tall, intensely blue, wild forget-me-not. China's big guns boomed, big cream puffs swam up from the dust between two of the deathly villages; out in the centre of the telescope, quite clearly now from their hiding-places of willow, sprang the little white figures in cotton . . . so little, so unterrible.

I know this is what impressed me about the only Japanese I ever saw in actual fighting. They were running away. At a distance of perhaps two li they seemed so near one could have dropped a penny on them, and they looked little and unterrible.

The Japanese soldiers, close-up, were not at all Japanese-without-tears. Within limits, one would not expect them to be, and in the Hsuchowfu district, as in others, they far exceeded those rules. As for being little . . . Chinese in Hsuchowfu were funny about that, some of them felt so disappointed. For many years they had reckoned the Japanese as dwarfs.

Now they said, rather mournfully: "These ones are not so little."

Such a beautiful view through the sweating hot eye of the telescope! Silent fields and villages now, the green erect, no longer waving, as if it breathlessly waited for something. I never saw white clouds ride higher or more splendidly shining in the sky . . . like great galleons, like everything white and majestical man has ever known, but this measured to the scale of unknown gods. Is it always so quiet at your front? Well, the ten thousand who died on, below, and near these slopes some few weeks ago, made a bit of a row passing out, Lady.

The shimmering heat sends you fantastical. Soldiers lying in the dug-out shadows, their arms flung wide open in the prostrate helplessness of sleep have the best of it. And we have to go down from the hill now. Because two women have turned up at the front, General Chien Yi-chih smiled and says: "I will parade all the troops I have here."

Photographed sitting on the carcass of another slaughtered record: in a way I wish we were both good, simple-minded peasants, though the polite Generals say it cheers the soldiers up to see some women about the place.

However, we had just got back to the camp, when the Rain Prayer settled all this about troop parades. The shining, toppling clouds took less than ten minutes to dull their lustre. Everyone became uneasy . . . not only the people in the little wooden room, but a couple of American new-corners, one a leathery-looking Colonel attached to the Hankow Legation, the other a likeable-looking newspaper youth.

General Chung Yao-ming said, watching the clouds, he must ride back; General Chien Yi-chih said that in that case he also would ride back. The men were quick on their horses, and Miss Chang Yi-lien miraculously managed to skate her narrow blue gown up her legs, riding astride and well.

I was very far behind, because the little donkey was justly rather put out by all that had happened, and not even a feed on top of it. But it was glorious, watching the clouds break, water and lightning stream together, and half a mile ahead the tails and manes of horses stream out. I like it when Rip's giants bowl ninepins. A terrific crash brought three men down, and one of them dragged, with a broken arm. He was part of Escort, and the break, I suppose, would rank as a Chinese 'Blighty' one.

Among the sallow discontented wheat-roots, rain hissed and seethed, and out of the green, which lifted up many heads and was magnificent against its summer, came flying hundreds and hundreds of ridiculous, warty-backed little frogs and toads. At the bridge my donkey took it upon himself to make trouble, toppling me half-way off his shoulder before, in a sort of fireman's crawl stroke I should never have thought feasible, I kicked back again into the string stirrups, and thanked God the string was good.

At the camp everyone was tearing off wet uniforms, Chang Yi-lien putting on a dry one, her little fan-face smiling. I did the same: our streaming pants, tunics, and puttees occupied the best clothes-line, shamefully filched from a white-haired old Mother Hubbard whose own washing had been hanging out to dry, and who came out to scream at those soldiers like an eagle. But she had a twinkle in her eye.

It's extraordinary how placidly, and in how amiable a spirit, the villagers accepted us all—General, military, Press. The basket-maker's hut, when I got in, was already full of the people of the courtyard, who evidently considered they had proprietary circus rights over that minor circus, their foreigner. The old lady who smoked a cigarette coming out of a small pipe was particularly affable. She lighted a cigarette in her volcano, affectionately patted it into shape, and placed it between my lips.

I would like to know how a funnily-clothed, still moderately young female of any foreign species, who doesn't speak the language, looks to an old peasant woman who has stayed in the same village all her life, and who isn't whipped by fear or hate. I think it (the foreigner) must look like a doll or a baby.

Why are you so kind, human beings?

For a short time we are all hanging about peacefully, sitting in the cool but not unpleasant darkness of earth rooms, loafing on matting beds, holding scrappy conversations, when we aren't too lazy to talk, or the rain makes it impossible to go out through the new green. Another General, the important Kwan Lin-cheng, has arranged a sort of command performance for us at his headquarters, half-way back along the road to Yun Ho, and we are waiting his word for the time when it is convenient.

Paul Yuan at our courtyard supper talks about the book I am supposed to be writing.

"It will be like a big movie . . . everything in it, unrolling . . . up on the mountains, those guns, the forget-me-not, the soldier falling off and getting his arm broken, us sitting here, the moon coming up."

"Seems to be an awful lot of it."

"Oh, that is quite all right."

"The first thousand pages will be the worst."

"What?"

"Joke. Special for you!"

Lee Kai-sheng tells me that the Chinese name for the forget-me-not is almost exactly the same as ours, and there is the same sort of romantic legend behind it. I am learning quite an ambitious amount of Mandarin, not from Paul, but from Mr. Lung. Mr. Lung says now he can go back to Siam and his newspaper soon, "because my country is successful. If my country is not successful, I made plans to stay a long time at the front."

When I first met him he couldn't put three words of English together, but it was there, curled up in his mind, only waiting the most casual conversation to open out again of its own accord.

I wish my Mandarin would do the same. Our method is simple; we write down on bits of paper sentences in English, opposite them the nearest approximation to their pronunciation in Chinese. He then repeats them, and at the time I can echo him so beautifully that he is always prepared to be proud of me, at a moment's notice. But alas, the parrot is a dumb bird after all, and Lee Kai-sheng always remarks: "Say it in English." Nevertheless our written vocabulary, and the variety and mileage of questions and answers we manage to work in, begin to impress the others. It is only I who remain unimpressed, knowing flatly: 'As soon as his back is turned, I will forget how that is pronounced.' I like him, sitting there quiet and luminous-eyed. 'My country is Mēelia.'

One night the two Generals both make writings, I think for the whole party . . . and that, if the brush is used instead of the fountain-pen, is a long task. The writings, when they appear in the morning, are so beautiful that I don't want to fold them over, and keep them perfectly flat as long as possible . . . black and scarlet on dead white.

The guns talked all night, loud and angry, muttering, muttering. . . . It was hard to go to sleep. Next morning we were early on horseback (in my case, donkey-back), and all photographed again and again, sitting on our prancing beasts, smiling in made-up groups, saluting . . . very cheerful publicity stuff. General Chung Yao-ming had a little camera, and snapped a roll away.

Wave, stumble, cross the creek, wave again. Does it look ridiculous to wave any more? Little Horse, Field, Plough, Small Moon, and Miss Flower-That-We-Eat . . . not a lollipop among them. That seems a shame.

CHAPTER THREE

The Way Back

BUT THE PIHSIEN ROAD, in these few days, has become different. That's obvious at once; but the brain receives so complacently any comforting, likeable truth that when, almost immediately afterwards, something like a contradiction of that truth appears, it thinks: 'Oh, nonsense! Inflammatory stuff!'

The difference on the Pihsien road, all the way from Landmark I, Peanut-Seller, who is still there and doing trade, may be summed up in terms of oxen, donkeys, slanting wheelbarrows (which have no barrow, just three wheels, handle-grips, and planks), stumbling women, old men in blue, naked little boys and girls with a bit more on, besides bundles and torn-off branches. The road, during the night, has been terribly cut up, and the deep ruts of lorries are too slippery to use. We have to keep to patches of grass, sidling from one side of the road to the other, as some old peasant's ox-team humps dejectedly before us.

Once there are wounded men, flat out in an ox-cart, looking abominably uncomfortable. On this road my donkey has a distinct advantage over all the large horses, who are inclined to slither all four legs in different directions.

The peasants know little except that they're running away; for a long time they wait, affable, apparently quite unfrightened, cracking a bit of a joke with the round-faced boy soldiers who never have quite enough to eat; then a moment comes, or a tip from somewhere, and running away becomes the thing to do. Perhaps, a few miles down the road, word will arrive that the bombardments have stopped, and they'll run back again.

These were not the people of our little village. But up there life is all little villages, thousands of them, built in the formation I have described, usually one on each side of the road. The space between belongs to fields. There was no dug-out or any kind of bombproof shelter in the village of General Chung Yao-ming. The people stick to willow boughs. Two or three villages are successfully bombed almost every day. For this, nobody except possibly a few villagers lamenting afar off seems to blame the soldiers . . . or even the Japanese.

"If a building has some people in it," solemnly queried a black-whiskered Japanese officer at Hsuchowfu, "and if then some soldiers come into it, what can we do but drop bombs?"

But while China had no 'planes over Japan, no air defence to be taken seriously outside Hankow and some strategic points, I still felt that question and answer game was Japan's baby, exclusive, born of the virgin Bushido.

Kwan Lin-cheng's headquarters were neither ordinary village, small wooden building, nor stately house. The place was a very large and prosperous farm, with a series of farm-houses and buildings all squared off inside the one high wall, many people still making their small living on the farm, donkey-trains bringing loads of flour and grain, and in some of the dark houses, the beautiful grains, orange, grey, white, and black, piled high in wicker baskets.

Kwan Lin-cheng's quiet secretary, who arranged guest-matters, immediately placed two rooms at our disposal. One was furnished in a civilized way; the other was a grain-store, and had three camp-stretchers and a Goblinesque tapestry which I didn't appreciate at the time.

Spiders, making themselves immense and at home in the pointed roof, sat up there; and they grew and they grew, and from their bodies the webs dripped and they dripped, covering every inch of the ceiling, floating out in a dreamy, off-hand way from every patch of the walls.

I said nothing, except, "Well, neither God, man, nor beast is going to persuade me to sleep in that room," which I thought, as a hint, might be enough.

Outside was the earthly smell and sweetness of a small paved garden, where the last roses were all but spent, flowering, but chrysanthemums were being budded off in small pots, and among the rocks were flowers whose English names I knew. The door of the other room was good plain carving . . . very simple, a panel showing a bird and some roses, but good.

'Willow, *yang liu!*' Mr. Lung and I walk across the courtyard, then outside, to pools where Chinese soldiers can't catch even the smallest fish, and naked urchins are calmly catching any number, in a pond not ten yards away.

"Very little fish," said Mr. Lung, deprecatingly. This time he was right, they were; a hatful wouldn't make a frying-panful. But the Chinese are sometimes capable of saying 'Very little,' in a deprecating murmur, about a building as large as a western university, and ten times as good-looking, and of which they are proud.

"We are ashamed, because now we cannot build as our ancestors used to build."

That very night, at midnight, when on the verge of strong hysterics (partly induced by the spiders) I was busy telling General Kwan's secretary that I would sleep anywhere else he could think of, only not with the spiders, he knocked me out with one clear blow.

"Of course," he said, "know it is very little and very dirty."

The spiders had it.

In the afternoon, when General Kwan received us, he gave me a dead Japanese officer's sword. I know the officer was dead, because I asked, through Paul Yuan, who was there as my interpreter, General Kwan speaking no English. Mr. Lung was with us, the idea being that he and I, in turns, should ask questions, But he saved time by writing carefully-prepared questions, while I had an interesting interview on the strength of two queries, only one of which the General answered.

It was a good sword. I never saw one of the famous Chinese 'big-swords' which were used with such wildly telling effect in the last onslaughts at Taierhchwang, but this weapon had a hilt less like that of the western kind than those worn by Chinese officers. The haft was strong, bound in white shark-skin, over which criss-crossed narrow bands of brown silken braid. There was a top circlet on which small gilt flowers clung like bees. Then the blade was not straight, but of a good long curve, not quite so long as the leathern sheath, which formed a little open snout where it touched the floor.

The room, like the other rooms in headquarters, was very plain, except that behind the General's head was a big glass cabinet, with coloured birds and plants in a pattern. The General's hair stood up straight, like a black bush, from a round, plump face, which was somehow a bit like a schoolboy's face, and when he laughed his teeth were very white. He asked me if I wanted to interview him later, and I said: "Yes. Would you tell me the story of your life?"

Then he stared for a moment, and said something to Paul Yuan, who said: "General Kwan says, we must all come back here to-night, and he will answer Mr. Lung's questions. Then he will tell you everything, with the exception of a few things that are secret."

I got back to the other room, feeling excited about the sword, though there is no doubt at all that I got it, as a man in one of Ernest Hemingway's stories put it, for being a foreigner. But in that case the man had at least got wounded, and I had got nothing, except either spider-bite or hives, neither received in action.

Our next meeting was after dinner. General Kwan offered us *pai ka'rh*, in the big goblets, and I had some, but not very much, because Kwan Lincheng drank nothing at all, and the two other men just touched their glasses. This was about nine o'clock, the General having first answered Mr. Lung's written questions.

I asked him two; the first was: "Will you tell me the story of your military life?"

It was a little after midnight when we left the room with the handsome glass cabinet. The General looked fresh as a daisy, but I was feeling tired, and nearly wept when I discovered that Paul Yuan, Mr. Lung, and I were, in spite of all representations, going to sleep in the room with the spiders.

Our interview had gone off fluently. One day I may publish the full text, perhaps, under the title 'Chinese Mars.' From 9 p.m. till something after 11, General Kwan had been killing Communists. After that he killed Japanese, but with a little less enthusiasm. This was not because the General was afraid, it was because he had ordinary good sense. In his days as Director of Anti-Communist activities, the Central Government troops he swung against soldiers and villages in Honan and Anwhei provinces, and along the borders of the Yellow River, were very much better off for mechanized equipment than their opponents. In one critical engagement, he had been able to use bombers. Fighting the Japanese put the boot on the other leg. The Japanese as far outpaced his troops in mechanized equipment as ever Kwan's Own had outpaced the Communists.

And yet he fought them; Kwan Lin-cheng being a Chinese version of that frequently discussed, yet seldom encountered, phenomenon, the born fighter, the man who fights because, quite literally, he is bored to tears when he tries to do anything else.

At the beginning of the interview, he said something a little pathetic. It was, perhaps, Kwan Lin-cheng's article of faith.

The General had been born in Sian, and started out as a normal Chinese schoolboy there. He got as far as the Third Municipal Middle School of Sian, and then a book interrupted the course of his career. It was Sun Yat-sen's book, *The People's Principles*.

'General Kwan decided then that he would give up his hopes of a university education,' translated Paul Yuan. 'He would fight for the Republican Government. He wanted to fight against the old, rotten governments that had upset China before.'

This may very well have been true. But by the time a young Sian soldier of eighteen (Chinese reckoning) had gone into Chiang Kai-shek's military academy of Whampoa for training, emerged from tussle after tussle, collected a skinful of bullets, fought so lame that he had to be hoisted on his horse and then had the horse shot dead beneath him (a Communist did that, and Kwan spoke of it with feeling), the old and rotten governments of the Manchu dynasty and five-barred flag had, temporarily, gone underground. Kwan Lin-cheng, looking about for something against which to lead his troops (he was a commander of troops at an age when the average western youth is somewhere between the sunset rays of Humbert Wolfe and the blinding dawn of Spender), could see nothing but Communists. Chiang

Kai-shek, by virtue of his young men at Whampoa Academy, already the military mind of Republican China, also saw Communists.

In Kwan Lin-cheng's military youth (about April 1926), the Kwangtung Communists, who were breaking up at the time, made a little mistake. About ten young men, of whom Kwan was one (and, in 1938, the Chinese Ambassador in Berlin was another), were strolling light-heartedly along a road, taking their military duties less punctiliously than usual. Communists, without the slightest difficulty, slipped down and captured the lot.

At that time the Chairman of the Province was a friend, a member of the Kuomintang. Kwan Lin-cheng lay for some ten days in a prison, not much healthier than the Shanghai gaols were for Communists. The conviction that he would be bumped off deepened. Then the Chairman of the Province brought some arguments to bear, and he was released.

He didn't go far. The Communists themselves, he felt, had gone too far. With a friend who also wanted revenge, Kwan Lin-cheng stayed at an hotel in the province, and finally, in disguise, went back to a Communist centre.

"What kind of disguise?"

Paul Yuan interpreted: "Oh, the General put on civilian clothes and wore some dark glasses." The two friends probably had some rather wild idea of a raid on a Communist leader's person, but after thorough exploration of the strength around them, they gave it up and went home.

After that, it was feud. Presently Kwan Lin-cheng, promoted from command to command, still lame but extremely tough and hardy, sat his horse and looked back on a private army, answerable only to Chiang Kai-shek. At moments, situations were critical, Chiang Kai-shek a long way off. General Kwan was then answerable to General Kwan.

He fought against the Japanese in the first war of the Great Wall. But no sooner had the Japanese made their peace, than he was off to challenge two northern generals, who had lifted their horn against the Central Government.

The Japanese could not get to like him. They asked the Central Government, very politely, to get Kwan's troops and others a good long way out of Peiping, and as the Central Government was just then playing to placate Japan, Kwan took his veterans to Loyang. But he couldn't rest. Communists, for him, sat behind every bush.

Clashes, successes, encirclement tactics, drives as far north as Mongolia, 'planes, machine-guns: Kwan Lin-cheng thinks his troops had a good reputation with the Communists, and his chief criticism of his former opponents was their habit of forming a scratch plan at the last possible moment, taking advantage of some chance luck to pin a fight on it: he did not deny that this impromptu fighting often worked. But was it war?

After fighting in the north he marched to Mongolia. "There was a political event in Sian at that time." But there was no fighting, and after the political event of the Sian *coup* ended in Chiang Kai-shek's release by the Young Marshal, not much time for argument. The Sino-Japanese war began.

Japan, after all, had during those years of inner conflict a long time to sit and think.

7 August, incident at the Marco Polo bridge. General Kwan took charge near the Pinghan railway. He was sent, to cover a line 75 kilometres long, three units and a high General of the 25 th Troops.

Unfortunately, the Japanese units were of superior size, numerically working out as four against Kwan's three, and including one unit of cannon, one of cavalry. Other Chinese troops in the same sector were as depressed as his own men. For some time they fought, then retreated.

Kwan Lin-cheng was in the front lines for four days, without food, without water, without sleep.

"After this, General Kwan could not sleep. He thought about it always, and his heart ached. General Kwan telegraphed to Chiang Kai-shek and the others, asking them to punish him. At last they all forgave him, and gave no punishment. General Kwan's retreat made his troops undisciplined, so he took them to Weihoifu, to re-train and organize them.

"He had only arrived there four days, when a place called Chang Ho, near the Pinghan railway, became very dangerous."

Kwan swung his still badly disorganized troops with the 89th Division to beat back the Japanese; and a few days later, Chinese Generals in the vicinity could spare time for a moment's more cheerful consideration.

Their losses were heavy. On the other hand, the Japanese were in retreat.

"We did not have any cannon, otherwise we might have finished them off then. We used our men instead."

Their next battle was at Taierhchwang, otherwise South Shantung. On 17 March 1938 they were in bleak country, arrived near Hanchuang (some forty miles north of Hsuchowfu) to garrison the Grand Canal.

And between March and early April, the flame ran up. A Japanese army was driven in retreat to Yihsien (that place on a stud-marked map which the Chinese were always about to capture during my stay in Hankow), and about 30,000 of the Japanese were killed or wounded, with approximately the same number of casualties on the Chinese side. What mattered was less the recapture of Taierhchwang . . . a flattened mud mess, containing approximately 7000 houses to begin with, and less than a dozen still standing when the fighting was over . . . but the conclusiveness with which the ill-equipped Chinese defeated the Japanese. Military experts declared that neither in the Russo-Japanese war, nor in the Great Wall engagements, had the armies of 'Dai Nippon' received quite so pointed a knock.

It was not, on the Chinese side, the knock of a well-equipped force.

"Sometimes, at Taierhchwang, it was so cold that our men could not hold their guns. Then, fighting the Japanese, they became so desperate that they just bit them."

I remembered Shanghai, and the Japanese leather beaks.

Yihsien was not so cheerful. The fact is, Chinese troops had a bad time at Yihsien, where Japanese reinforcements from Lini came along fresh, and threatened to upset everything, driving part of the Chinese forces north-east.

For Tang En-po and Kwan Lin-cheng, the position was well retrieved. Coming along, out of a bad jam, to find more mountainous country for their troops, on 10 April they arrived in the Chinese lines at Pihsien, finding the soldiers without trenches or cover. For the better part of a month they fought it out with the Japanese, and won.

"For ten days, the fighting is night and day: all kinds, from artillery to hand-to-hand fighting. The Japanese had 60 cannon, of range from 50 to 70 li. For a while the cannon-balls are like machine-guns. Very hard. Hundreds of houses burned and fell down, in the circle of the cannon. Aeroplanes bombing us. Tanks protected the Japanese, but our men advanced in face of the tanks. Chinese captured a Japanese leader, member of 5th Troop, Panyuan's Troop. He said the Japanese were two-thirds killed dead. Taierhchwang made the Japanese washed out. Retreating from Taierhchwang, they tried to break through at Pihsien. If they do, they will come back in force."

Now this interview is over, I am nearly dropping with fatigue, and with the bother of thinking too many things at once. But I ask Question Number Two:

"Is fighting the only thing that has ever interested you?" General Kwan laughs. He doesn't answer for a moment, then he says to remember that his school was the Third Municipal Middle School of Sian.

He liked horses very much. One of the things that really disgusted him, after a battle with the Japanese, was to come upon over a hundred horses, hastily shot, even hacked about, but few of them finished off. One of these, with two bullet holes in its carcass, he bandaged up in an extraordinary arrangement of splints and slings, and adopted as a mascot. He gave me the horse's portrait, which I have kept.

Paul Yuan, Mr. Lung, and 1, had the spider-room, the Tass party having grabbed off the other. It seemed a long, troubled time before waking up: but when I got there, Mr. Lung was smiling, and Mr. Yuan, deep down, comfortable, gruff beneath the bedclothes, demanded: "Do women sleep in the same room with men in New Zealand?"

I told him something close to the truth. We all breakfasted with General Kwan, who looked in the best of spirits, and afterwards had his photograph taken with us many times over. Paul Yuan took most of these snaps, promising to send me prints at Canton. I never got them. But then . . .

I sent home my exquisite little donkey, feeling it was only fair to return him to the dispirited owner. Then we were all in a stinking, grunting lorry, disputing over what to do next. The Tass party were off to Hsuchowfu, without delay. Mr. Lung and I rather thought we might stop for a few hours at Yun Ho, then go on by rail to Taierhchwang.

About half an hour down the road, the lorry screamed to a halt. We were all out in the fields. Two villages, one not a quarter of a mile ahead, climbed up in flames and smoke while we watched. When the 'planes departed, we got along to another village, and heard from a few frightened peasants that since seven o'clock this morning the Japanese had been bombing the road. Almost the whole village population was in flight across the Grand Canal.

This was the first time we'd been so near to a bombed village, and we wanted to see what was happening inside. The 'planes had wheeled away, everything looked safe enough; we came out of the wheat, into the village, which was quiet, slowly and lonesomely burning up, not in any melodramatic sea of flame, but with individual outbursts crackling from one hut after another. Probably the bombs used had been small ones. A peasant, just about to scramble over a wall, told us that in one of the burning houses were a woman and her family of seven, all dead. And there were two fox terrier pups, playing together, perfectly clean. I remember that, because you don't often see foxies in the Chinese interior, certainly not such clean ones.

Then we were all running, quite blindly. The 'planes had come back and seemed right overhead, their whirring louder and lower than usual. Chang Yi-lien cried out. She had planted a shoe into the belly of a donkey which sprawled across the path, its brains and entrails oozing out. I began to swear. Obviously I couldn't get to the wheatfields before the 'planes dropped another bomb, but in front of me, right on the edge of the village, was a crater large as a young pond. I slithered into this, finding it bottomed with filthy-smelling jellied mud.

I wasn't the only one in the pit. Plastered flat, clinging against the mud slope like a bat, hung an old blue-gowned peasant with a skullcap. His little eyes, though bright as an animal's, were quite blind, quite dazed. Dirty sheepskins lined his gown.

"All right! All right!" I began to talk to him, and when the 'planes circled off, tried to make him get up and come into the wheatfields, where the green hoods are better cover and don't stink like that mud. But he just clung: there in my mind, transfixed for ever, he stays plastered where the war left him.

Through the wheat Chang Yi-lien's blue gown came on to meet me, serenely, moving in none too great a hurry. But we had just met . . . fan-face, mud-face . . . when our dignity evaporated, and we clasped hands and ran, the 'planes over us roaring back. We lay behind a grave-mound, plastered close, talking and eating the small wild peas which swarmed among the wheat.

She said: "I hope you will write a book and tell the world about this," and though all I wanted to do was curse, I said I would. I didn't say: "The world will worry, Chang Yi-lien, I don't think!" because at that time I thought the world really would worry, if it understood.

What happened next was only what one might have expected. War is so simple.

After we had got back on the green lorry we slid a few yards farther down the road: but it was hardly worth while, because the 'planes came back and we ran for the wheat. A few minutes of that and then the lorry started up, and we straggled in.

Paul Yuan was standing there on the road. He waved his arms and shouted: "You can see what it's like now all the time here."

I thought he would get on at the back again. A hundred yards down the road, suddenly like something striking at the heart, there were the still red and yellow roses of Yun Ho station. Paul Yuan was running over there, making for the station. I hadn't even said 'Thank you' to him for what he had done, which, apart from acting as my interpreter, was to treat me as a friend.

Before we came to the Grand Canal, Mr. Lung, who was outside on the back of the lorry, jumped off and started back to Yun Ho. But it happened in too much of a hurry, and I couldn't get out. We were down by the Grand Canal. Here also the villages were eyeless and deserted, everybody shouting and arguing as to how they could cross the Canal. And every few minutes the white beautiful wings of the 'planes sang, ripping the morning as they circled back. There was an old ferry, which certainly didn't look as if it could transport a lorry. The road on both sides of the Canal was black with people, young men pushing old women on wheelbarrows, because of the bound feet. Just the same, some of the old women were making a few copper cash, selling bowls of tepid water.

Hot and thirsty. Yes, anyhow, that's true. I didn't know whether to go on or to walk those few miles back. The point was not the bombing: it was whether Paul Yuan and Mr. Lung would think me in the way.

I think now that I should have gone back. After all, people in a hurry don't let you be in the way so much that it hurts. If you've got to be killed, they let you be killed, and otherwise they park you somewhere until the fun is over. But at the time it seemed I would be adding to everybody's troubles.

We crossed over. For a long time, after another scare, we sat out in the most poisonous-looking valley I ever saw. It was crawling with black insects, only some kind of cricket, I suppose: but even there a little peanut and hot water stall functioned across the road.

I had the sword, trailing it like an iron tail. For the moment that seemed more comic than anything else. We got to Hsuchowfu wearily, too tired to do anything but climb into rickshas and wave good-bye. Mr. Lee Kai-sheng said perhaps he would be going back to Yun Ho in a couple of days. If he could find Paul Yuan and Mr. Lung he would thank them for me.

At the mission I walked in on a prayer meeting, retreated, and lay down upstairs.

Dr. Nettie came up in a little while and slipped an arm round me.

"Honey, we've all been praying for you."

Too dusty, Cora. The wheat had gone slim pale yellow, the hollyhocks were wide, the irises dead. Too much to happen in the course of a few days, and the dust grows sometimes weary beyond the use of prayers. She was a dear, though.

I wrote Paul Yuan a letter, thanking him for acting as my interpreter. About three days later (during which Hsuchowfu's own conditions had changed) we got some news from Yun Ho, though not from Paul.

It had been bombed almost to pieces. I don't know whether they got Tang En-po's headquarters, but I know what happened at the station. They got the dug-out, a direct hit, and one of the officials killed was the station-master who had given me his bed.

About Paul Yuan and Mr. Lung, about the friendly Chinese officers who had given me the trophies which wounded men and bombed women in Hsuchowfu found so encouraging, I don't know. Dr. Nettie would say: "God knows," but all I can say is that I don't. I tried every way I could think of, but never heard of them again. It's a big war in its way.

CHAPTER FOUR

Interview with a Ghost

Q. WHAT HAPPENED on 10 May?

A. In the morning the bombing was very heavy, and though the hospitals were in the safest part of the city, and never scored anything worse than a few bricks knocked off Dr. Nettie's chimney by a bit of shrapnel, the patients were badly frightened and the staff nervy on account of the way the 'planes, flying very low, kept crossing and re-crossing the compounds.

This was the first time it had been so bad. I should say they crossed at intervals of no longer than fifteen minutes at most, over a period of several hours. During part of that time Dr. Nettie was operating on a little girl who had an eye blown out and a leg almost torn off.

I was helping, both because I wanted to help and because the state of nerves over at the main hospital demanded more attention than usual. It was pretty bad, because of the recurrent low flying of the 'planes, and the fact that the bomb hadn't left quite enough skin to cover up the baby's knee, which had to be cut twice. But by a rather incredible patchwork Dr. Nettie covered up the knee all right, and for a moment looked cheerful, as the baby had been screaming about her knee, not about her eye, and we thought the eye might be there under a flap of skin.

But it was just a hole, with blood welling up.

Dr. Nettie said: "This child can't live, she can't possibly live. The splinters of the eye-socket are driven into the brain, and there'll be infection setting up in there directly. If she does live, she'll be hideously disfigured. I hope she won't live."

I wanted her to shoot in enough morphine to let the baby go before she woke up: but she woke up, and Dr. Nettie translated what she was screaming.

"My eyes are killing me! I can't live, my eyes are hurting me so!"

Her mother had been wounded too, and was waiting on a couch in a room off this ward. It wasn't a theatre; the baby was blown so filthy with dirt and grit they dared not take her to the theatre in case other people were infected.

I went into the room where the mother was. She was sitting up, blood running from a wound in the leg, and tears running down her naked breasts., She was trying to answer the baby's shrieks in some reassuring way. But then the morphine took effect and an old lady's body was taken out of the mortuary and laid on the grass, so that the baby might have some place to die.

The men carrying the old woman's body passed the men carrying the baby as she moaned and slept.

The corpse problem was already getting serious, as the *ching pao* was on so long in the daytimes that the relatives were afraid to come for their dead. The baby problem was worse. Rows and rows of pregnant women, and they always seemed to have their babies in the middle of the night, waking Dr. Nettie up again. But some of the country bookings were too scared to come in at all, and she used to worry about them.

Q. What was your own impression?

A. That having babies of the men, for the men, is a funny business, but it's working towards its own solution. That doesn't matter.

Q. Did anything else happen that day?

A. Yes. In the afternoon, bombing up by the East Gate, the 'planes got a total of several thousand clay houses—an area of approximately three-quarters of a mile deep by one and a half miles long being wiped out without the exception of a single house—killing 220 people.

They were trying for the station, but I don't think a miss ought to be as good as one and a half miles, or 220 civilians die the way that lot died. A kind of heavy explosive bomb was used, not the small thermite incendiary bomb, but one resulting in huge fires.

A party of us, including the Franks, Dr. Nettie, Dr. Mac, and an American military attaché, went over the whole of this area very shortly after the bombing, while the roads were still stinking heaps of hot soft ashes. The Colonel said he considered the bombs had contained sulphur and phosphorus.

Anyhow, the houses were wiped out, blackened, charred, and so were the majority of those corpses the Red Swastika monks. (Buddhists, great chaps) were digging out of the ruins.

Kid lying in the gutter, with a few leaves over him . . . head off, trunk blackened.

Little boy with the bone a beautiful clean white, snapped off and sticking up from the blackened skin.

An old woman of ninety, charred.

A man carrying by a girl's head, shoulders, and naked breasts, roasted red like a pig. There wasn't any more of her.

And the weeping It was the road of weeping. The women, tears streaming down their faces, filthy, distraught, going down on their knees and knocking their heads . . . if you'd only come to see *their* dead. They were already destitute, you see, they had lost their husbands or sons or other unconsidered trifles, and though they weren't consciously begging, they hoped with their streaming faces and all the fear of their bodies that now the God of the Christians was going to help.

Dragging at you. I went with one woman up a hill-side. There was her boy, lying face down in the dust, his face a little flattened against the dust. About eighteen, in coolie blue, with short-cut hair. His entrails were blown out, lying in coils in the dust, and over them crept the flies.

Some of the old Chinese Christians have taken shelter in the basement of the fine Memorial Church, which is damaged. One of them, very old, is unhurt, but keeps saying her stomach feels sick. Her share in this world's goods was one-half of a tiny room. She made her living picking up dropped coals and cinders on the railway tracks, selling them again. Out of this sparrow's bread she gave regularly to the upkeep of church, pastor, etc., has been doing so for many years, is probably doing so still.

The Chinese preacher, Pastor An, a young blue-gowned man, with ten children, was sheltering in a dug-out with his family. Just beside the dug-out is a very deep, narrow hole. One of us starts to pry into this. The Colonel: "Let that alone, you fool! Down there is an unexploded shell."

If the shell had exploded, Pastor An, wife, and offspring would undoubtedly have been blown sky-high.

Bats on the air, soft and fluttering, solid dark in liquid half-dark. Down the skies, lightning flickering. If that had come a few hours ago, real lightning, real wrath! Too late, Jehovah.

Q. Did anything else happen?

A. Yes. We went home, and in the candle-lit room, over food, told God our hearts were very heavy, but we knew He had done this for His glory, because otherwise He would not have done it.

Q. Have you any opinions of glory?

A. They don't matter.

Q. Did anything happen the next day?

A. Yes. Next day the ancient drum-tower was burning, and it was either on the 11th or the 12th, I forget which, that the worse damage was done to the new Memorial Church, which had already been badly knocked about. It was really a fine building, stone, with a big rose window and curving stairs. . . . The Americans claimed against the Japanese for total loss, which I don't think it was.

But that wasn't what Dr. Nettie was thinking about when she hurried along a half-dark road to see. Mr. Frank, who had been in Hsuchowfu nearly as long as herself, was with us, and she kept saying, holding his arm: "Oh, do you think his grave will be all right?"

That was her child's grave. It was untouched—a little stone slab in among bushes and quiet grass.

Mr. Fortunato was struck across the forehead by falling masonry in the big bombing of the day before. We met in a street, were hunted off by a *ching pao*, and took rickshas to get well down west of the town. We sat in a tea-shop and talked for the last time, and he gave money to a poor shivering devil of a soldier, half dead with malaria; we then went back to Dr. Nettie's, where he heard for himself the full account of the bombing.

He was pleased, because any damage done to foreign property in China makes news for the foreign press, while nobody cares a god-damn what happens to Chinese property, unless it's the Chinese. He sent out and got some good pictures, but they never reached Hankow.

The Hsuchowfu post office was still trying to function. But those pictures, with other mail, were still there when the Japanese came in. The Japanese ripped them up; a gentleman of our party (not Japanese) walked in when the sentries weren't looking, and retrieved the lot.

When last I saw him, Mr. Fortunato was just off for Nanshuchow, where a Roman Catholic mission had been bombed. Actual fighting, for which General Li Chung-jen had promised me a pass, was going on near there. I never got my pass, which hardly seems regrettable. Mr. Fortunato, who expected to be back in a few days, was lucky to get out alive.

By the way, our Hsuchowfu Roman Catholic mission, a Jesuit order, also got their packet of eight bombs on 16 May. Bishop Philippe Coté, sheltering in a basement, had plaster and masonry crash down over his head, and the whole place, when I saw it, looked like a battle-field.

Q. How were the various missions working for refugee purposes?

A. On the whole, very well, though they had their worries, which became much more serious during the next few days.

The arrangement was that the Roman Catholic and Presbyterian missions house protect and give medical aid to Chinese refugees of three classes—women, children, men over the age of fifty-five, who had never acted as combatants. Tokyo had agreed months before to recognize these camps, provided that, besides their national flags (American and French), they showed also the Blue Cross.

For some extraordinary reason, however, the missionaries seemed to have expected only a few hundred refugees; they got a few thousand, and to make matters worse, the bombing of the Catholic mission seriously upset accommodation plans. I'm not sure it was before or after this bombing that the Sisters associated with the Catholics were evacuated into the country until some considerable time after the occupation of Hsuchowfu. Naturally this made operations more difficult for Bishop Coté and his small company.

The Chinese Red Swastika monks had a responsibility almost heavier than the Christians. They had to feed the refugees and bury the dead.

Already there was a good deal of grain ingeniously hidden beneath dug-outs (about all those rabbit-holes were good for); more was distributed in village hiding-places, but getting it in proved no catch. Harvesting had begun, and continued in the face of almost continual air alarms. The Christian missions wanted to open the refugee camps, but the Buddhists resisted, saying that until the last possible moment not one single person must come in.

One day there was a scare that the whole Red Swastika organization had evacuated. So they had—they were blown out of their headquarters, remained away for the one day, reorganized, recamped, and were functioning again. When I left Hsuchowfu, they were still at work. They wore navy uniforms and caps, with the swastika stitched on. I need hardly mention that the Buddhist swastikas were no relation to Hitler's.

The missions settle policy and all important questions by joint meetings, at which all three organizations were represented.

A very serious difficulty, once the refugee camps filled up, was the appallingly bad water supply, never adequate for cleanliness, hardly sufficient for drinking purposes, and gritty, unhealthy water at best. No mission can be blamed for this. The good wells were all at a distance, and the Chinese water-bearers were, quite legitimately, afraid to go out and fetch it. This was hard on the wounded as well as the refugees. In addition, the refugees were nearly all housed in three-story school buildings—deathtraps, in the event of a serious fire. One place right under the nearest camp caught on the first day, but a Chinese bucket-brigade had it out in no time.

Q. What about medical and hospital arrangements?

A. Fair to disastrous. That they weren't still worse was a matter of luck. The Chinese, until the last fortnight or so, had maintained excellent Red Cross hospitals, with the result that though the American women's hospital was looking after a lot of bomb cases, the men's hospital had only an overflow of thirty-seven wounded Chinese soldiers, and all the rest were cared for by the Chinese. But once Hsuchowfu's fate was certain, the Save-the-Values policy was adopted, and these hospitals completely deserted by their staffs.

The Chinese still made great efforts to dress the wounds of their soldiers (Dr. Nettie and Chinese nurses from her hospital giving some help here), and to evacuate the wounded westwards. A party of young Chinese from Hankow, mostly medical students, did not withdraw, and were still in the city after the occupation. Their lives were in danger, especially as their leader was a cadet officer from Chiang Kai-shek's Whampoa Military Academy. I understand this young man telegraphed Chiang Kai-shek himself, and received the answer, 'Remain until the last possible moment, this is as important as any other military work.' But I don't believe the party were candidates for suicide; I think, like myself, they postponed 'the last possible moment,' and got cut off by the sudden break of the Lunghai line, southwest.

A second handicap in the functioning of mission hospitals and clinics was the complete destruction, by bombing, of the power plant. This cut off X-ray facilities, and all lighting but candles and lanterns. Our candles were severely rationed. Time and again, woken up after midnight, Dr. Nettie operated by lantern-light, or attended to some difficult confinement.

As the bombing became more severe, this night work increased. All day the Chinese were terrified to bring their sick and wounded any distance, and I don't blame them. Once the *ching pao* sounded, you were supposed to stop exactly where you were, even if you had no cover. Usually the young Chinese pickets were decent about that; but their actual military orders weren't to be decent—they were to shoot.

Dr. Nettie did have one major stroke of luck. On the last train which brought Hsuchowfu anything at all came her delayed consignment of medical supplies—a good deal of stuff, all in order except a few leaking bottles of castor oil. But, generally, the wounded soldiers' requirements, especially such things as splints, bandages, ether, morphine, cotton-wool, were cruelly and disastrously short.

We were lucky in having plenty of smallpox and other vaccine. Up till the time I left, there had been no serious epidemic, though the millet and corn gruel which was almost the sole diet in the refugee camps threatened a bad show with dysentery among herded women and children.

Q. Any special criticism?

A. One American man doctor, over sixty; one American woman doctor, seventy; two Chinese doctors, whom I didn't meet, and whose names I don't know, though I heard they stayed on in the city. An original population of at least 200,000 ; when I left, on 16 June, a refugee camp population of approximately 7300, living as I have described. I don't like this Savethe-

Values stuff. Anyhow, who *are* the Values? In wartime, the ordinary common or garden soldiers are my pick. Also, if the position inside an occupied city would have been too dangerous for Chinese doctors, or if their work might have been rendered useless by restrictions, what about sending a few doctors from the International Red Cross, to act equally at the service of Chinese and Japanese? I doubt if the Japanese could have afforded to kick: on a single day, I saw a number of their wounded estimated at 2000 come into Hsuchowfu, and those were just the beginning.

The young Chinese nurses (few of them even in their twenties) were aces. I was under a bed with one, in a gate-house full of dirty red paper lanterns and nothing else but this absurd cast-iron skeleton of a bed, on that last afternoon when, to add to the delights of bombing, Chinese and Japanese big guns were cracking at one another across the city.

Nurse Lee lay, every now and again peering out, to giggle. She was carrying a basket of medicine bottles, and got them back again to the American hospital, unbroken. If there weren't so many Miss Lees in China, even in Hsuchowfu, this might do for a belated bouquet. Anyhow, little Miss Lee . . . I haven't forgotten how you giggled.

Poor old Mrs. Ma, the stout hospital matron, who was simply run off her bound feet, had a slight stroke a few days before the occupation, but pulled around. By the way, Brownie, the large lady-dog without any pups (such an example to us all!) was nervous during air-raids, and the nurses, believing in the audibility of her great splay paws, made her very thick raid-sox, to muffle her. Brownie, sulky at first, finally took to this like curry-combing, and used to come whining for her sox when the 'planes began.

Under the stairs in Dr. Nettie's house was the favourite place for retreat when a bad raid arrived. There was a dug-out of sorts, just behind the hospital, but it was rather inaccessible, and nobody seemed to fancy it much.

Q. About dug-outs in general?

A. Oh, those. They weren't much worse than the tin umbrellas now sprouting in London backyards, but there's not a great deal to be said for them. They were this bad. If you put your top end in, your bottom end stayed out. Thousands of such clay holes were scooped in the old execution grounds, in yards, even in the streets.

I hope I've given a clear picture of the crazy-cobblement and circuitous ways of those streets. One straight, broad road did cut through from the Clock Tower to the station. After that the fun began. About three years before, the cobbles had been flattened out a little, but the general plan wasn't altered. I think I could count the number of Chinese automobiles I saw there on both hands.

I did see one dug-out that looked high, wide, and handsome—General Li Chung-jen's, near a little pavilion at his military headquarters. By some miracle, headquarters was never bombed. Summing up the dug-outs, give me a willow bough, or some lovely green wheat.

Q. How would you describe the mental state of the people generally?

A. Restive, shaky, scared, still humorous, not yet disposed to real mass flight. When that came, it was quickly over, leaving no time for the common symptoms of panic—incendiarism, looting, and so forth.

And the Chinese organization in that city was good. On the evening of 13 May, there was a grand torchlight procession and an open-air meeting at the Sun Yat-sen Memorial, mainly for *recruiting* purposes. Recruiting, when for days our skies had been just one bombing 'plane after another, and one very short-ranged anti-aircraft gun to answer back! Round-headed kids plunging torches about, officers shouting gallantly from the platform, and the only musical instrument available, an elderly victrola, offering the crowd, 'Chi-lai, Chi-lai!' Then the harsh, bitter-sweet wailing of a sing-song girl. The little red plums of torch-ends dropping from their twigs.

God, it was weird! Dr. Nettie and I were the only foreigners present, invited by a Mr. Pao, a young staff officer of Li Chung-jen's. He had been at Geneva for years, and spoke far better English than I do. His wife, he said, was an authoress, now in Hong Kong.

Everybody, including the missionaries, was extraordinarily optimistic. (I was never even told that the missionaries had made refugee camp arrangements with Tokyo . . . or not until it was rather late in the day.) From all accounts, Hsuchowfu was to be defended both with a necessary force of Chiang Kai-shek's best, and with attacking 'planes.

We all knew that however brave the existing forces might be, reinforcements were needed. There weren't any Chinese tanks, and stories of the Japanese tanks were Hsuchowfu table-talk.

As late as 17 May, young Mr. Wong, the husband of our girl soldier, whose swollen knees were still resting upstairs in the women's hospital, and who himself was in close contact with General Li Chung-jen's staff officers, came in elated, with a definite report that Generalissimo Chiang Kai-shek had sent word: 'Hold out till the t8th, reinforcements will arrive!'

It was afternoon. We looked at one another, and said: "It's the 17th already."

Poor young Wong! His eyes were shining under his eternal, odd Panama hat. I don't know anyone in Hsuchowfu who was in a more damnable position than he, and in the course of another day it became still worse. There was not only the fact that he had his crippled wife and little Lo Ti on his hands. (He had made one attempt at getting them away, but all the conveyances were gone, and after hobbling about three miles, she broke down. When he brought her back to the hospital, she said only two words, heartrending words: "I'm spoiled.") Besides that, his close association with general staff was a terrible danger in the event of occupation. I don't know precisely what his game in Hsuchowfu had been, but I can guess. He was a member, anyhow, of the progressive societies in Hankow, and once, in a moment of despair, said to me: "Too many people know me round here."

Summing up, I think the state of Hsuchowfu's nerves was very shaky; but except for those bombed and starving, few despaired. Before 17 May, many thousands of refugees had fled, but most remained in the nearer villages, ready to come back if Chinese luck changed. Those whose little huts hadn't been wrecked or burned carefully fastened the doors with big wooden bars.

I saw Japanese soldiers, on the hunt, smash open those doors, one by one, along our little Chinese street.

Military precautions were tightened up, though in no way affecting the foreigners. On the last day, over one hundred spies were shot. Again I felt this was either too late, or a mistake.

Q. Aircraft and anti-aircraft defences?

A. That was rather interesting. Hsuchowfu had no anti-aircraft defences worth mentioning. No 'plane ever flew less blithely on its way because of anything the people below could tell it, and I've explained about the dug-outs.

In the absence of defences, there were the Chinese pickets, of whom I speak from personal experiences. One had to decide whether to stay indoors or to risk the *ching pao*. There was little enough that I could do at the hospital, unfortunately. So for a part of every day I went out on the streets, to see and hear everything possible.

The pickets were young soldiers, just kids, with tin hats, rifles, bayonets, and Mausers. Those big Mausers were the most accurate shooting equipment the Chinese had, the sighting on every other kind of gun, big or middle-sized, being as wild as a turkey. Along guarded streets were small waist-high embankments of sand-bags. These weren't for the pickets, who had no cover. They were for possibly innocent pedestrians.

Outside headquarters, I have sat more or less comfortably squeezed behind such a refuge, while a picket child-soldier, carefully removing and concealing my hat because he thought it too visible, then (in case I should be scared to death) reached down his hand to me. He and his mate, a few yards down the street, cracked mild comments at one another, while above, in beautiful dual formation, came flying the black crows and the white falcons.

Those were the colours used . . . dead black, silvery white, and on both the Rising Sun: they never came all at once, but in two flights, or more. They flew as low as they liked—what had they got to stop them? And you never saw anything more beautiful, or more heart-breaking, but that's beside the point.

The fleet that day numbered sixty 'planes. They were looking for headquarters, crossing, re-crossing, circling. They were coming daily, in fleets of from thirty to sixty 'planes, though one day Hsuchowfu had the honour of a visit from two hundred of them. A lot of their flying looked like sport. Beautiful exhilarating sport it must have been, the god's way of riding wind and sun, stars and moons shooting past.

This was intimidation—getting on the people's nerves without wasting too many bombs. But when they bombed, they bombed.

They got a Chinese Red Cross hospital, formerly packed, but then housing only a few poor devils left behind. Those were mostly finished off. The street leading to the Catholic mission was one mass of uptorn cobbles, boulders, wildly tangled telegraph wires. Against this glory, against the coming of these lords, who owned the skies and could do what they liked with them, stood looking up, cracking jokes and grinning across at one another, nothing more impressive than Hsuchowfu's kid-soldier pickets.

Q. Did you ever do anything like work?

A. Very little. Learned to vaccinate Chinese kids, but the supply, unfortunately, gave out. Helped to dress the wounds of some soldiers; they got bayoneted by the Japanese next day. Saw bomb-cases; I was slow, though, having no training and no Mandarin. Wrote articles until and after the postal system collapsed. When the real crash came, I tried to employ young Mr. Wong (girl soldier wife, little Lo Ti for daughter) as my interpreter. I could only have paid him about a couple of dollars a week, I hadn't enough to offer the missionaries a decent board for myself, but I thought that the small degree of protection offered might be just better than none at all.

However, the missionaries wouldn't hear of it. They were now terrified of their girl soldier, because she had worn a uniform; equally of Wong, because *he* had worn a uniform. (Wong, by the way, was the one who took the trouble to come at midnight, 14 May, and warn us of the breaking of the Lunghai line.)

Anyhow, seeing there was no chance for himself, he asked the hospital to keep his wife and child in safety. They refused, because he couldn't produce a financial guarantee. (I don't suppose many of the young students so ardent about their patriotism had a penny behind them.)

Every Chinese patient in the mission hospitals, every person entering the refugee camps, was supposed to pay up or to have a guarantor. So I was informed by one of the mission staff.

Apart from Wong's penury, I think it was his wife's uniform —formerly the mission's pride—which turned the scales. At midday, 18 May—less than twenty-four hours before the Japanese army occupied Hsuchowfu— Wong carried Lo Ti out of the green hospital gates, a bundle on his back; Mrs. Wong, limping, limping, limping. They were making for Hankow. I gave them a card to Edith, to be presented if they got through, but the card never appeared.

However, that is again beside the point, except that I not only failed to help the unlucky tribe of Wong, but got myself disliked for it.

Fortunately we were all too busy to spend much time on likes or dislikes. The same afternoon we were dressing the wounds of castaways whose filthy mats, dumped in an empty school-house, were alive with maggots.

I used my shoes to tread on the things—then thought, with sudden clearness: 'These shoes were bought for walking in the streets of Kobe.'

Feeding refugees is a funny, ordinary, little job with some amusement in it. They bring their rice-bowls, mothers, children, old men, and the game is to scrape down the sides of the bucket with your huge wooden spoon, scrape again and again, extracting every lump. Then, perhaps, the rice-bowls are filled twice, instead of once.

The kids are lovely, and besides that, my not knowing Mandarin is actually a bit of an attraction. When Mr. Liu the Good tries to teach me a few sentences, and I use them, infants, male and female, stand about with their tummies protruding, sing-songing: "I-don't-speak-Chin-ese!"

They never got tired of this. It's too awkward at the Sunday services on the lawn. I don't like going, but go. And always a bunch of bad infants, wriggling about, chant in whispers, "I-don't-speak-Chinese!" The red bag, dangling at the end of the long stick, is poked under the noses of refugee Chinese by Christian Chinese. From Dr. Mac's hospital a few of the wounded soldiers, awkward and bulky in their white hospital jackets, have come over on their crutches. I don't notice whether or not they drop something into the collection bag.

Q. Why stay in Hsuchowfu?

A. The Japanese, through dropped leaflets and also through some prisoners, had said that if they couldn't take Hsuchowfu on 15 May, they would go back to Japan. Not a very truthful people, I'm afraid. Anyhow, we knew there was no chance of their taking Hsuchowfu on 15 May, but Dr. Nettie and I both thought there might be a terrific bombardment on that day. I decided to wait until 15 May passed by.

As a matter of fact, on 15 May we never heard the *ching pao* until evening, when eight 'planes came back from bombing the Hsiaohsien road. But at midnight on 14 May we heard, through young Wong, of the breaking of the Lunghai line.

All vehicles, especially the rickshas with the big copper butterflies on their backs, incontinently vanished. No other train left Hsuchowfu. Walking was the one way out, and at the time I didn't think I could walk the several hundreds of miles involved—though later I changed my mind, and tried it.

In addition to my pass from the Generalissimo, General Li Chung-jen gave me a safe conduct through the Chinese lines, in case a chance came when I could use it. It was all he could do, and really I can't see that anything was to blame, except the lamentable haste of the Japanese.

What did they get by it? The Chinese had dug huge pits, like lion-traps, here and there outside the city, and the Japanese were in such a hurry that on 17 May seven of their green tanks lumbered into the pits, where the Chinese overwhelmed them—sheer weight and courage of man against machine.

To come back to myself, there was nothing I could do, for the moment, but wait. Even the ranks of Tuscany (ourselves) didn't forbear to cheer, though, when Hsuchowfu's Chinese bankers (who commandeered the last lorry, and hadn't a spare seat) saved the bank's specie, after a wild run through to Hankow.

The Franks bagged a donkey for flour-grinding, maize-grinding; unfortunate moke working a twenty-four-hour shift. I think we acquired a donkey later. Certainly we acquired the refugees, especially old Mr. Hsu, our milkman.

Old Mr. Hsu arrived, bringing a very large family and kids, a huge belligerent white nanny-goat and her kids, an old lady with her fortune in the shape of two pigs, and a very fair response in poultry. The Hsus' personal kids climbed the trees and broke them off in bits, the Hsus' other kids ate all the leaves and flowers.

And the din!

Hollyhocks, gendarmes with dark red hats, concealed my sword: which, however, I took away before the occupation, and disposed of in a less compromising and more secure resting-place.

Mr. Han, a young Chinese mission teacher, who reached Hsuchowfu only to be injured by bomb wreckage the moment he went indoors (thus losing all his baggage and acquiring a blood-soaked head-bandage) remarked to me: "Do you know, this is interesting. In English, a hen clucks, a sheep bleats, a kitten mews, a dog barks, a cow moos, and so on. But in Chinese, everything yells. A chicken yells, a goat yells, a cow yells, a bird yells, and so on."

In the mission compound, Mr. Han was surely right.

The missionaries were all proud of him. He was tall, well-dressed, good-looking. The Japanese hardly got into Hsuchowfu before they offered Mr. Han a decent job in a Ta-tao office, which he, greatly to his credit, refused.

Yes: but I was jealous of him, for the sake of poor Mr. Wong, who was not a Christian but merely a Chinese; Chinese enough, probably, to go out and get his throat cut, or be burnt up in one of the villages, along with his crippled wife and Lo Ti.

On the afternoon of 18 May the city stank of burning uniforms, as the remnants of trapped or wounded soldiers tried to get rid of incriminating evidence. Mr. Frank consulted General Li Chung-jen as to the feasibility of transferring both missions to the hill-sides, to escape from the racking shellfire. But they gave it up as a bad job.

Chinese observers had literally seen the balloon, or balloons, go up. Four huge green sausages, gently swaying from mooring-ropes, and on them glaring visible the spot of the Rising Sun. In the street outside the hospitals five wounded soldiers in hospital jackets, apparently part-recovered men, turned out lest they endanger the others, hobbled about, be-crutched, be-bandaged. They were hopeless, but quite uncomplaining. Another, tearing open his jacket, showed his swollen belly: he was a bad case of malaria.

One queer thing happened at dusk, while refugees were still leaving. Down the cobbled street slanted past us the huge, mangy gold figure of a camel. Dr. Nettie gripped my arm.

"It's the first camel I've seen in Hsuchowfu, in all my thirty-eight years."

We slept: or else we lay down, and felt doped. Kept thinking, with disproportionate anger and misery, about the Wongs, and of those soldiers whose wounds we had dressed. They lay on clean mats now, with two old men to look after them in the night: but the first thing the incoming Japanese did was to bayonet them, and God knows, left out on the battle-fields for days, their fractures still unset, pus running from wounds crusted with a green glaze of flies, those men might have wrung pity from anything calling itself human.

"Two days ago, I was a fine, big man. Look at me now!" That one had both his eyes blinded, and the worst was, we hadn't enough water left to sponge the infected blood and filth from his body and face.

"Cursed be the hand that fired the shot. . . ."

A lot of gunfire very early, rifles now, as well as the bigger stuff. The Franks had arranged to go out from their badly-exposed compound and meet the Japanese, showing the American and Blue Cross flags. I don't know whether they did or not. First, I watched while the cook-boys burned my uniform and other things—it would have been unfair to keep them longer, in case of a house-to-house search—then went upstairs and made lint swabs. I was making lint swabs, like the well-conducted maiden cutting bread-and-butter, when the Japanese entered the city.

In the end curiosity got the better of me, and I went down and watched through the hospital gates' excellent cracks. Sturdily-built, shortish, red-tabbed soldiers, first on the rangy Australian cavalry horses, then marching in a great company, next at least twenty green caterpillar tanks (there may have been more, before I came down, but I'm certain about the twenty), then more cavalry. A taggle of foot-soldiers came after, smashing in little Chinese doors, fixing up what appeared to be a telephone wire. In its way, this finale was a relief; though almost unbearable when they routed out one old Chinese civilian from his childish hiding-place.

'Maybe they aren't going to do anything to him,' I thought,

Maybe they weren't.

Dr. Nettie was in the hospital, looking after her women. After a time we went up to the attic, and in turn climbed to the top window, watching the smokes of incendiary fires lighted *after* the occupation. We counted eight smokes.

It was a fine day. The observation balloons still swung there, glistening green. For some hours, three bombers straddled the Hsiaohsien pass, not circling, just sounding crash after crash, bombing the fleeing remnants of Chinese soldiers. I hope the little picket-soldiers got off, they were so good.

Q. The foreign population were perfectly safe?

A. Perfectly. Didn't they have their arrangement with Tokyo? But that night—19 May—five or six drunken Japanese soldiers broke into the refugee camp directly behind the women's hospital, dragged out an eighteen-year-old Chinese girl, and raped her in the alley. Dr. Nettie and I went across, with young Mr. Han.

It was pitch-dark. At first the puzzle was: 'Find your Japanese.' When we found one, he was squatting down in a dark corner of the grounds, pointing his rifle at us, and he wasn't a man with a sense of humour. Not finding him polite, we left. Then we ran into the rest, who were rather excitable, and, of course, spoke no English.

One of them slightly cut Dr. Nettie's hand with his bayonet. I don't think he meant to, I think he was a drunken man with a bayonet, who wanted to wave it around. But as easily as not, he might have planked it through the doctor's middle.

"You mustn't do that," I remarked, with imbecile distinctness. "This is a very old lady." Another big Japanese then became affectionate with me, in a drunken way. But Mr. Han, with real courage, went out, grabbed a Japanese officer, and got him into the compound, where the officer induced the brethren to leave.

This was too late to make much difference to the Chinese girl in the alley, though Japanese soldiers obligingly went and fetched her back.

I should like to say that in Hsuchowfu I never heard on reliable authority that any of these outrages were committed where officers were near enough to have intervened, and also that after the first night the missions were treated well enough. But just one slip of that drunken oaf's bayonet, and the chances are that every foreigner in Hsuchowfu would have been murdered. To kill one, and leave the other seven hanging about, would have been too silly, especially when everything could have been blamed on the common scapegoat, 'retreating Chinese soldiers.'

Q. What was the general significance of Hsuchowfu?

A. It was a Chinese key-position, well defended for far longer than anyone, Chinese, Japanese or foreign, had expected. Later, it became the starting-point of a strategic retreat, whence an army of at least 200,000 soldiers escaped the Japanese trap.

That word retreat! Of course any fool can see there's no such thing as leaving Hsuchowfu. Hsuchowfu is China's.

CHAPTER FIVE

Harvest Bird

YOU ARE LOOKING very well to-day.

Thank you. You look well yourself.

Yes, we're all beginning to feel like ourselves again. But look at you! believe you must have grown at least another inch since the last rains. At one time I thought they would never come.

I haven't grown any taller myself, my time for growing is well over; but the child must have grown, it feels so heavy. Perhaps it will be born to-day. I do feel remarkably well, ready now to face anything. I, too, was worried over the late rains.

Now it's full sun-up. What a colour you have, a real sun-colour, amber and dark brown, and with the jewels the sun hangs in your precious ears! Wheat, you are looking very Chinese to-day.

What else should we look? Listen, they've begun. It's a sweet noise, I like it, the noise of the big scythes in the centre of the field, working nearer. I suppose that is how the bees' murmuring sounds to the flower. The men are working hard. Yesterday the noise was away at the far end of the field, but now, if everything goes well, they may reach this corner before nightfall.

Then we'll be cut down.

As if that mattered! After that our children will be born, our sons and daughters, the grain.

I shall only have a daughter, ignorant and ugly, but you will certainly have a fine son.

You are laughing at me. But taken all together, I certainly think we give them a good field. To-morrow, perhaps you and I will be threshed out, and lie with our heads together under the stone, while the donkey marches round and round in darkness.

Yes . . . sometimes it seems a pity. You look very handsome where you are. A shame that you should be cut down!

If we don't have our children, how do you suppose we can feed the people who planted us and are cutting us down? It is almost wicked, the way you talk, but I know you don't mean it.

Men, men, always to feed men! Are they the only ones? Doesn't it sometimes seem to you a trivial destiny?

And if we don't feed men, whom do you suppose will sow the next crop of wheat? You are getting confused. You must see that the whole thing lies in the wheat. The trouble is, men don't plant half enough wheat, and also, owing to droughts and other troubles, our children aren't as fine and strong as they ought to be. The thing for us to do is to feed the men without the slightest complaining: the more of us there are, and the better, the stronger the men will grow. Then they can plant more and more wheat.

What good will that do?

The men will grow taller and stronger in every way, and have good sons and daughters themselves, just as we need to do. Then they will plant still more wheat. Perhaps this very field, though it has had such a hard time, and was certainly nothing to boast about a few years ago, may produce wheat as fine as any in the world, and the best grain.

Taller wheat, taller men. So that's all we are supposed to know.

It's all we need know, but there is another thing. Often we used to hear the trains on the railway track. They run to another place, down in south fields, not a wheat country but a country for rice and millet, and there the people who come out to the railway trains sell little patties, made in the dirt. On one side a character says 'Ground,' and on the other, another character says 'Sky.' That is what we do not know, but there is some meaning in it, ground and sky. It's what we are all made of, men and wheat. Not that I want to claim any monopoly for wheat, the millet has done as well as ourselves this year, and look at the bean-shoots, already climbing.

Yes, the bean is always pushing. Can't wait to see us fall, before he sings out: "Look at me! I'm alive, climbing!"

Well, you know, these little fellows, when they are creeping along the ground in our shadow, can't really believe that they will ever have their own time of growing, and their own say in affairs. They grow quieter as they grow higher. Besides, the crops are in rotation, it isn't as if they interfered with our grain.

Then you don't ever feel, 'I'd like to put out my foot and stamp on that cock-a-hoop?'

The summer would have a bad time quarrelling with the autumn. We all need one another too much to start arguments.

Stop talking, listen to the scythes, they are so near. If this is our last day, I am glad it was like this . . . so warm, so golden. That old fellow in blue has brought out his water-bottle, and the cracked earthenware bowl that he will tip up and drink, trying to cool himself with brackish water when the sun is right overhead. But why aren't the women working in the fields, as they always do?

Because they are afraid. You know that, as well as I do.

Yes, I have nostrils, like anyone else. One doesn't like to think of it, and if I could, I would always stand looking the other way. He has lain there now three days, poor fellow. Why don't the harvesters come and take him away?

Well, they are mostly old men, and they feel afraid of getting into an argument. Then, after dark, when they shut the doors of their huts, they never know just what is going to happen, and the world outside seems strange to them, as if it had been all changed by water. You know how it seemed to us, until we found the wheat could keep on growing. But men take longer to get used to things than wheat. Soon they will know their way about again, in darkness or light, and when they do it will be their own way, not anybody else's way. We are the wheat, and people may think: 'Those peasants are too ignorant to know anything!' But we know our way about.

Look how he lies. His blue clothes are torn and bloody, and the flesh, which was our colour a few days ago, is a horrible colour. Ants and beetles scurry in little black streams into the pits of his nostrils and throat. I suppose you will say: "It is all right, he has only been cut down?"

No, not in his case. Can't you see how young he is? How could such a boy have done his work in the world? It is not good, it is the most terrible, the most criminal thing on earth, when the young are cut down before they have borne their fruit and given of their seed. But since he couldn't do it in that way, he does all he can. That body you seem to despise is coming back to earth. He is given to ground.

What of sky?

The sky is a big ear. It hears and records a lot. But that is none of our business.

What about the others, who did it? The people who make our people afraid, because our people are women now, or mostly helpless and old?

They will think they are right, and know they were wrong. They will justify themselves completely, and the man who does that accuses himself. He is his own prosecutor and his own defence, and when he has done clamouring, there is the wheat to judge him, and the testament of ground and sky. It is true those others have had a difficult time. They are a sun people, like ourselves, but beneath them burns the savage, destructive fire of the volcano. It is very hard to be trapped between two burnings, two mighty passions, but only those people themselves can find a cure for that, and they will not find it by defiling another man's wheat.

Let us be tired, let us forget to pretend that we have voices or thoughts, and sink into our own speech, the slow rustling murmur of many laden heads, meeting the keener voice of the scythes. Can't you hear the harvest bird calling, early this year? He never forgets to come to China. Some of our people say he sings: "Work now, work now," but others say it is "Worship now." I will be wise for once, I will tell you what you are going to say. You are going to say "There is no difference, Ground is written on one side and Sky on the other."

Go to the green gate, persuade the old silvery-shaven doorkeeper to open it, step out, nod to the Japanese sentries, whose uniforms are woollen and a pretty good colour, with red tabs and yellow flannel stars on the shoulders. They have also large bayonets on their rifles, but usually they are good-tempered, and let you go without argument to the corner. Turn the corner of the alley, and you find some more sentries, and after those the first shop opened up again in Hsuchowfu, a barber's, which also acts as a teashop. The Japanese, both officers and soldiers, are continually in need of a barber, for instead of shaving their heads bare, like the Chinese, or else growing it thick and long, they have what I am sorry to say is very like a prison crop . . . run close all over the skull without any parting, and in too short a bristle for you to be able to see what kind of hair it is, good, bad, or indifferent.

Their features, though, vary a great deal, though they are generally classified as types by people who have been in Japan.

If you say anything about a Japanese, they ask at once: "Was he an Aquiline or a Flat-face?"

Flat-face sounds ugly, and isn't; the Flat-faces are nearly always (though not without exception) the best-looking, with smooth skins, not so dark as the Aquilines; also they are the gentlest and best-educated, the only ones who speak or understand a word of English. The fable about the Japanese being superb linguists is purest nonsense: the English are bad enough, but the Japanese are worse than the English. One would have thought, if they were going to have a war with the Chinese, they might at least have spent a few sen learning the language, but they can no more make themselves understood by the Chinese than they can by the foreigners. Another thing about Flat-faces *v.* Aquilines is that the Flat-faces in Hsuchowfu all seemed to be young men, as young as the majority of Chinese soldiers. But the Aquilines, with their strong noses, dark skins, small wiry build and challenging looks, equally seemed to be veterans; a fair number wear heavy whiskers and beard, and as the Japanese whisker and beard is not merely jet-black, but also comes out in the world's cornpletest wiry frizz, they look no canary-birds.

But the Aquilines aren't all so tough. Major Fujita was an Aquiline, whiskers and beard complete, and I rather liked our Major Fujita, though most of the others did not. Possibly these hirsute growths made the Aquilines look older than they were, for Major Fujita, who came from Tokyo and belonged to the Soong (Pine Tree) Company of Foot-Soldiers, told me that he was thirty-eight. He looked ten years older than that, and nearly all the heavily-bearded men looked between forty and fifty years of age.

Besides these two, there was a third type, not numerous, quite different, and not so good-looking as either, perhaps because of the mop of greasy black hair tumbling to the shoulders. They had small features, and were fairly light in colour. I think these may have been Manchurian or Korean members of the Pacification Corps which followed on the heels of the army, and set up at once, with the jobs of winning over the citizens (those they could catch) popularizing the old Five-Barred Flag, de-popularizing Generalissimo Chiang Kai-shek, and also opening a Japanese refugee camp for Chinese, as a rival to the foreign refugee camps. This was another idea not very popular with the Chinese, who said that whatever the Pacification Corps might intend, the soldiers took no notice of them.

Incidentally, although those picturesque hair-crops did take a little getting used to, the only two Long-Crops (that will do for a name) that I ever talked with were both not only exceptionally polite, but exceptionally interesting young men. One of them was the station-master at Taihan. He couldn't quite believe in a woman without a degree (in China, also, many women are Doctors of Medicine, Law, Philosophy, and what not), so to please him I gave myself an honorary doctorate of Philosophy. I was feeling philosophic at the time, for many reasons. It was a rash bet. He talked me under the table in about five minutes, and I could only save myself by saying over and over again, with an agonized look: "Yes: will you please tell me, where is the toilet? Yes. Please, tell me where is the toilet?" He was a little injured. I still have his card.

Once past this little barber's shop, where there were always a score of soldiers lounging about in the back-tilted chairs, being luxuriously barbered by an old Chinese whose ancient razor must have harboured a multitude of sins, and drinking little cups of their black sweet tea, the going was usually easy.

Turn down a filthy cobbled alley (where I saw one of the few opium-smokers, an old man who sat laughing with his white hair blowing about in the wind, quite crazy) look warily at the wary people who are beginning to creep back to their gardens, most of them wearing the Red Spot armlets; turn again to the creek, cross the rickety bridge.

You are now at the place where we cheered the Pihsien soldiers. On one side is the hospital where Chinese wounded men had a bad time when the Japanese bombed it: the building must still have been worth taking over, for now the Japanese themselves have a military hospital up there.

On the other hand, the bridge crosses the green and scummy creek where an ancient peasant woman slaps at her washing, grumbling loudly. There is a cluster of houses and small shops near-by, and though the shops aren't open, Japanese soldiers always hang about them, watching with no friendly eye. In the hospital alley, they've got used to us all, and sometimes, even when they are practising martial law and the street bristles with bayonets, hand us along, only saying something like "Man-man-ti, man-man-ti," which I take to be "Slowly," or "Carefully."

But these others, typically, are very suspicious. I like that, feeling quite glad to be hated, and to hate back.

Cross the bridge, meet a young Japanese soldier who is playing with a Chinese kid, and has a hollyhock in front of his tin hat. Yes: but what about the beggar-woman in Hsuchowfu, pressing the crumbling rose against her withered old face?

There is a sentry posted next, whose duty it is to search the Chinese (sometimes the foreigners) in case they are going to kill the cat. Two old Chinese men in front hang back nervously, waiting for me to catch them up: killing Chinese in front of a foreigner is bad, because the foreigner reports it.

If you don't think Chinese get killed (and without provocation) the Wan Tzu Hui (Red Swastika) men, who pick up and bury the bodies whenever they can, are the people to tell you about that. Fourteen in one day, and the youngest with his head kicked in, battered to death by soldiers' boots.

The Chinese have nothing in their baskets, and the Japanese sentry lets them pass. Just behind that sentry lies the field where the Chinese used to keep their transport lorries. It was never bombed successfully until the last day; now nine great green Japanese guns, long and heavy, point their snouts at the sky. They are always there, covered partly by tarpaulins, but each day I count them, to see that one hasn't been moved, because it seems that if only their whereabouts could be known outside, and if a surprise attack of bombing 'planes were feasible . . .

And this is the old execution ground, where the grave-mounds are now green, and the *yang liu* green, and I can sit on a grave-mound for a moment, thinking, how funny all that is! Plots and plans, plans and plots! You would do this, you will do that; but as a matter of fact you can't do anything.

Just in the gully are the last bits of the three dead people I met, the first time I came this way. Two men had been carrying a woman on a stretcher. She was underneath the stretcher, but her legs and part of her body stuck out. The others were swollen black, their blind heads full of maggots. I went back to a sentry, pointed them out, and tried by gesture to indicate that they ought to be buried, but he only grinned.

Anyhow, it wasn't necessary. Either the dogs, or quick action of decay itself, got rid of them. The execution ground is full of fat slinking dogs. There is nothing to worry about in a few scattered bones, one of them a human jawbone.

Nothing but hard and insolent eyes . . . nothing but the silvery light on the under-faces of the swinging leaves. Time to go on. The road turns bright and sunny, yellow, Hsuchowfu's true colour, with a weedy stream full of croaking, bubbling frogs on one hand, and on the other the partly harvested fields, where the harvesters move slowly about, and the harvest bird, a child of the cuckoo tribe, sings in Chinese: "Work now!" or "Worship now!"

There are a few old grave-mounds, one real hill. This I climb, restlessly, sitting down under a mimosa whose brushes are beginning to colour. There is no clover in this grass, but there are small pink and yellow vetches, running wild like a very young child's laughter, and later on, at the Franks' place, masses of coreopsis and sunflowers.

"Worship now!" But if I could only work out a whole sentence, a whole thought; I can't, any ability to write leaves me completely, dragged down into caverns by the savage eddies of dream.

It is getting better in the city now, but worse in the villages. We know that, both from reliable Chinese, and from Mr. Frank, who goes out almost every day into the country, taking the little car with the American flag and some Red Swastika men, who collect hidden grain, radishes, fruit, and once even some meat.

We've had no butter, sugar, eggs, meat, floury things, for weeks, and not many vegetables. Our cook-boy is a very good, faithful boy, but none of the mission boys will put on the Red Spot armlet, and in their Blue Cross ones they don't feel safe on the streets. I'd love to go on these country trips, but am never allowed. In the first place, they want men who can carry things. Besides that . . .

They are all working hard. I think Mr. Frank's job is the most dangerous; there's always a chance on those lonely roads that he might run into something he wasn't meant to see. On the other hand, Dr. Mac has thirty-seven wounded soldiers on his mind, and though Major Fujita says they will not be murdered, he also says they must not be discharged without his knowledge. What happens when their wounds and fractures heal up?

We all know that through the agency of that filthy little spy, Mr. Liu the Bad, a Japanese-bought native of Tienstin, the Japanese were on the trail of a wounded man in the hospital, said to be a high-up officer in disguise. But a few nights back, one man escaped over the walls. He wasn't an amputation case, so unless they strip him, how will they know? They can't strip all Hsuchowfu.

"Now," said Major Fujita, more in patience than in anything else. "Of course, he will be caught, and, of course, he will get shot. If any of the others try the same thing, of course they *will* be shot. We cannot guard the whole of these walls at once."

But the wounded man, soldier or officer, got clean away, and for the first time since we saw the Pihsien soldiers go through, we felt like cheering. All the same, this makes things harder for Dr. Mac, who is worried and down-hearted. The almost constant presence of Mr. Liu, hanging about frightening the servants and even the nurses with his questions, is no encouragement for the persons responsible to be anything else.

Dr. Nettie simply continues with work, night and day, heartbreaking work. The nights are the worse. She can't get out for walks, as at first, because she will not leave the women's hospital. That is for fear of the Japanese. As a matter of fact, within the hospital premises, and referring strictly to those Japanese who came there, there have been no difficulties worth mentioning after the first night.

Major Fujita turned up, with his black frizz, apparently pacific intentions, and solemn demeanour. The first time he and his staff went into the hospital premises, all the nurses got down on their knees and started praying for dear life . . . not to him, of course, but to God.

The Major was taken aback.

"What are they doing?" he demanded. Dr. Nettie told him, "They are praying, Major . . . they are all afraid of you."

The Major's lips twitched a little.

"Oh," he said. "Tell them they must not do that, they mustn't!"

That was all very well, as far as he was concerned. Dr. Nettie then took him (and two Japanese doctors) through the ward where the raped Chinese women and girls lay, some of them savaged by gangs of men, some waiting to see whether they would have a baby. I don't think the Major stayed very long. He came and he saw, but there are places where one cannot expect to make any further conquests.

For the rest, our Japanese visitors were unfailingly civil, though a bit long-winded. They came partly to practise their English, partly out of curiosity, partly because they were in love with Dr. Nettie's good piano. On this they insisted on playing rather home-made little songs of patriotism, which the children sang in their schools. They all had snapshots of their homes, their gardens, their Fujiyama, and usually of a wife and children.

But the word about Dr. Nettie's piano nearly brought her very bad luck. A high-up Japanese General was shortly coming to visit Hsuchowfu. He was intensely musical, and never travelled anywhere without, a trained musician, a Professor of Music, a graduate at the University of Tokyo.

Desperate perplexity of the Japanese: where in Hsuchowfu would they get him a piano? Their hints became louder and louder. Dr. Nettie at last agreed to lend them hers, for a few days; it was retained for a few weeks, and when *her* hints about its return became louder and louder, that was not so good. She did get it back, but scratched, and without even a card of acknowledgment.

Before this, they had tried to bag the mission car, which bore Mr. Frank about, with one large American flag stuck in front and another painted on top.

But the loss of the car would have been awful. Mr. Frank had the courage to refuse, after which he was not quite so popular with the Japanese. The petrol situation was desperate at both missions. Before the fall, the Roman Catholic mission, whose car was just a baby, borrowed a couple of gallons from the Americans. After the fall, they drove up to return it.

"How much have you got left?" asked Mr. Frank. They showed him . . . about a pint.

They were sent back with their two gallons intact, and perhaps later the Japanese may have replenished them. *They* had plenty of petrol. The number of automobiles they brought into Hsuchowfu's impossible streets, not counting the tanks, but counting lorries, heavy cars, and small staff cars, all painted muddy brown instead of China's muddy green, was really remarkable. When I told a famous Chinese lady in Hong Kong about that, she objected, "But they couldn't have. . . . Hsuchowfu has no such streets!"

Hsuchowfu, before the fall, had such streets that if a car wanted to get out from an alley, it might have to toot its horn for ten minutes before the rickshas and pedestrians allowed it, at dead slow rates, to proceed. Hsuchowfu after the fall had streets still worse, many of them torn up, though automobile traffic had now this huge advantage . . . ricksha traffic was completely at a standstill, and the few Chinese pedestrians crept quietly, listlessly, about the streets. But partly counter-balancing that was the large number of cavalry soldiers, and the continual tank movements through the city, both east and west . . . this last feature proving beyond doubt that our little city, though isolated from its war, was still very near its war.

Internal preparations showed that even more clearly. The Chinese had never had barbed wire in their streets. Many streets in Hsuchowfu were now a mass of barbed wire entanglements.

From the Catholic mission we got our first news of guerilla activities, and it was straight, because two priests, in their little car, had run slap into it. At a small spot called Pehsien (where they were probably attending to parishioners) they came to a gate, where to their amazement they were faced by some Chinese soldiers and a machine-gun. Instantly the machine-gun began to pop, the soldiers, of course, having mistaken the Catholic baby car for one of the slick little Japanese staff cars.

The priests wasted no time in explanations. They did a lightning twist, and beat it up the road. We were sorry to hear they had been in danger, but so pleased about the guerillas.

The first time Mr. Frank had his car with the flags out in the streets, he wrote down in his diary: 'City 100 per cent looted. Not a shutter unbroken, though I drove everywhere in car with American flag. Many bodies lying in the streets, all civilian.'

Getting better in the city . . . getting worse in the villages. I think there is a definite policy-reason behind that, apart from the fact that the villages are, of course, helpless and wide open to attack.

But the villages can harbour guerillas: the villagers may harbour disguised stragglers from the last retreat, and the Japanese are now a great deal more jumpy than when they first came to Hsuchowfu.

So I think the reason why village girls and women are brutalized, and village men murdered for nothing (five in one tiny place, where the peasants were now afraid to go out and finish bringing in their harvest), and their oxen taken, and even ten-cent pieces looted, is only in a secondary way a reason of brutality or licence. It's firstly a reason of fear. Get them back to the city!

But in the city their homes are burnt, smashed-up, rubbish-heaps. In the country, while they have agricultural implements, a bit of land, and harvest from what they have sown, they can hang together and, in a communal way, just manage a bare existence; until, of course, the rains come with August, when they may have to cope with some floods. In the city, refugee camps or no refugee camps, what can they do but starve?

Refugee camps! From the gates of all refugee camps in this city they're being driven off in scores, pressed away . . . faces of hunger and fingers of hunger. What about the young girl the Franks' mission simply couldn't take, and sent over to the Catholic mission, and while she was waiting at the gates, the soldiers ripped the clothes off her back?

The small pagoda still dreams there on its hill-crest. That is where I would like to live now. Both the Chinese hotels are badly damaged and closed, nowhere else is possible, but I would like to go away and live in the pagoda, and then perhaps just one sentence would make itself clear.

The Chinese are so good. The first time I came to sit under this tree, Pastor Wong or Pastor Tsai, I forget which it was, came hurrying after me to make sure about this murder-and-rape business.

I was beginning to feel better, and he bust it up. But immediately, pulling out a newspaper bundle, he said in his stammering English: "Some of this . . . look, sausage *very* nice!" and extended the remaining end of a large liver-coloured sausage.

It was funny, too, when the Chinese killed the old lady's two pigs. They thought she might object, so they did it privately, in the Ladies Only of the nearest refugee camp. The blood ran out by a gutter into the street, and hearing wild shrieks, Japanese soldiers came tearing in with fixed bayonets, thinking we were having a nice little revolution. If anyone's going to do any throat-cutting round here, it'll be us. . . .

The big silken banner was tied round my waist for three days, then burned. The sword was safe. Dr. Nettie goes every night to visit the sick girl from Nanking, who is a Christian worker for the Kuomintang. She hasn't got a thing wrong with her twenty-year-old shapely body, except cancer of the uterus. The Japanese have questioned her more than once.

She knows approximately when and how she will die, and her face smiles when she discusses it. Her old mother, who doesn't appear to be a Christian, sits beside her all day.

This is all nonsense. Sun past meridian, and I'm going to Charlotte's for lunch, only a little farther along. The clay track by the wall is narrow, with the frogs still throating through green where the stream follows. They hop up like bubbles of tapioca.

At the gates the Japanese guards are very happy because Charlotte, after Chinese infants had furnished the whole outfit with fly-switches, responded to their pleadings, and gave the guards switches too. Behind them, smiling, are always a couple of Red Swastika men. The wild coreopsis and sunflower flame over the compound, where the American and Blue Cross flags are made with pebbles, enormously and exactly made by children. The bombers, it was thought, couldn't miss that. They only just did miss it, their bombs lighting in the field on the other side of the wall, cracking up the mission glass a bit. . . .

Charlotte has a big hat, and under it a pleasant, comfortable, motherly face. She can be quick-tongued, coming from way down south (Mr. Frank comes from way up north), but she is the most human of the outfit.

The hollyhocks are gone, but kids are forking up the hay into stooks.

'Worship now! Worship now!' A great column of water splashes up over the trees. Mr. Frank goes out to find what is happening. He comes back grinning.

"Guess what that was?"

"The Japanese soldiers are dynamiting for fish."

"But how did you guess that?"

"Because that's exactly what people used to do in New Zealand, especially during the depression years."

The flies get in, and it's slap, slap, slap, but a classic feast. There's some pork for dinner. Also ice-water. We just eat. . . .

Round the building is a sort of moat. Though you'd never guess it from the summers of Hsuchowfu, that freezes over in winter, and the children used to go skating there. One of them, a little boy to her, but really in mid-teens, is in Shanghai now, waiting to start for America, and Charlotte wants to get a pass in order to see him.

I want one too, but the Japanese aren't having any. So instead of going to Shanghai, we walk quietly across the fields to the foot of Cloud Dragon Mountain. This mountain would have been a real dragon; but when it was made, the spirits who made it feared to put so perfect a likeness of the dragon into a hill, and its head was cut off. But on cloudy days, often its head changes into the dragon-head.

In the near distance is another hill, made by men. A great General died and was buried in Hsuchowfu, and his men marched past his grave and as they marched each man flung a barrow-load of earth on the foundations. You would never take that immense tumulus to have been made by anything but nature.

Here in the lower part of the cemetery are slender stone pillars, raised to the memory of faithful widows who refused to marry again: there are large, curious, circular graves, covered all over with a sapphire blue wild gentian.

Charlotte is a little worried about climbing the mountain, because there are so many soldiers. But it's a sunny day, and she feels warmed up and comes, and the soldiers, sitting about everywhere drinking small cups of tea, are most courteous. They bow, and want to snap-shoot us, many of them having little cameras, but Charlotte won't. We scramble down the other side, long mounts of stone steps taking us to the Cave Buddha, who is a Buddha of importance, being the third largest in China.

Within the cavern, where still the bowing wands of incense make their red sparks of sweet fire, Japanese soldiers are side by side with Chinese Buddhist priest; over them both stares out the immense calm face, carved from the living rock, gilded all over, lacquered, and wearing still the crown of blue snails. I looked for the figure of Kwan-yin, but didn't find her. She, perhaps, was in another place.

Buddhism is not only tolerated but encouraged by the Japanese in China, though probably the Shinto shrine will also be introduced into occupied areas very soon. It is a religion of tranquillity and peace. It is the religion which, according to a Mongolian delegate in Hankow, has weakened Mongolian will to resist.

O thou Jewel in the heart of the lotus! Well, God knows we are tired enough.

Wild melon-vines at the bottom of the hill. "Well, there you are! It was all right."

"They were certainly very kind."

Inside the compound Mr. Frank looks white as death, shaken and stricken. We get into the car and go to see.

"The worst of it was," he repeats, "I saw something happening, but I didn't know what was going on. I might have been able to help."

Nobody now can help the five men on the yellow clay of the little yard; they have all been run through with bayonets. Under the mat that covers them they look crumpled and bloody, and at the bottom their big bare feet stick up in the sun.

None of them is young. The thing was, a party of artillery men got hold of an eighteen-year-old married woman, daughter of one of these men, niece of another. They were dragging her away, and one of the old Chinese kowtowed to the Japanese, while another appealed for help to the gate-guards, who had been useful once before.

This infuriated the artillery-men, who let it rip with their bayonets. Three other men, coming along, either made some comment, or were killed as witnesses.

'Worship now! Work now! Worship now!' Well these old bare feet have done all they could. One can't ask them to plod farther.

In the notes I made I used a kind of phrase shorthand, very simple, unintelligible unless I explained it myself.

For instance 'ear-rings' means the case of a woman carried in, raped by seven Japanese soldiers. They thrashed her husband and made him look on. She begged him to cut her throat, and he tried, but either couldn't or wouldn't succeed. She then swallowed her sharp-pointed ear-rings, and was still in agony, as, owing to the complete breakdown of the X-ray equipment, Dr. Nettie could not perform an operation.

A name written next is that of a sixteen-year-old girl; she was carried in, crying in agony, after a night with the soldiers.

'Diphtheria' means a rather hard case. There was a young mother at our refugee camp, whose little son showed signs of a diphtheric throat. There was no place where they could be isolated, except a small hut inside the wall of the Franks' compound.

She cried and begged so, and the little boy howled so hard, an old woman was found to stay with them. But when the soldiers broke over the wall that night, and outraged the woman in front of the child, they just shoved the old lady out of the way.

If anything is wanted to make this story complete, the little boy's diphtheric throat never was a diphtheric throat.

The word seventy, repeated twice, means that the old raped lady mentioned before now had another companion, of approximately the same age, to keep her company. Another girl, who hid for days under a bed, starving and thirsting, was found by the soldiers after all; they dragged her out and treated her in the same way.

These are only a few of the cases that can be authenticated by every missionary in Hsuchowfu . . . not to mention Major Fujita, and the doctors.

After all, even if there's another Nanking, what, of it? There's already been one Nanking.

And this was only a clay city: also, it is perfectly true that not a hundredth part of what happened in Nanking was duplicated here. And, Hsuchowfu or Nanking, what am I writing about? The Far East!

I think I am tired. I shall write no more to-night, except of Bishop Philippe Coté; and little enough, unfortunately, I know of him. I didn't meet Bishop Coté until after the fall of the city. Bishop Coté, Father Lelong, a Chinese priest whose name I remember, perhaps incorrectly, as Father Fan, and a young Canadian priest were working at their mission for the relief of refugees, in much the same way as the Americans. Aside from the bombing of their mission, the Catholics were terribly handicapped because the Japanese wouldn't let them open their new 18,000-dollar building, which was intended to be an orphanage.

Again it was a case of successful spying: the Japanese had got hold of the deed under which this property was bought from the Chinese, and discovered that the transaction had not been completed when the 'incident' broke out. So far, they were refusing to recognize the ownership of the building as valid, though they may by now have changed their minds.

I went to the Catholic mission some days after the occupation. There was a dead horse in the street. The coffin-shops and little broken-shuttered places reeked with rotting human flesh, and I retrieved a blind weeping kitten, and got the dirt out of its eyes, a silly thing to do.

Refugees at the iron gates begged to be taken in. The walls were pitted, but inside the place looked worse . . . every plaster roof fallen, wood, partitions and fixings still in hopeless chaos, a swivel-eyed picture between a broken and a straight one, and, passing the chapel, a brief look from white painted lilies.

I liked Bishop Coté, who gave me a glass of Liqueur du Couvent, and wore an amethyst on his finger, purple as a Canterbury bell. He looked kindly, as well as serene. He told me about the Japanese officer who came there and burst into tears, because he didn't want to be in North China, he wanted to go back to Nikko, Nikko, his own place, Nikko! His wife and his home were there.

The bombing had interfered a great deal with refugee arrangements, Bishop Coté said. But the missions were working well together with the indispensable Red Swastikas. The Japanese never stayed long at his mission. They didn't like the look of it.

Li Ai Tang came from the Red Swastikas. At one time he had been a president of something important in Hsuchowfu . . . the Chamber of Commerce, I think it was . . . and he must have been over fifty-five years of age, for he spent one night in the refugee camp.

Then the Japanese sent him a red-spot armlet and safe-conduct, and he was next heard of as heading the Reformed Provincial Government of Hsuchowfu.

At the first meeting, Mr. Li Ai Tang was ingenuous enough to express himself, quite plainly, upon a point of importance. The Japanese then showed him where he was. It must have been a hard thing for an old man. I think it is too early to judge many of these puppets.

The quaint thing was, perhaps, that he left his wife and daughter-in-law in a Christian refugee camp, coming to visit them in his red-spot band. If, through fear, a mother brought in her little boy wearing one of those armbands, it had a short life and a merry one. There were always such little difficulties, explaining brotherhood to the bombed.

I said I wouldn't write any more. It drifts, drifts one picture after another. The small American chapel, used as a stable for horses. An officer showing me his sword, which is the living image of my sword. . . .

Letter from Mr. Ueda. I still have the original. Mr. Ueda was a young soldier going to Nanking.

'Miss X.

'UEDA.

'I will take with me your letter, and I will send to the British Consul. If you have other news, I will take also.

"You feeled, "Is not Japanese soldiers good of woman?" but Japanese soldiers is kind of woman. So it is in the battle now. I want (you) to understand my heart.

'It is dangerous you will go out this city alone. If you will leave this city to Hankow alone, you will be a dead for bad men.

'If the war of Japan-China shuts up, you will be safe to go out this city, and you can return to the native-land. I hope that you will be good health and happy. If you returned to the native-land, I want (you) to give me good news of New Zealand.

'Japan have many beautiful views, and good peoples live in. I want (you) to visit Japan, if you like. All Japanese are kind for all foreigns.'

Well, good health and happiness for you also, and a safe return soon to the native-land. However, this letter notwithstanding, on 30 May I picked up my little handcase, left my blanket (poor Edith's 'Good-bye, blanket!'), and went.

There was the suspiciousness of Mr. Liu the Bad, who hung about the hospital grounds and frightened the Chinese. Many of his questions referred to me. There was the little question of how long guests at missions should remain, while the refugees eat gruel, get dysentery, and never have enough water to wash. I couldn't write, and wasn't allowed to send out one word to say whether I was alive or dead. There was the desperate sick feeling of lying broken on the floor of a pit: I wasn't so good at accepting summer as the Chinese. Finally, there was no possibility of retreating uphill and living in the pagoda.

Getting out was quite easy. I just walked with Mr. Liu the Good to the east side of the city until we got pretty close to the station. He couldn't safely come any farther, but I knew where I was by now. Nobody said a word, and like Felix, I kept on walking, soon to strike the old rails of the Lunghai line, and beside them the sunken clay tracks, easy walking, and cool because of willow and acacia.

CHAPTER SIX

On the March

WHAT HAD HAPPENED HERE, about three miles along the tracks, was obvious. At intervals of a few hundred yards the railway tracks and clay border-paths vanished, replaced by sleeper-bridges over little dry ravines, and these had slowed the Chinese soldiers up as they ran. They hadn't been bombed, all had died from machine-gun or rifle fire; they had died some time on 19 May, and this was late afternoon of 30 May, and here, a few miles from Hsuchowfu, the harvesters were working in their fields, with nothing to intimidate them beyond the occasional swooping song of three 'planes, which every now and again whirred and glistened above the fields and the willow trees.

The dead soldiers wore shabby blue uniform of the padded jacket type, and from some the jackets had been stripped off, the quilting torn out and scattered. It lay in white masses like floss candy, the heavy downpours and dew with which it had been soaked making it shine gently. I counted over one hundred of these dead, in places stepping across them where they lay huddled by the tracks. The villagers, I thought, are afraid to come and bury them: that may have been true, or it may have been only that the villagers, working among their brown grain, were very content to leave the dead lie, if they could hope for a little peace and safety themselves.

The only other killings I saw were very close to the tracks. Both on the Lunghai and the Tsinpu lines, main stations are ten miles apart, but there are small station-houses half-way between. At the first of these there were three bodies. Either the officials had run out, or had been killed first and dragged out. They lay face down, and for hundreds of yards down the tracks were scattered papers, records, letters in the narrow black-brushed envelopes, books with their pages torn out, and one which spoke in English. Its cover said: 'New Maps of the World.'

Rogoff: 'Wounded books crying out for help in the different languages of the world.'

Not long afterwards I walked past the first station where there were Japanese soldiers. The larger stations, as I found, had interpreters, but here the garrison of no more than half a dozen men had only a few words of English among them. They were extremely jovial and friendly, and inclined to shower me with food. I ate one of their sweetstuffs, done up like a tablet of chocolate—a dark, soft jelly, tasting of iron and raisins. Then it was little pink sugar-cakes, and then they insisted on filling the mug slung round my neck first with their black, sweet tea, then with huge crystals of sugar. It was darkening; they made gestures which seemed to mean, 'Stay here for the night,' but I thought now I had had enough hospitality, so I shook my head, thanked them, and walked on. I knew how to say 'Thank you!' either in Chinese or in Japanese, but no other Japanese except a polite form of saying 'Good-bye,' which I had picked up from a book.

The edge of dark, quiet and alone, dark ringing out softly, like the circles in a pool when a stone has fallen: an old man, last out in the fields, has come to fetch something, and I call out to him. I want to know if the next station-house is very far along. I can repeat all the names of the stations for some considerable distance, and also have them written down in Chinese so that villagers can direct me.

The peasant comes up by a path to the line for a moment, and then, round a corner, a good way off, there is a vivid flare of lights. I can see quite plainly what it is—one of the small open trucks or trolly-cars used for running up and down the tracks, filled with soldiers. In front, they have a rather glaring light. Probably they are perfectly tame: but the old man, scared, gives me a push. I guess, a long time afterwards, that what he means is: 'Get down, there's some trouble coming.'

But not at the time. The bank was really very steep, and having lost my foothold, somehow I didn't save myself in falling. Perhaps the handcase got in the way.

Once in the night I woke up. I could see then, for a few stars, clear as drops of ice, remain imprinted on my memory. I think I had been stunned, hitting the side of my head when I fell, but wakening up was too tired and weak to do more than go to sleep again. It was full daylight when I woke next. I could see out of my right eye, though it seemed misty. The other eye was quite blind, and in the eyeball a sharp point of pain. The bank down which I had fallen was covered with acacia bushes, and set among the leaves were the long rosy thorns. I had a thorn in my eye.

The first time I stood up, I fell down again, but I heard something coming along, and half clambered, half dragged myself up the side of the bank, calling out: "Please! Please!" in Chinese. The thing coming was another trolley, like the one the night before. The soldiers stopped and picked me up, but if they said anything I don't remember it. As soon as I was out in the full light of the sun I couldn't see at all, and didn't feel capable of making any effort. Doubtless a good deal of that was mere shock: and for a while, at the mission, everybody had been living on very short commons.

When the trolly stopped (it was at the second station) I was helped across to a corner of some yard. I lay still, and remember clearly of the next ten hours only two things. Lifting my hands, trying to push away the flies from my mouth and nose. Then once a soldier came over. I didn't see him, but he placed a water-soaked pad over my eye, and the cold was a great relief.

Towards evening, when the sun's heat died out of the air, the last effects of the shock or the blow on my head, whichever it was that laid me out so completely, passed off. I could think, and opened my right eye, which was quite all right. Very cautiously, I tried the other two or three times. That was blurred, and to open it hurt me, but I could see: even when I shut my right eye, still I could see.

I had simply accepted the fact, 'I am blind,' and now that I knew I wasn't, I felt overjoyed, light, not tired in the least. Coolness and the shadow . . . those two blessed things, soaking into one, like the soldier's cold-water bandage!

I got up and walked over to the station, where the soldiers were, trying to tell them I could see. During the day, except for the man with the cold-water bandage, I don't remember that any of them came near me, but now they were quite friendly and gave me some tea. One of them showed me a pocket mirror. I said: "Aiyah!" for my eye was hideous, the white covered in blood, the outside black and swollen up a good deal. But it now seemed funny, because I could see.

In point of fact, I escaped blindness twice over. There had been a haemorrhage inside the eye, but the retina wasn't touched. So much I learned in a few days. But the doctor who told me that was unable, through a defect in her own eyesight, to find the little thorn still embedded in my eyeball. Three weeks later, in Tsingtao, a German doctor got the thorn out with his instruments.

I wanted to go straight on from the station, but it was dark, and the soldiers would not let me leave, whether because of the night, or because I was still a little groggy in walking. They cleared a stretcher for me in a corner of the station. About ten o'clock, troop trains came in from the Hsuchowfu direction, and a Japanese doctor came running over. He spoke good English, but was in a state of much agitation. "What has happened to you? What has happened to you?"

In a moment I realized that he was blaming my damaged eye on Japanese soldiers, and laughed.

"It's all right. I fell down, and have hurt my eye."

His relief was intense, and he put some drops in my eye, but was anxious for me to go back on a troop train to Hsuchowfu: about the last thing I wanted. I thanked him for his drops, and he was gone, those trains soon rumbling out of the station. Early in the morning, before the sun had begun its blind white and yellow glare, I left the station.

And walked on: and walked uncommon badly. An annoying thing had happened. I had completely lost my nerve for crossing the sleeper-bridges. Every time I came to a bridge I had to scramble down, cross, scramble again up the other side. I had no food that day till evening, though some peasants working in the fields obliged with warm water out of their kettle.

The fifth station along, a place called Tim Hsien, was near the home of two old-established German missionaries, Dr. and Mrs. Kuhlmann, where I hoped to find shelter for a night. I drew the sign of a cross on the ground, repeating the mission's name over and over, thinking that perhaps these villagers might know of a short cut. They argued a bit, amiable, talkative, interested, finally coming to a decision among themselves. Two grinning boys appeared with a wheelbarrow and motioned me to get on, which I did. Once mounted on a wheelbarrow you can lie on your stomach or lie on your back, but to sit up is difficult, and it's a vehicle which, besides being undignified, hurts the foreigner in backbone and ribs.

It was all a business transaction. "Five dollars!" said, with sudden and perfect intelligibility, an elderly man with shaven skull. Five dollars, in China, is a scandalous price to pay anyone for doing anything—except, of course, in high places—but the sleeper bridges annoyed me too much for any bargaining, and that villager, probably much to his own surprise, got five dollars. The wheelbarrow boys then fastened rope halters round their necks, and started off at a jog-trot. But they never got me anywhere near the Kuhlmanns'. Probably I mispronounced the name of the station, and nothing was clear in their minds except: 'The foreigner wants to go to some place farther along.' They kept to a path close enough to be in sight of the railways: but when we passed some soldiers on that line, they became doubtful, had a chat, and unslung themselves from their halters, grinning, smiling, dripping with more or less honest sweat.

I didn't know enough Chinese to be rude to them. I could say 'I'm not afraid,' but they knew better, and had reason to. They shook their heads, smiled in the pleasant Chinese way, and were off, for which at heart I did not blame them. The lift they had given me, short though it was, was a lift. If I can hang on till I get to the Kuhlmanns' place, maybe they will fix my eye up and tell me how I can make a detour round to Kaifeng, I thought. In Hsuchowfu, we had not heard of the battle raging around Kaifeng, and to the best of our knowledge, trains were still running from Kaifeng to Hankow.

At the next station, Huang Kou, I began to suspect that there was military action in progress somewhere, because the Major's interpreter was a bit cross, filled with a baffled desire to shoot me. It was silly to walk into that station: but I wasn't thinking well. I was thinking only: 'This must be another li,' 'This must be another li,' and wishing the sun were not so hot. Also, nobody had told me: 'Huang Kou is a much larger station than the first two; better look out for trouble,' so I walked full into the biggest caterpillar of Japanese troop trains I had ever seen. They were stationary on both lines, and from them the soldiers had dropped off like peanuts, and were wandering around.

"You should not go on till dark," said one of the Japanese soldiers politely, "it is very dangerous. You had better sit down. I will fetch somebody." There was a wooden box, so I sat down, and leaned back, nervous. Enough soldiers are enough soldiers: these were too many soldiers. The polite one came back, not with 'somebody,' but to fetch me within the station, where the Major was a swarthy Aquiline who scowled and spoke no English. That would have been no difficulty: the trouble was with the interpreter, who was a perfect little rat, very dirty and disreputable in appearance (though not so bad as myself), and who spoke beautiful, fluent English, with what I imagined were traces of the Oxford accent.

I thought it would be better not to tell the Major (the interpreter called him the Major) any lies, because obviously the interpreter knew so much English that he would only find them out. So I told the truth—that I was a reporter, had been up at Hsuchowfu and got caught short, was now walking back to Hankow as a refugee. Nobody liked reporters: the Major, through his interpreter, wanted to see my pass, so I showed him my pass, which was, of course, a Chinese pass, issued by a Chinese gentleman and soldier not so popular with the Japanese. Also my British passport.

"The Major says," declared the interpreter, "if you were a Chinese woman, we would shoot you."

He was savage, but the point seemed past discussion. I wasn't a Chinese woman.

"Or if you had a gun," he continued, "or a knife."

He was too big a temptation, and my eye and feet and temper were all so sore.

"Why don't you give me a gun, then?"

"We need all our guns for our own men," said the interpreter, crosser and crosser on the Major's behalf. "The Major says you are to get off this railway. You cannot walk here. It is highly strategic."

"I am sorry, but where am I to walk? I don't know the village paths, or enough Chinese to ask the way from the villagers. Besides, as you can see,

I am hurt."

This failed to strike any chord in the interpreter (or the Major). The railway line was highly strategic. Mr. Liu the Good would have said that the interpreter was very 'un-polite'; (his unfailing description of Mr. Liu the Bad). The end was a military escort, not very amiable, which, after leading me through a largish village, squalid and unkempt, a place that looked as if it sat in dust and ashes, took me a mile or so beyond, and there left me. I didn't use my polite way of saying 'Goodbye' or 'Thank you,' but waited until they were out of sight, then struck back slantwise towards the tracks, coming out well ahead of the troop trains. There was nothing else to do: the villages, without a knowledge of paths and of the language, were plainly impossible.

It was getting dark again, and I felt sorry for myself, though with a haziness that made things impersonal. Along the road I met three privates, carrying some poultry and eggs, probably acquired from unlucky villagers. They were quite good-tempered; one of them dropped three bantam eggs into the enamel mug which was still slung around my neck, as if I were an orphan kid bound for a Sunday school picnic, but I had no way of cooking eggs and the thought of eating them raw made me sick, and one after another these little round objects rolled out of the jogging mug and broke themselves on the road.

At the next village I thought: 'I will go in, and perhaps I can get some food and a sleeping-place.' It was smaller than the Pihsien village—a mere cluster of clay huts, without any larger building among them, or any courtyard plan; at first nobody was in sight but a dog or two, and some children, but soon a couple of women came.

I tried my painful Chinese on them, and they brought me not only hot water, but one of the little loaves I had eaten before. The village was full of Rising Sun flags—white background, round red eye. A number of men came back from their work, and one brought out a long straw mat, so that for a time I could lie with that between me and the ground. But friendly and gentle though these villagers were, they would not give me a bed for the night, and from their looks and gestures, I thought I could pick out why: these people were afraid, too much afraid. They had every reason to be afraid, and I had not. A Chinese could be shot, but the Japanese weren't shooting foreigners.

After a time, I could not think of anything to do but say "Thank you," and go on. I did not get far, not more than another half-mile. All this country was flat, without sleeper-bridges, but I dared not walk in the dark in case I came to another broken stretch, and besides, I was tired.

I climbed down a low bank into a field, and lay there, among the same sort of bushes as had left a thorn in my eye, but on warier terms. The stones, pitch-forked out from the fertile stretch of the field, lay heaped on the edges, and I couldn't sleep. Slowly drizzling rain fell, wetting the leaves, wetting my coat, but not lashing out to full strength . . . the slight, uncomfortable half-rain of a half-dream.

I must have slept towards morning, and on past sun-up, because I woke to see peasants working in the fields, and stood up at once, calling out to them. This may have been a bad mistake, and frightened or antagonized them, for they didn't behave like the people from the other villages. (I could see their village, rather a long way back from the road, behind some trees.)

A number of them came up, men and women. I tried to talk; it must have been exactly like a scarecrow risen out of their earth, and talking gibberish in their field. They argued among themselves, then they caught hold of my arms, though without violence, and took everything I had away from me—hat, stick, handcase (containing my papers and handbag), sunglasses, coat. That left me the clothes I stood up in.

They weren't bandits: even at that moment of utter dejection, I could see, anyone could have seen, that they could not possibly be bandits. None of them struck me or tried to frighten me, none of them even shouted. They just took, down to a couple of rings I had on my fingers. Then they went away over the fields to their village. Except for my stick, sun-glasses, and papers, I hadn't lost anything of material importance. The money I had was about thirty dollars Mex., and unless for paying the wheelbarrow boys, I hadn't found out that money was any use in these parts. But I minded unreasonably, especially because I had lost my papers. I had no sense of humour about it. Instead, I sat down in the field, and cried.

And they came back, which seemed so queer that I cried still more. Nearly all my things they returned to me, putting back the rings on my fingers, opening my case to show me the contents were still there, trying to reassure me. I can't hope to explain the sheer awfulness of this, nor how, instead of making me feel better, it made me feel, 'Oh, this is past the limit!' I couldn't understand what they were doing, what they wanted; they were equally unable to understand me.

Later on in Tsingtao, I heard that several foreigners in lonely parts had met with similar adventures. But if they returned later with supporters, and asked the reason why, the villagers apologized civilly and said: "We thought you were a Japanese."

It was quickly at an end—scattered. A boy with a wheelbarrow, a strong, bright-looking young fellow, came up, and made signs for me to get on. I hesitated, trying to stop crying and see what he meant, also scrawling more crosses, this time with the toe of my shoe, and repeating the name of the Kuhlmanns' station. He nodded vigorously. But I was too slow in making up my mind. Some more soldiers came along the lines, and looked curiously down. The villager also hesitated, then, with something which sounded to me like a Chinese curse, went away.

The soldiers called down, then shouted, and I went up the bank. They weren't, apparently, annoyed, but insistent. Not a quarter of a mile down the road, gently asleep, lay the long black hulk of another troop train, with its soldiers head and shoulders above their loose-boxes, or sitting with legs dangling from the covered iron cars at the back, empty except for their mats. There were a couple who spoke some English. They said: "Get up," while I argued that I must get on my way.

This seemed quite intelligible to them, and they said it would be all right, their train was going through that day to Tsingtao, which had a big foreign community.

I got up, but as soon as I did, they quietly took my case away from me, and went over it with the meticulousness of monkeys looking for fleas. The English of those who spoke some English didn't run to the written word, and those papers they hardly touched, but read the Chinese ones.

There was no sort of fuss. They seemed more curious than anything else. I sat back, and felt sick.

"You are a reporter?"

"Yes, a reporter."

"You write for the papers?"

Talking to a council of intent eyes, carefully listening people, who, except for a few phrases were quite unable to understand. All the foreigners in Hsuchowfu had been searched, some more than once. Any Japanese sentry who took it into his head would even stop the American car, make the missionaries, male and female, get out, and feel about them for weapons. I had been in the car on such occasions; but there wasn't the same curiosity in those searches as in this. One soldier pulled out a couple of yen and offered to buy a ring. It had a red stone which appealed to him. But when I shook my head, he made no attempt to force the sale.

I don't clearly remember leaving the train, anything except sitting in a covered car which drove in at a gate. I was afraid, because at the back of my mind I knew something I dared not let myself know. The place we entered was one of thick stone gates and courtyards, and right in the middle of one gate was suspended a cage, with a singing canary. Soldiers lounging in a guard-room, laughing and joking, offered me food and tea, but I couldn't touch it any more.

In the evening a Japanese officer came in. He not only spoke perfect English, but seemed to understand it, and to understand as a western person would, without any mental translation to quite other terms, quite another inward significance.

I asked him, and he said: "Yes, I have travelled and lived a long time in the west." After a time, I put the idiotic question whose answer I did know, but was too tired and too sick-hearted at wasted effort to admit.

"This place isn't Hsuchowfu?"

He answered immediately: "No, no, the name of this place is not Hsuchowfu. We will take you in the morning to the British Consul." He started to talk about the war then, about what he called the sovietization of the villages. I stopped him at that.

"The villages here! Have you been into them? How much sovietization have you found among these people? They are people who work hard and are terribly poor, like any other peasant people."

He said: "About the villages, yes, that is right. But it is the soldiers."

Incorrectly, I said: "The soldiers are the same people as the villagers."

The Japanese officer did not say anything more about the Chinese soldiers, but asked about my eye, and I told him I could see better now. He said, quite kindly: "To-morrow it will be a little better still," and went away.

In the morning, I went out past the singing canary, and looked into the street, seeing the three-tiered yellow tiled gate with the bronze dragon-heads and little bronze bells—one of the few ornate gates left in the poor man's city. Then there was no more sick struggle of argument, and I only felt 'Well, I will have to start all over again.'

I didn't see the friendly officer of the night before, but another one with an interpreter, in temper and technique rather comically like the one at Huang Kou. He shouted (per interpreter) that I must get out of Hsuchowfu.

"I'm doing my best," I said. "But it's a long way to walk, there aren't any trains, and your men lied when they brought me back in the troop train. They said they were going to Tsingtao, straight through. I would never have agreed to come back to Hsuchowfu."

No impression: loud roars from the Japanese. A young Catholic priest, one I hadn't met before, came in at the gate, and I said to him, rather incoherently: "Well, what do you think of him? How do you like him?"

He replied: "I dare not tell you what I think," and then I left, going out through the dusty streets towards the East Station, with an idea that though I could not walk another ten miles, somehow I might be able to get a lift on a troop train to Tsingtao. Tsingtao was farther than Hankow, that was why I had chosen to attempt the Lunghai line first. But fighting on the Tsinpu line, so far as we knew, was over: it could no longer be called 'highly strategic,' and might be easier going.

Anyhow, one thing (I thought). At least I will never believe a word spoken by any other Japanese.

The old Chinese men with sunspot armlets. (said to be sold at five cents) at first looked in their black clothes like feeble overturned beetles: but now you've got used to them, though the swanking, grinning little hooligans bragging their sunspots under the noses of the Japanese are a pest. Just kids, really, alive, wanting to be normally free and happy kids. You see, you're a westerner, and therefore expect patriotism from a platform, religion from a pulpit. You'd expect one of the old men or the rowdy brats to go up to that Japanese having his hair cut, make a Sidney-Cartonesque speech on short wavelength, bite the Japanese ear and die. The majority of peasants and workers in such districts as Hsuchowfu did not yet recognize 'my country' as a political or sentimental abstraction. To them it meant literally 'my country—this bit of soil I'm prodding with a two-pronged wooden fork I grew specially by making a crotch of young branches on a growing tree.'

This day, in some ways, was the worst I ever spent—a day of being pushed about in filthy streets. The same thing, and worse, happened daily to many Chinese. I think my black and crimson eye and disreputable looks largely accounted for it. The Japanese did not think I was British: it is uncommon for anybody but a White Russian with or without a Nansen passport to look quite as bad as that, so they guessed my nationality as Russian.

For a while I sat on the station, seeing there what I never hoped for or expected—Sidney Carton. He was about nine years old, and was he mad! He was helping Chinese labourers, who slowly, bossed by the Japanese, were rebuilding the brick station arches, which had been bombed. They made a good job of it, smoothing mortar with care, and the dust of their concreting flew down to mingle with the other dust, litter and filth, which an anxious old coolie with a huge broom again and again pushed off the platform.

In some way, the job got on young Sidney Carton's nerves, and he flew into the first real Chinese temper I had ever seen. Turning, he simply shrieked at everybody, yelled at the top of his voice things which sounded really picturesque. He didn't get killed. One of the soldiers gave him a cuff and pushed him out of the way, and he cleared off, knuckling his eyes.

Presently Charlotte, who had heard I was at the station, came over with some cookies and a bottle of ice-water. I thought if I stuck it I might still get to Tsingtao. Having made the break, it was hard to go through it, and involve other people in it, all over again.

So Charlotte went, and I drank, but gave the cookies to the soldiers, hoping this might bribe them into taking me on the troop train. They ate the cookies but did nothing about the troop train, for which I can't blame them.

The old coolie went on sweeping and sweeping. A story was being written that day in Hsuchowfu, written by a Chinese man in Chinese dust, while above him other Chinese men rebuilt the bombed arches. But they did not build for themselves.

Having given the cookies away, I lived instead on Roy Campbell; comical though it sounds, I believe that beautifully grandiloquent, beautifully simple poet helped me to stay alive. One of his verses just fitted Sidney Carton's thin naked shoulders:

'Who, on that brow, foresees the gems aglow?
Who, in that shrivelled claw, the sword that swings
Wide as a moonbeam through the farthest regions
Carving a blood-red pathway for the legions,
Making amends to every cheated crow
And feasting vultures on the fat of kings?

This is that Tartar prince, superbly pearled,
Whose glory soon on every wind shall fly. . .'

Foreign *pai ka'rh*, of course, nothing reasoned about it; but a good rum ration in an emergency.

The Japanese station-master got rid of me by sending me to a military headquarters for a permit to travel. At the gates a sentry, large, cheerfully tough, showing off to a crowd, shoved his fist into my face and sent me staggering back. I offered him a swig out of the water-bottle, with as much impudence as my damaged eye would permit, and when he made a wry face, tasting nothing but water, the crowd simply yelled; after all, only a bit of very human fun.

The little tangle of streets lost me. By now the Japanese forces had brought down from Nanking the first civilians after the Pacification Corps allowed in Hsuchowfu—Japanese and Korean prostitutes. Our Major, in answer to protests about the rape of Chinese women and girls had promised these some time ago.

"For a few days it may mean some trouble," he said, "but after that there will be other women brought in."

Dr. Nettie said that they wouldn't be Number One prostitutes, or they would never be risked so close to the fighting. But those I saw were pretty, dainty and dumpy little things, in their kimonos and expensively embroidered obis. Most of them were inside a shop, or crowding about the door, on which were slung empty beer-bottles. One dropped her bundle of clothes. "Aiyah!" squeaked a soldier, imitating the voice of a frightened Chinese girl. There was one woman wearing violet, sitting alone in a broken-shuttered empty shop. She looked out and smiled at me. I didn't look back, but later wished that I had.

At dark I went back to Dr. Nettie's. The cook-boys were at first perturbed, because of the refugee kitten from the bombed building, which, despite all prophecies, had lived for days on milk administered with an eye-dropper. On leaving, I had given them five dollars to feed the waif, which they, very naturally, had no time to do. So it had starved to death.

"Now," they said to Dr. Nettie, "the cat is dead, and she has come back. She will want the cat."

They needn't have worried. The kitten was the kitten. It would have been nice if it could have stayed alive, but that might also be said of the Chinese soldiers rotting along the Lunghai line. It would have been nice if everybody could have stayed alive.

The day before, the Japanese had held a flag-day for the inauguration of their Reformed Provincial Government of Hsuchowfu, and the streets were strewn with the remnants of thousands of paper five-barred flags (the old pre-Republican Chinese flag), which the Pacification Corps had festooned everywhere.

Dr. Nettie was upset because in one big refugee camp, dear old Chinese Christians, whose eyes had simply glistened when they listened to the sermons of the Chinese pastors, had appeared to listen and glisten quite as much when the Japanese proffered candy. She didn't seem to connect this with 'glycerine tears.' But of the other camps, several had behaved with marked independence: in one the children refused to speak or accept any gifts, and in another the women took a similar stand. I don't think this encounter, or the flag-day in general, can have carried with it much feeling of enthusiasm, though the Pacification Corps produced something very novel—a brass band.

The Japanese refugee camp was now stated by the Pacification Corps to harbour about two thousand Chinese people, but no foreigners were admitted. The Chinese most strenuously denied the figure, and said that villagers were being tricked by Japanese soldiers, who told the women and girls to go to the camps supported by the Red Swastika men and the missions for safety, and once they had arrived in the city conducted them to the Japanese camp.

Activities in country districts were by that time more important than anything that happened in Hsuchowfu itself. The old skeleton societies were stirring, the first traumatic stage after the bombings and burnings quickly passing off. It was learned from fairly reliable sources that guerilla forces to the number of about four thousand were massed within less than fifty miles of the city. I remember one missionary's look of mingled anxiety and relief, as he exclaimed: "They say we're completely encircled!" The barbed wire entanglements were little thickets of thorn, the green tanks came and went. Already the guerilla movement, which a few months later, helped by organizers from outside, evolved as a practical re-conquest of Shantung and penetrated Kiangsu as well, had started.

Hsuchowfu, now a key-point to the Japanese, as formerly to the Chinese, held, of course, a garrison of great military strength. But even in the stumbling attempt along the Lunghai line, I had seen one exposition of Miss Yuan's telling phrase— 'We can cut them across the wrist at any time.' Stations could be left with half a dozen Japanese soldiers as garrison. Miles followed where, in spite of occasional patrols, Japanese were chance-met. Truly the guerillas could 'cut them across the wrist,' and did. The blowing up of bridges and railway tracks by Chinese guerillas had begun by the end of May, the same month in which Hsuchowfu was occupied.

Strange tales kept drifting in from the smaller towns, which had lain, as it were, at the end of spokes, with Hsuchowfu for hub. One place, Hsiaohsien, was by eye-witness account the scene of one of the most heroic little episodes in the war. The story was first retailed by two well-known young Chinese, who came in, having lost all but their lives. They had gone out of Hsiaohsien into the hills, trying to escape a frightful bombing.

Now the Mayor of Hsiaohsien (yet another Wong) and his Chief of Police had for garrison and picket purposes 200 soldiers: and both Mayor and Chief were men born in that *hsien*. When the Japanese were coming, the Mayor swore that he would die sooner than surrender the city. And lying in the hills the two young people saw an action of great valour. They saw the city gates shut, after the Mayor, the Chief of Police, and the handful of soldiers had come out of Hsiaohsien and disposed themselves where they could make the best possible job of a battle . . . against an army.

It is perhaps unnecessary to explain how the two hundred would be armed, or what they would lack in means of organizing a mechanized resistance. But this is how they fought, as we heard again and again from reliable sources, including one of the Chinese pastors who went over directly after the fighting to see if he could find traces of some Chinese Christians in the city. Of the Chinese soldiers there was no survivor, and both the Mayor and his Chief of Police were killed. But as many Japanese as Chinese had fallen, some said even more.

There was nothing to stop anyone from entering those fearful and curious little remnants of streets, for the occupying force, who had put Hsiaohsien to the sack after overcoming its resistance, had left no garrison. Nobody could have lived there; not the craziest old waif of a peasant had drifted back. The stench of corpses was so bad that Hsiaohsien was left quietly to its dead. The Chinese pastor was looking for an old Christian doorkeeper, 'Fatty.' 'Fatty' was found, with his belly slit up; he was a huge dropsical ancient, whose sickness had kept him in bed for some months. A boy with the pastor found his mother's body, her throat cut. She was an old woman. Somehow the soldiers had missed ten dollars pinned in her petticoats, which became this boy's sole inheritance.

Now there were plenty of Japanese civilians, mostly dapper little men of the shopkeeping type, coming into Hsuchowfu, picking about at the ruins and rubbish-heaps, and looking, in general, rather woebegone. Also Chinese people were coming back, not only the old, but young mothers carrying their babies in their arms. Always the young tried to get in at the missions, and almost always they had to be turned away from the overcrowded, overloaded buildings, where lack of proper fire exits was a constant anxiety.

The old, when they came, also picked over the rubbish-heaps. One can't even imagine what they hoped to retrieve, but forlornly and gently, hope they did. Nearly all, perforce, wore the Japanese armband which was their only protection, though on the hospital premises sat one old gentleman who said he would stay there until he died before he would be seen wearing the badge. But his daughter, a very young girl, was one of the rape cases in the women's hospital.

Charlotte told me of a rich old man, an armband, and a house. There weren't so many rich people in Hsuchowfu, and certainly few stayed to meet the Japanese. But this old man had built his family a fine-looking house, and until the last moment (when it was too late) his avarice and the roots of his life could not bear to be torn from their native soil. So he was caught. Charlotte met him, wearing the armband, bringing in his women to the refugee camp. Suddenly the tears ran from his eyes.

"Shame! Shame! Shame!" he cried, tearing off the armband.

"These people do not know what is good for them," said our Major. "Now they have broken the dykes at Kaifeng. It will only mean that a lot of them must get drowned."

Still patient, if a little fed up with things, he came now and then to the hospitals, camps, and missions, and was allegedly trying to get Shanghai passes for Mrs. Frank, Dr. Mac, two of the Catholic priests, and myself. The missionaries at last had an interview with the anonymous Japanese General (charming and cultured, they said) and were promised the passes. They had taken Mr. Han along, and he, in an inspired moment, asked for a pass himself. Greatly to his surprise, he was promised too.

Slowly, one morning, Major Fujita took the passes out of his pocket. Mine he kept to the last.

"Some of the officers did not want this one to be issued. They said: 'England should not sell China all those munitions.' "

They said! It didn't much matter what they said, and I only wished England were selling China as many munitions as the Japanese believed— or pretended to believe. This Major Fujita, who was a soldier, quite understood, and did not mind in the least. Since the world must divide into friend and enemy, he was not a bad enemy. A man with some sense of humour seldom is.

For a day we wiped the sweat from our faces, almost happy.

"It's the piano that did it," declared Dr. Nettie.

Then we discovered that the passes (permitting their bearers to travel via Tsingtao to Shanghai) were for the time being, at least, hardly worth the paper they were written on. The station officials, acting like little gods, refused to recognize them, or to entertain any idea that foreigners might travel on the troop-trains, though by now plenty of Japanese civilians were coming and going. There were, of course, no civilian trains, and by no persuasion could we get at a date when exit might be allowed.

Afterwards, Mr. Han told the missionaries he was afraid my pass was no good, as it lacked something the others had—a special identification. This may have accounted for some trouble I had later. But I don't think the pass was a deliberate 'phony.'

The crimson was nearly gone from my eye. Painstakingly I bathed it every day, but somehow couldn't wash off a look of general' disreputability. My clothes, when I washed them, went into hundreds of minute holes. The rubbers had flapped loose from my shoes, and though I hacked them off with a pen-knife, now the dust came in at every step. Both the Americans and the French-Canadians had been allowed by the Japanese authorities to send their Ambassadors a reticent telegram (worded by the Japanese, and with no personal signatures) informing the world that they survived. I, being unofficially there, was never allowed to send a wire at all; which, though I didn't know it, provided grounds for a little newspaper fussing.

No way of getting out; but Dorothy Clawsen and her Chinese doctor got in from Nanhsuchow, a little place about twenty miles away, and finished the last lap on a Japanese tank. The doctor's broken arm was their pretext for leave. He had tumbled off a ladder, fractured himself nicely above the right elbow, and, as he was a surgeon, naturally wanted to be carefully repaired. So Dorothy Clawsen (an American missionary, brown-haired, sweet-faced) tackled the Japanese authorities and got three-day permits for absence. The poor doctor was upset at finding what had happened to Hsuchowfu's X-ray plants, but as he was the only medical man at his station, he had no choice but to turn back.

Just for the day of Dorothy Clawsen's visit, the mission and its people seemed young again. She was a quiet-spoken girl, but had a will and a way with her. Dr. Mac made almost historic ice-cream in his freezer, and we laughed over the way Nanhsuchow had dished any thirsty Japanese on Occupation Day. Mrs. Lee, their mission housekeeper, had remembered in time about the vats of grain spirit kept in one village, and thither, on the run, went the mission staff. The owners were distressed at wasting good strong liquor.

"But," they protested, " this is nice to drink!"

They were over-persuaded, the liquor slopped hastily out of the vats— gone where it did much less harm than in the collective blood-stream of an occupying force.

It took her forty-eight hours to get out of Hsuchowfu, once having got in. "Your lot," she remarked, after twelve hours of sitting in the east station's sun-glare and grit, "aren't a bit like ours." But she said they would get back, and they did. She had been a sort of festival day, Dorothy Clawsen. . . .

The Franks and I reached a vague understanding that since I was determined to have another try at moving on from Hsuchowfu, if I failed again, and got back intact, I should try my hand and my appalling Chinese at one of the refugee camps, giving up all idea of leaving Hsuchowfu. In fact, I thought that to reverse policy, stick like a limpet and wait for the Japanese to throw me out, would be no more than poetic justice.

The Tsinpu line, running north to the coastal city, Tsingtao, looked peaceable; it hadn't been the scene of recent hostilities, and though to get a lift from Hsuchowfu itself was apparently impossible (the Japanese station-master could hardly have expressed himself better on that point), I thought that twenty miles up the line things might relax a little. They did, but not as I had expected.

Charlotte wanted me to stay on for a few days, waiting for the missionaries to make another concerted attack. But I had lost faith in promises, and they, too, were discouraged. For the second time I visited Bishop Coté, who looked tired and worn. His priests were still waiting for their Peiping passes to be recognized.

I had the actual pass, which gave permission to travel to Tsingtao, and nowhere added 'bearer must travel by train.' It was issued by the anonymous General, whom I had never seen, but Major Fujita had told me: "With this in your possession, no Japanese soldier will molest you."

This was the time when the melons were beginning to form, presaging the dysentery season, which worried poor Charlotte because of the cooped-up refugees, whose numbers never grew less. Apricots were in season, also beautiful Chinese peaches, though I never saw these in Hsuchowfu itself.

Hsuchowfu was still living hard, dying hard. Its streets still looked a hellish and terrible dusty mess, many of its rows charred rubbish-heaps, nobody having recovered the energy to tackle the devastation in a serious way. Things were still getting better for the Chinese in the city, worse for the Chinese in the villages, and two-way troop movements were very frequent. The blunt-headed old stone carvings of the east river bridge slept on, while naked alien soldiers splashed about beneath them; but the bronze cow of Hsuchowfu had shut her mouth.

That is the last I can say of Hsushowfu, except for one purely sentimental thing. In a few weeks, it had become something past forgetting. I left it, and found that this was an illusion, a trick with mirrors. There is no such thing as leaving Hsuchowfu.

It was a poor man's city, but there was something about it. Yes, it will live again.

Major Fujita, who did not know I was leaving, tried some time before to lend me ten yen. I said I had plenty of money; but looking mildly at Dr. Nettie, he insisted: "She has no Japanese money," as if this were a serious deficiency. Feeling as awkward as a woman offered a five-barred flag in a refugee camp, I refused the money, but he marched out, leaving it on the table.

Dr. Nettie said: "Don't let that man think he can bribe you, honey." I said: "Certainly not."

But I didn't think he was trying to bribe me with ten yen.

I thought he was being kind. However, in order to annoy nobody, not even myself, I put the Major's ten yen note into an envelope, and addressed it to him, with a polite note of thanks, to be handed over by Dr. Nettie after my departure on 16 June.

CHAPTER SEVEN

Soldiers and Apricots

A CHINESE MASON OFFERED to guide me to the north tracks, which I didn't know. All went well as far as the outskirts, where we nearly came to grief, halted by a Japanese sentry who, instead of making the usual public and perfunctory search for weapons, shoved his bayonet at us, and pulled me along into a shed. The Chinese, who was the likeliest to get that pretty toy in his stomach, should in common-sense have taken to his heels, but he followed.

The sentry, meeting us so early in the morning, and in a lonely part, had the floor to himself, and was by a long way the most unpleasant and familiar soldier I had met. When he started thrusting his hands inside my clothes—not searching for weapons—the Chinese looked shaky, but stuck. However, the pass Major Fujita had given me impressed the sentry, and he turned us loose. A very short walk along clay paths (we were dodging the station), and the Chinese pointed out where, if I climbed a bank, I would hit the railway. From the top I waved good-bye; he promptly went back to the mission, and, as I found out later, told the missionaries that the sentry had treated me abominably, and he was afraid that by this time I would be dead.

No shelter trees along the Tsinpu line, and as the sun got up I was broiling. The second main station, Liu Chuang, was near a dried-up creek.

Everything looked quiet, and I passed on to where the dry and stony bed of the river ran under a sleeper-bridge, apparently a substitute for the real bridge, which had been blown up by guerillas. Half-way across, concentrating only on not slipping, I was stopped by a Japanese soldier who didn't need to say: "Halt, or I fire." He was kneeling on a little truck or trolly-car, and looked up, smiling. If I didn't stop, the truck pushed me into the creek, where I would break my neck. So I got aboard the truck instead, and the soldier rattled back to the station. Here another soldier, black-frizzled, seemingly in a perfect fury, grabbed me by the arms and ran me inside.

But this man's bark was worse than his bite. He started to laugh, came back with another soldier, inspected my pass, and after some talk between them they gave me a lift on the trolly some distance down the line. Here I was told, by gesture, to hop up into the mail-car at the back of a troop-train.

It was sheer luck, the luck of dream-come-true; and when, at the next station, Likwoyi, the Japanese station-master there yelled for me to get down again, examined my pass, waved it away with contempt, and would not allow me any further mail-car luxury, I felt disappointed, but far from broken-hearted. This was the third station—good going in one day, and with still an hour of waning light left.

What followed, I have tried to piece together a thousand times, and might better have dropped it at the first attempt. I'm no nearer putting it together in any form that might be intelligible to both sides. I was a strange woman, shabbily dressed, walking alone through a dangerous terrain which had been a battle-ground a few weeks before.

Yes . . . but whatever my personal ideas about the Japanese (which had not, since 10 May, been altogether the ideas of a neutral), I was technically a neutral. A neutral may be a spy. Yes . . . but I had the pass from Hsuchowfu, not the pass of a civilian official, but of the chief Japanese military officer in that city. . . .

Bushido, the language difficulty, the well-known fact that one Japanese military force is often jealous of another . . . those things are small pieces of a puzzle; I pick them up, look at their colours and shapes, know they fit somewhere, but can't decide where. There's nothing to do but throw them down again.

I walked on from Likwoyi, and had gone about another li when a Japanese boy in civilian clothes came after me. He had a few phrases of English, and told me to come back.

"Very dangerous!" he kept saying, waving at the fields beyond which lay the villages.

I had shown the station-master my pass, and had nothing else to show, beyond the papers in my handcase, in which the boy took no interest at all. The Chinese villagers certainly didn't frighten me. I asked: "Who are you?" and the boy replied: "I am Japan schoolboy."

That was all very well. On the Lunghai line, the Japanese soldiers at the first station has also wanted me to stay the night. But I wanted to get on. After the other walk I felt used to sleeping in hedges. So I kept moving, until a couple of Japanese soldiers arrived, who had no English at all, and needed none.

I showed them my British passport, complete with Chinese travelling visa and Japanese chrysanthemum, then the Japanese pass from Hsuchowfu, and finally a letter of recommendation which the British Consul in Hankow had had brushed out for me in Mandarin. No good. Still, I didn't think they meant much beyond a little questioning. One of them kept smiling—a Flat-face, a particularly decent-looking young fellow. They had my arms, and were urging me along, but without fuss or violence.

However, the group at the far end of the platform, well away from the station-master's office, weren't there on a goodwill mission. They were about a dozen privates, with no officer in charge, or in sight.

Neither my polite way of saying 'Good-bye!' nor 'Thank you!' seemed suitable here, and I forgot 'Banzai!' There can't be anything stupider than a Pecksniffian flourish of passports and passes, but since they couldn't speak English, nor I Japanese, I couldn't think what to do but show them these documents once again.

One man thought of something better to do. He was small and leathery, getting on for forty, and had a white towel tied round his head. Somehow he looked as if he had to do with horses; anyhow, he was certainly of a manual occupation.

There was a game we used to play in my childhood called 'staring out.' It was an intensely irritating game, for which the best prey was a policeman. That was what this man did . . . walk up close, stare and grin; rather like a couple of unblinking dolls in the kids' game.

I did nothing practical—I couldn't, two of the platform soldiers held my arms in a good grip behind me—but either he didn't like my looks (neither did I, very much) or one of his mates chipped him and annoyed him. He hit me hard on the face. He didn't wait for any cheek-turning, but smiling, lifted his other hand, and swiped hard again.

For about twenty minutes he kept that up—smile and slap—while I did my best to smile back, and kneeling on the ground, other soldiers went through my papers and the few things in the handcase. They couldn't read English, and the only items which might have interested them in any way were, I had thought, the scrappily written and unintelligible English notes. But I was wrong about that.

The soldiers holding my arms picked up the face-slapping gentleman's cue, and started in, like overgrown schoolboys, twisting my arms. I felt that: but if the man who was slapping my face hurt me, I never knew it at the time, I was too much annoyed with him. The Flat-face boy I had thought so decent-looking knelt on the platform, shuffling papers, over which the others were exclaiming, "Spy-a! Spy-a!" I stared for a moment at the nice-looking boy, meaning: 'I didn't think you would enjoy this.'

He understood. In answer, he picked up one of the Chinese cards I had kept, held it carefully so that I could see it, and ran his mouth up in a quizzical way, meaning: 'If you can't explain that, you'd better take it.'

The card was printed in Chinese, without any romanized equivalent. I had no idea at all whose name it mentioned—probably that of some officer

I had met in Hsuchowfu, or at the front. And I had kept the cards because, those days having passed in such a roar of waters over our heads, so much that was friendly and hopeful having been swept away, I simply couldn't bring myself to destroy them.

The person who counted most was the face-slapping gentleman, who, after making my head feel queer for a moment, changed over and started to use his boots. But nothing hurt, except my arms, which I wished they would leave alone. They didn't think they had found enough in my handcase, so the kneeling group yelled to the others, and I said aloud: "Well, my girl, this time you're for it."

They ripped my clothes off, looking for papers which weren't there, wild because they couldn't find what wasn't there: but when they came to the little bag in which I now carried my dollars, an accident or lucky shot finished things up. I got my hands free, had the money out, and threw it, together with the valueless old rings from my fingers, hard into the face of the man with the towel.

Everything stopped completely, Joshua and the Rising Sun.

The Japan schoolboy, who at a safe distance had been dancing about crying: "They don't speak English!" advanced and said: "Japan man not robber."

I said: "Shut up," and as nobody picked up the money, touched me, or seemed to know how to proceed, got some clothing on, though not much, said: "Well, what do you think you are going to do now?" and walked down the steps, trying to whistle, a thing I never could do.

There is a creek running under willows opposite Likwoyi station. I walked into it, but finding it to be no beautiful fathomless depth (in which I would cheerfully have drowned, at the moment), I didn't feel equal to lying face downward in two feet of stinking mud, and crossed quickly into fields.

An old peasant was working in twilight, and I thought he'd gone crazy, because he knelt down, and started to kow-tow, knocking his old head against his old, hard, mother earth. Then I saw it wasn't my fancy dress which had deranged him. Half a dozen of the little red-tabbed forage caps had come up behind me, and I was sick of them, no longer angry, just sick of them. Also scared they'd bayonet the old peasant, for being there as a witness; but they didn't, they only ordered him off. They took my arms and fetched me back again, but once on the station didn't touch me, and let me put on my things, excepting some which were ripped up. My hand-case had been broken, but was neatly packed, and on top were the dollars Mex. and my papers, still safe.

The papers, though there was nothing in them of military significance, merely notes which I might have been able to reconstruct from memory and the rough MSS. of a couple of short stories (one of those, yes, very anti-Japanese), eventually travelled by safe hand between two Chinese ports.

One British officer said he couldn't understand why the Japanese didn't destroy them all, in case of accidents. But that is easy. I only wanted to insult them, in return for their own insults, when I threw my money in one Japanese face. They never realized that. They thought I mistook them for robbers, which touched their pride, and also convinced them I wasn't a 'spy-a.' So they felt ashamed of themselves for knocking me about, when I was nothing but a poor fool of a refugee, scared of robbers.

I picked up my handcase. They made gestures, indicating that I ought to stay at the station, but I went on. Another soldier (I don't think he took any part in beating me up, or if he did, I hadn't noticed him) took my bag and walked beside me.

"Why did you do it? What good did you get out of it? Don't you see these things only make such a lot of trouble for everybody?"

Talking against the tides of language. I wished I could feel angry again, feel anything but hopelessly sad. A hundred yards down the track was a disused building, and I wanted to sit down, so turned in, sat.

The soldier went out and got some rice and stewed apricots, which I wouldn't eat. Then he fetched a lantern and some straw. There were tears on his cheeks. It should have been funny, only that it was terrible, and made me wish I could die. A lot of them came back and started talking, and I said: "Go away. He is good, he brought me apricots." But the end of that unintelligible gabbled argument was sleep.

Somebody who did understand a little English must have translated the bit about apricots to the other soldier, the one with a towel round his head. I should have woken up next morning in a sweet peace-making mood of love for all fellow creatures, but didn't; I was cross, sleepy, fagged out. For the moment I didn't recognize him, then the towel, his build and his nut-brown smiling eyes fitted together again. He had brought me some apricots, little, dusty, and half-ripe.

I threw them at him, having apparently developed a habit of throwing things at this man, and he went out without a word, having done nothing, first to last, but smile.

Later I remembered what Lafcadio Hearn wrote about the Japanese smile. Also, by the way, what the same author wrote of the Japanese deity, Jizo, who once came down and took a woman's shape, in order to save her from what Lafcadio calls 'the shame of being stripped in public.' However, there was nothing to be done about it, once it had happened, any more than when the lorry moved on past the still roses outside Yun Ho station. It is done, possibly paid for.

All that day I walked. Once I went into a village to lie down, and the good-hearted villagers gave me rice-gruel and a mat to lie on. An old man wanted me to stay on, but a poor old woman with a red patch stuck on her underlip came up and said how much they were afraid. One could hardly be surprised about that. Farther along, just before the rain started, I went through another village, burnt out, ashen dead, no living thing among its roofless charred walls. Ashes and silence together, and the first great spots of rain.

Rain turned everything into a hissing bog, though it probably got me over the next ten miles without interference. All this district was once very bad bandit country, and its doubtful reputation lingers on; but the rain made bandits seem companionable. To walk was just better than to lie down. I wanted a warm place to sleep; presently I could do nothing but keep saying to nothingness: "Please give me a place to sleep, please give me a place to sleep." What I got, probably after midnight, was the blackened shell of an in-between station house, burnt right out. It was better than nothing, but I couldn't sleep, and lay shivering, my arms wrapped round me, trying to warm first one patch of my flesh, then another. My body seemed like a thing apart, for which I had somehow become responsible, and it was alive, cold, and painful.

In the morning light, everything I had was filthy with ashes. Remembering something, I took out as many papers as possible, including all the Chinese ones, spread them flat, and thrust them down under my girdle. Then the walking began again. Midday, I tried to get two young peasants to take me on their wheelbarrow behind the next station, Lincheng, but though they started, before we got close to the station they quite rightly asked for their pay, and made off. I had company, though—a Chinese boy, no more than seven, who declared sturdily that he wasn't scared, and swinging his basket of vegetables walked through without turning a hair.

We were nearly out off Lincheng, a big junction on the Tsinpu line, and also the place where some bandits ambitiously bagged a Rockefeller, when the Chinese kid saw the usual couple of Japanese soldiers halt me. He strolled on, swinging his vegetables. They took me down a street and some steps, into a barrack-room full of soldiers lying on mats, and through a sacking curtain into another room, Minoru Koide's room.

I don't know Minoru Koide's rank: but he was a big-sword officer, and spoke patchy English, not very much of it. The whole time (I was there about thirty hours) I thought: 'Yes. Soon you'll begin about my handcase, and probably continue as the soldiers did at Likwoyi. Or on general principles anyhow, you'll start yelling. Or you will promise me the moon, and go away, and back will come another Japanese officer, who will start yelling.' I didn't like the peculiar bulge made by the papers in my clothes, and spent much of the time lying on my stomach, for camouflage. Minoru Koide must have thought this very odd and ungraceful. There was a bed to lie on, his bed.

On the wall hung a big print of snowy Fujiyama, also a coloured one of some famous French painting whose painter I forget— 'Mother and Daughter; we had the same thing, in the same colours, at school. He gave me some whisky (Scotch) and some beautiful canned peaches (Tokyo). There was an air-cushion pillow to his bed, and also hanging on the wall was his big sword. After asking me questions for a couple of hours, he gave me the bed, and himself sat up in an arm-chair, where I doubt if he got more sleep than I did.

Once we got tangled up, because he was asking me: "Haven't you got an umbrella?" and said it so badly that I thought he meant 'Emperor.' I didn't want to talk about Emperors: now, I thought, he is leading up to Mikado. I kept stalling, until another chance remark revealed the innocent banality of his question.

Fantastic! He made me want to laugh and cry, because it was all so fantastic, because our lives are so madly, solemnly fantastic! At dusk he took a harmonica, went outside into the dark courtyard, and started to play 'Humoresque.' Our piano, among thousands of others, cherub-chirruping that in New Zealand!

It was funny, but after becoming dog-tired you reach a stage where funny is no longer funny, and think that people, if they value their own safety, had better stop. He said he'd get me a berth on a troop-train for the rest of the way. What I thought was: 'If you, or some other Japanese officer, don't make things extremely unpleasant and start yelling to-morrow morning, you'll send me back to Hsuchowfu.' I liked him, but didn't believe a word he said. Next day another young officer came in, and asked questions for hours. He was sociable, maybe, but he harped too much on the looks of the Chinese women and what was in Hankow.

I answered as I had heard Chinese people do, when they didn't mean a word of it: "It is very little and very dirty. There are no pretty women at all, except for a few in Canton." At that time, I didn't suppose any Japanese soldiers had a dog's chance of being in Canton.

After a little morning drill, the garrison soldiers lay on their sacks in the same stuffy, tired trance as we did, Minoru Koide jumping up now and again to Flit the room. The sanitary conditions at the post were enough to have brought on it a variety of epidemics. We couldn't think what to do, only to talk, lie still, talk again. Now and again, another soldier thought he'd ask questions. Usually the first, scrawled on paper, was 'Have you got boy?'

Wait . . . only to wait. . . .

At dusk, just as he had promised, Minoru Koide got me off in a troop-train, with a short-sword soldier named Nishinomya for body-guard. Nishinomya spoke no more English than I did Japanese, but somehow I understood when he asked Minoru Koide about this. Minoru Koide replied in Japanese: "She can say 'Arigato.'"

I'd been so sure that the whole thing—Scotch, canned peaches, 'Humoresque,' 'Mother and Daughter,' thy need for a bed is greater than mine—was trick from start to finish. Now I didn't know, still don't know. Anyhow there was nothing to say; nothing to do but go on.

Lying in the iron box of the troop-train, which pulled up for a very long time near water, we were plagued to death by mosquitoes. The men lit small coils of incense to keep them off, the red sparks eating down and down, in spirals, just as I had seen in the stalls where the bridges cross from Canton city to Shameen.

But for Nishinomya (who persuaded another iron box filled with fourteen soldiers on their mats to take us along), next morning I would have been ditched in a biggish occupied city, whose name I didn't know. Azaleas and a yellow pagoda. I saw no foreigners pass. But as it was, I lay on a mat like the Japanese, and Nishinomya put his pack and great-coat under my head.

The Japanese soldiers sang nothing as stirring as China's 'Chi-lai! Chi-lai!' But there's a near-tuneless, sad little refrain, sounding like a Japanese ' Mademoiselle From Armentieres,' which holds them together. You feel, without the link of this three-word chorus, they would roll apart like pebbles.

Most of the fourteen are middle-aged men, stripped down to their white under-suits, the others very young. One of the young ones knows for a certainty that I'm a spy, and smiles bitterly, ostentatiously drawing his blanket away so that it won't touch the mat on which I am lying. If I move, he raises his eyebrows and stares. It is good to be young like that. Nishinomya might be anywhere between twenty-five and thirty-five: he has gold teeth in front, the Japanese crop, and good, honest eyes. He keeps producing rations—steamed rice with the pickled plum, two kinds of canned meat and vegetables, biscuits, aerated water, all from Tokyo factories. An older man chucks over two big juicy Chinese peaches, which taste clean.

At stops, little witch-like, haggard children, almost naked, run along outside the wires which cut off the tracks, holding out their cans: and the soldiers, living on the fat of Chinese land, in Hsuchowfu district even killing off the peasants' oxen for fresh meat, throw them scraps, sometimes a few copper cash as well.

At last a glorious golden sunset streams up, near the bottom of Taishan, that wild and holy mountain. The guerillas are up there now. If you could see its purple rock-crests and sacred dragon-heads, you'd know its perfection as a natural fortress.

It was here a long-cropped station-master, distressingly polite, made me come down and talk about philosophy. On his walls a woman danced with an urbane skeleton, a Hollywood siren pouted fat red lips. He kept pets—a magpie, tied up, which cried shrilly, sticking out its pale little tongue, a tiny dog. To drink any more aerated water would kill me. . . .

The rifles are stacked up in a corner of our iron box. Everybody thinks: 'The guerillas may be coming down.' I have persuaded a soldier, as a joke, to show me how to use a rifle. The same flat, dropping little chorus is chanted on, one group letting it fall, two or three more taking it up. Gently the last of the sunset lingers away, islands, domes and lakes, clear gold in clear green, before Tsinanfu, which the Japanese call 'Si-nan.'

Japanese military headquarters: Nishinomya explains me to some important-looking officers. For some reason, a squad was called in, an order snapped out, and, of course, I said an inward farewell: but this had nothing to do with me. The soldiers tramped out again. I had heard there might still be a British Consulate at Tsinanfu, and asked about this.

One English-speaking officer said: "Yes," and went to the telephone, while another gave me wine, toothbrush, toothpaste, soap, all made in Tokyo.

'Nishinomya is a great help,' I thought, and asked: "May the soldier come with me to Tsingtao to-morrow?"

This pleased them: they smiled, and consented.

In came a slender gowned Chinese, to whom I was introduced.

"This is the British Consul," said a smiling Japanese.

'Oh, yes,' I thought, with keen recollections of Mr. Liu the Bad, 'Ta-tao, of course. Another of the same.' He, for that matter, seemed none too pleased to see me, and was snappy about my passport.

No wonder! Probably he was disappointed and hurt to see anyone technically under his charge drinking wine with Japanese soldiers. What had happened was this. When Han Fu-Ch'ü, the great warlord and Governor of Shantung province, withdrew without defending Tsinanfu, there was nobody but this Chinese official left in the big British consular buildings, which had never been fully occupied. Until the last possible moment, he communicated valuable and immaculate reports to Tsingtao, and still preferred to remain on in this doubtful, lonely place, where few foreigners at that time were permitted to make their way.

The Japanese never called Hsuchowfu by its name, but something like 'Joshu' in English phonetics. I can see the Consular representative now: "Joshu? Joshu? What do you mean by Joshu? Are you talking about Hsuchowfu? I am a Chinese!"

After some conversation, he informed me I was going for the night to a Chinese inn, and in the morning to Tsingtao. He then disappeared. I had no means of saying to him: 'I am very glad there are some Chinese.' Nishinomya took me to the inn, small, friendly, dirty, full of mosquitoes. Night-long, feet tramped on sentry-go outside my door.

Next day much the same, only longer: also, though it was a military train, there were a few Japanese civilians aboard, including two women. There were seats in our carriage. Nishinomya fixed me up as well as he could with his kit and coat, but as the day wore on he wasn't satisfied, and went away, fetching back a couple of wooden boxes so that I could lie with my legs stretched out. I shut my eyes, and for a while felt I might be able to die now. Real pain had only begun the night before, at the Chinese inn. A boy wrote in Esperanto: 'If you understand the Esperanto way, write back,' but I could make out only that one sentence.

With darkness crept into the air the smell of the sea. It was strange what a difference that seemed to make to us all—the sea. A curve of far lights, the black waves washing. We became silent, sat with darkness and the salt air washing a world away from our eyes and feet.

At Tsingtao it was heavy night. This also was an occupied city, entrenched, betrayed by Han Fu-Ch'ü and handed over without resistance. But at first glance, the war atmosphere seemed to have disappeared. There were plenty of foreigners, including some English people. I heard them talking, jovially welcoming one another, but they were on the other side of a barricade; I didn't even want them, they sounded so unreal. Nishinomya and I walked on, after he had made signs to ask if I wanted a ricksha, and in a short time came to another Japanese military headquarters, a very big place where I was taken upstairs.

There was more talk, a lot of talk, but only a little questioning. On the train and at all stops, every Japanese who could speak or write any English at all (many who cannot speak can write, in a round copybook hand) had asked questions, especially: "Are you a journalist?" "Have these soldiers hurt you?" "Do you like Japanese?"

In self-defence (since being a journalist meant that they wanted to shoot me or beat me up) I had left off being a journalist at Lincheng, and become a writer of romantic novels. Also I had a father in the House of Commons. That institution might have done worse.

After the talk, a Japanese chief wearing a large scarlet and white ribbon round his neck drove Nishinomya and myself round to their military hotel, the Grand, whose host, a small, clever and rather depressed civilian, spoke English with a thorough understanding and some amusing little colloquialisms.

Mutual smiles, large glasses of foaming Japanese beer. After this, casually, the host of the Grand Hotel asked me some more questions, including: "Which do you like best, Chinese soldiers or Japanese?"

I answered that one truthfully, telling him about the Chinese soldiers whose wounds we dressed on the last day; what, exactly, their courage had been, and what happened to them. The meeting dissolved for bed.

It is a beautiful place, Tsingtao, with a marine parade. All sorts of people, Chinese, English, German, Japanese, Russian, travel fresh as paint along the marine parade, blown about by clean-lipped winds from the sea. Yes, it has the winds and sea I love, the rose and white statice pinned against the wind, and an awkward new-born butterfly clinging there, afraid to travel on such limp wings. It does not look like a Chinese city: the Germans, who built most of it for a resort, used in building Europe's warm, heavy red tiles, an eccentric contrast with the thin little black tiles on yellow clay huts. Then the Japanese, during their occupation, which began in the 1914-18 war and ended only when world opinion forced them to return Tsingtao to China, started something quite novel—an afforestation scheme. Tsingtao has many trees, millions of small, sand-shod pines and green acacias. Blue and white, white and green, and everywhere red tiles; also the tan of the smart uniforms the Japanese have provided for Chinese Ta-tao police and traffic officers. It looks quite lovely, in fact, but not Chinese.

Nishinomya, having changed from uniform into a grey kimono, which made him barely recognizable, came into my room during the morning, and stayed there for a couple of hours, reading a Japanese book. He did not attempt to speak. I was tired, too, and kept still.

If it had been possible to summon one of the Chinese soldiers from Hsuchowfu, whether living or dead. . . . It's a pity the common soldiers can't discuss their wars, because apart from economic causes, which are a matter for adjustment, two things make wars—the art of the talker, the pride of the machine. Common soldiers usually have little of either. They are still the nail-iron . . . useful in a war, because so willing to be picked up and thrown away; and, of course, among the few castes it is reasonable to like. Otherwise, until such national welding of soldier and civilian as China is attempting to-day becomes the universal reality, the soldier, like western clerks and eastern coolies, is somebody who tends to get lost.

When Nishinomya had finished reading, he looked up, smiled at me, and went away, quietly opening and shutting the door. The hotel manager was taking me to the British Consulate in the afternoon, after which I expected to see Nishinomya again. But when I called back at the hotel he had gone, so neither 'Arigato' nor my polite form of saying good-bye came into use. I left, instead, a note of thanks, though I do not know if it was delivered.

In any case, what was there for a foreigner to say that would not have seemed hypocritical, sentimental, or both?

'My entire sympathies are with the Chinese. I thank you for your courtesy.

'I think your military leaders, your Government, whatever force has driven the
Japanese nation into waging this war of aggression against China, are tragically and hideously wrong. With all my heart I hope that their military adventure will be finally defeated, that the misery of a China dominated by Japan, before she has even had time to fill her lungs with that new air she is seeking to breathe, will be wiped out once and for ever.

'Long before the Sino-Japanese conflicts and recent events leading up to them began, I think that the western world, coming to the eastern world, was also tragically and hideously wrong. How can I say the greatness of that wrong?

'Our faults were mainly arrogance, lack of understanding, motives seldom beyond commercialism, an attempt, partly out of blindness, to falsify the integrity of eastern peoples.

'The results of these faults (though we, like China and Japan, are changing to-day) still show their heads in both countries. That is a matter for regret, the regret of a generation; and also, of course, inescapably a matter for payment in one form or another. But to sow more regrets, in the fields of a neighbour who is completely innocent, whose only excuses for your attack are that her spiritual growth has outrun her strategic strength .

. . you will find there is no revenge in that, really no satisfaction. Having made China hate you, with the best of Japanese intentions, you will find that you cannot use China to revenge yourselves upon the west.

One is sorry to see so many good people mixed up in this, on all sides so much suffering. . . .

But no. To say or write this would only have been ridiculous. Besides, among the strong and united to-day, desire to set injustices right has gone far beyond individual compassion. Too many countries have been betrayed with a few tears, strictly inexpensive words of encouragement.

They were more than ordinarily kind to me at the British Consulate, and later, when for a while I stayed quietly near the sea with a member of the Consular staff and his wife. I didn't think of much except getting on to Hong Kong. In Hong Kong were some Chinese people I knew.

The End